GW01090402

TROY HOUSE

TROY HOUSE

A TUDOR ESTATE ACROSS TIME

ANN BENSON

UNIVERSITY OF WALES PRESS
2017

www.uwp.co.uk

British Library CIP Data
A catalogue record for this book is available from the British Library

ISBN 978-1-78316-989-4
eISBN 978-1-78316-990-0

Designed and typeset by Chris Bell, cbdesign
Printed by Bell & Bain Ltd, Glasgow

For my dear parents, George Edwin and Sophia Haywood.

Contents

Preface and Acknowledgements ix

List of Figures xi

List of Abbreviations xv

1. Troy House Estate: an Enigma 1

2. A History of the Estate's Ownership: Identifying the Key Periods of Estate Development 13

3. Troy House: a Building History 73

4. Troy House Gardens: Location and Nature Across Time 111

5. The Walled Garden West of Troy House 145

6. Key Built Features of the Estate's Fieldscape 167

7. Troy House Estate: its Historical Significance 181

Appendix 1 Troy's History: the Existing Literature, 2015 187

Appendix 2 The Somerset Family Tree 192

Select Bibliography 195

Index 199

Preface and Acknowledgements

THE GENESIS OF THIS BOOK was the work for the dissertation of my MA at the University of Bristol (2013), under the supervision of Professor Timothy Mowl. In the subsequent years, I have pursued numerous new directions, as well as refining material presented at that time. I should like to thank Professor Mowl for enabling me to transfer my skills from my previous career as a science education academic to that of researching the history of houses and their designed landscapes. He generously continues to offer encouragement, support and a challenge to my thinking; I am particularly grateful for his reading of a draft of this book's chapter on architectural history.

My research would have been impossible without the support of those who own the different parts of the Troy estate. In particular I thank the Long family (Troy Farm), Gillian and Colin Davey (walled garden), and Peter and Kate Carroll (Troy House garden). Nicola Bradbear provided information about the estate's deeds and auctions, and the late Joan Ryan kindly gave me access to her photographs from the 1930s, when she lived at Troy Farm. Michael Tamplin has allowed me unlimited access to memories of his childhood and working life on the estate. I owe him a great debt for illuminating the architectural and landscape developments made during the time of the nuns' occupation; the Sisters of the Order of the Good Shepherd have also been supportive of my research.

I thank the Duke of Beaufort for giving me permission to access the archives held at Badminton House, and archivist Elaine Milsom for her expertise and kindness. Indeed, scholars would be lost without the guidance and assistance of archivists and librarians. I am indebted to the staff of the British Library, the Guildhall Library, the Lindley Library, the National Portrait Gallery, the National Archives, the Society of Antiquaries and

Monmouth Museum. I am particularly grateful for the assistance given by the reprographic staff of the National Library of Wales, often at short notice, always with good humour, and for the advice provided by Iwan ap Dafydd.

Staff at Gloucester County Record Office assisted me throughout my research. Tony Hopkins of Gwent Archives alerted me to two key theses; these significantly progressed my understanding of the history of the medieval period in relation to the Troy estate and I am most grateful to him. Richard Suggett of the Royal Commission on the Ancient and Historical Monuments of Wales responded to my request to have photographs taken of several elements of the estate; he has been a constant source of information, always willingly given, during my quest for Troy's history. I also thank Lisa Fiddes at Cadw for her accessibility and co-operation in identifying all of the information held on Troy at the Cardiff office.

There are specific debts to individuals. I am grateful to Professor Daniel Power for providing me with advice on genealogical records for chapter 2, and to Professor Maurice Whitehead for furthering my understanding of the history of the Jesuits in early seventeenth-century Wales. Professor Dafydd Johnston's support was invaluable to me when considering the information I might obtain from the works of the poets of the nobility and from medieval Welsh history in general. Also, Dr Cynfael Lake generously translated a previously unpublished poem at my request. Post-graduate archaeology students Christopher Waters and Emma Whitcombe are also thanked for their support with the demands of geophysical surveys and maps. I thank them all. The opinions expressed in this book result from their example, but any errors are entirely my own.

I thank Dr Mark Lewis of the Monmouthshire Antiquarian Association: his were the first words of encouragement to start publishing my research on Troy, which I did some three years ago as an article in the Association's journal. Local historians Peter and Trish Hayward kindly helped me locate the remains of the estate's original deer park wall. Friends have endured periods of my writing 'purdah' and offered support throughout; I am especially grateful to my friend and writer Dr Charles Moseley. My cousin and artist Margaret Cole has contributed to the book's drawings. Finally, I thank my son, Richard, for his patience with my IT skills and especially for steering me calmly through the trauma of Windows 10 suddenly appearing on my computer two weeks before final manuscript submission. I have long dreamed of producing a book from my research on the history of the Troy estate; I am fortunate in that, thanks to the support of all those named above – and apologies to those whom I have inadvertently omitted – it has become a reality.

List of Figures

1.1 Charles Somerset, Marquess of Worcester (1660–98)
1.2 Aerial view of Troy House, farm and walled garden, 1994
1.3 View of Troy House from the track that continues to Troy Farm
1.4 Ground plan of Troy House buildings
1.5 Steps leading up to the walled garden's ornamental stone entrance, 1992
1.6 Entrance to Troy farmyard, 2014
1.7 Troy Farm and the estate's woodland
2.1 The Lordships *c.*1170
2.2 The property of Monmouth Priory in the twelfth century
2.3 The church in medieval Gwent: Troy St John and Troy St Michael
2.4 Lineage of Sir William ap Thomas
2.5 The alabaster tomb of Sir William ap Thomas (d.1445) and his second wife, Gwladus (d.1454), the Benedictine priory church of St Mary, Abergavenny
2.6 Charles Somerset, first Earl of Worcester
2.7 Edward, fourth Earl of Worcester
2.8 Locations of Raglan Castle, Troy House, Chepstow Castle and the Cwm estate with connecting rivers
2.9 The first Duke of Beaufort and his family, by S. Browne, 1685
2.10 Elizabeth, wife of the fifth Duke of Beaufort
2.11 The eighth Duke of Beaufort, by Ellis Roberts
2.12 Troy Convent Laundry Service
2.13 Troy Special School for Boys, 1984–91
3.1 Detail, John Aram's map of 1765 showing the access route to a courtyard

3.2 Detail, Joseph Gillmore's map of 1712 showing the access route to a courtyard
3.3 Troy Farmhouse: above, during the 1930s; below, in 2015
3.4 Troy barn and detail of its corner post, 2015
3.5 The interior of Troy barn with the triangular arrangement of its blocked slit breathers, 2015
3.6 The original archway in line with the oldest route to Troy House (1930s), and the remains of the arch with the keystone on the floor (2015)
3.7 St John the Baptist Church of Troy?
3.8 The building lying on the western side of the farmyard in the 1930s, now largely demolished
3.9 The remains of an ancient window in the building lying on the western side of the farmyard (1930s)
3.10 Entrance to the south wing of Troy House from the farmyard
3.11 Three archway entrances to the current farmyard/outer reception courtyard
3.12 Medieval floor tiles: left, Malvern fabric sample; right, two Malvern fabric finds at Troy
3.13 Detail, *Prospect of Llannerch Park from the East*, English School, 1662
3.14 Footprint of historic Troy House: south wing (pale blue), north range (red) and rooms with ornate plaster ceilings (PC 1 and PC 2)
3.15 Detail, lead clock-face of Sir William Powell's 1607 clock-bell on the gable end of the south wing
3.16 Sketch of one of the south wing's windows with a metal grille, the latter broken on one side to accommodate a brick wall
3.17 The 'furniture door' in the east section of the cross wing, 1950s
3.18 Roll-moulded beams in the room entered from the 'furniture door', and detail of an end-stop
3.19 Visual evidence of a demolished section of building east of the 'furniture door'?
3.20 Troy building costs, 1681–4
3.21 The west elevation of Troy House in the 1950s showing the raised red sandstone window surrounds of the 1680s build
3.22 Footprint of historic Troy House: south wing (pale blue), cross wing and its conjectural projection (dark blue), 1680s build (red) and ground-floor rooms with ornate plaster ceilings (PC 1 and PC 2)
3.23 East elevation of Troy House showing the attached 1680s north range

3.24 Troy's main staircase of 1681–4 and, on the far left, the extra steps for accessing the older four-storey east section of the house
3.25 Plaster ceiling details in order of: ground-floor rooms, PC 1 and PC 2; first-floor room, PC 3 above PC 2 (1950s)
3.26 The oak room at Troy House *c.*1895
3.27 *A Panorama of Monmouth, with Troy House, c.1672*, by Hendrik Danckerts
3.28 Detail, *A Panorama of Monmouth, with Troy House, c.1672*, by Hendrik Danckerts
3.29 Troy House: a suggested building phase plan
3.30 View of Troy's stone staircase and the detail of its ground-floor doorway bolection moulding
4.1 Aerial view of Troy's 'yard'
4.2 Detail of Aram's 1765 map showing two enclosed areas and their probable uses
4.3 Thomas Hill, *The Gardener's Labyrinth*
4.4 Detail of the quadripartite garden, *A Panorama of Monmouth, with Troy House, c.1672,* by Hendrik Danckerts
4.5 Garden area to the east of Troy House and its attached chapel
4.6 Garden area containing several old stone walls to the east of Troy's farmhouse
4.7 Garden wall B of brick and stone
4.8 Gable end of wall A
4.9 Buildings at the end of wall A
4.10 Uses of land east of the farmhouse across time
4.11 Gillmore's 1712 map with its named areas
4.12 Annotated detail of Gillmore's 1712 map showing gardens east of the house
4.13 Annotated detail of Aram's 1765 map showing gardens east of the house
4.14 The nuns' exedra garden and alignment of garden walls, 1978
4.15 Overlay of the three areas' resistivity results with an aerial photograph taken during the nuns' occupation of Troy House.
4.16 Overlay of Gillmore's 1712 map with MasterMap
4.17 Overlay of the 1881 OS map, which shows the position of garden walls, with Aram's 1765 map
4.18 Stansted's exedra leading to an avenue of trees in the late seventeenth century
4.19 Part of the *parterre de broderie*, Tredegar House, Newport, south Wales

4.20 John Worlidge, *Systema horticulturae, or the Art of Gardening* (London, 1682)
4.21 Detail, the 1712 Gillmore map showing a rectangular feature, R, close to the river
4.22 Land to the north-east of the house
4.23 Topographical survey of the area to the north-east of the house
4.24 Detail, water feature on the 1845 tithe map
4.25 The Canal and 'Great Room' at Hall Barn, Buckinghamshire, 1730
4.26 Detail, Gillmore's 1712 estate map showing the north range and its garden area
4.27 The procedural entrance to Tredegar House, Gwent, a late seventeenth-century house and garden
4.28 Detail, *Troy House (view from the Wye Bridge)*, by Thomas Smith, *c.*1720s
4.29 *Newby in the West Riding of the County of Yorke*, *c.*1700, showing an avenue of trees lining the procedural route to the house
4.30 Troy House from the west, 1870–90
5.1 Relative position of the walled garden
5.2 Walled garden: entrances and access routes
5.3 The west wall's original entrance with pillars, infilled by the nuns to create a cemetery within the walled garden
5.4 View of the ornamental entrance from outside the walled garden, 2015
5.5 The moulding and ogee stop of the ornamental entrance's doorway, 2015
5.6 The pediment of the ornamental entrance, 2015
5.7 The barrel-vaulted roof of the ornamental entrance's lobby, 2015
5.8 View of the ornamental entrance from inside the walled garden, 2015
5.9 Detail of the ornamental entrance's classically inspired rusticated moulding, 2015
5.10 Rustic work: Sebastian Serlio on architecture
5.11 Vredeman de Vries: his use of rusticated stone mouldings in a classical setting
5.12 West-facing bee bole near the ornamental entrance, 2015
5.13 South-facing bee bole, 1953
5.14 Registration of Troy's bee boles, 1953
5.15 Detail, Gillmore's 1712 map and its key, showing the walled garden as a cherry orchard
5.16 Detail, Aram's 1765 map and its key showing the walled garden as a cherry orchard

5.17 *Prince Henry Frederick (1594–1612)*, by an unidentified artist, 1596
5.18 Resistivity results superimposed on a MasterMap of the walled garden
5.19 Aerial photograph of the walled garden, 1978
6.1 Locations of Keeper's Cottage (KC), brick kiln (BK), ice house (IH) and the deer-park wall (DPW), running along the eastern boundary of the woods
6.2 Cadw's 'game larder' seen from the south-east, 2015
6.3 Cadw's 'game larder' as it appeared in the 1960s
6.4 The north wall's window close to the barrel roof of Cadw's 'game larder', 2015
6.5 A comparison of the moulded string courses: above, Cadw's 'game larder'; below, the ornamental entrance to the walled garden
6.6 The two conduits on the 1765 Aram map
6.7 Overlay of enlarged sections of the 1765 Aram and 1881 OS maps
6.8 Coloured Mitchel Troy Parish 1881 OS map with conduit label and red water tanks
6.9 West face of what may be Aram's second conduit house
6.10 Pipe bringing water into the conduit house
6.11 Possible route of underground metal water pipes for Troy's conduit house
6.12 The conduit house at North Hinksey, Oxfordshire

List of Abbreviations

BL	British Library
CAWCS	Centre for Advanced Welsh and Celtic Studies
CCR	*Calendar of the Close Rolls*
CFR	*Calendar of the Fine Rolls*
CPR	*Calendar of the Patent Rolls*
CSP	*Calendar of State Papers*
GA	Gwent Archives
GGAT	Glamorgan-Gwent Archaeological Trust
IBRA	International Bee Research Association
MA	*Monmouthshire Antiquary*
NLW	National Library of Wales
NMR	National Monument Record
NPRN	National Primary Reference Number
ODNB	*Oxford Dictionary of National Biography* (Oxford, 2014)
PRO	Public Record Office
RCAHMW	Royal Commission on the Ancient and Historical Monuments of Wales
RIBA	Royal Institute of British Architects
TNA	The National Archives
VCR	*Victoria County History*

One

Troy House Estate: an Enigma

AT FOUR IN THE MORNING on 13 July 1698, Rebecca, Marchioness of Worcester, wrote to her mother-in-law, the first Duchess of Beaufort, from her cousin's house at Llanrothal (now on the Herefordshire border):

> Madam
> I am under so much trouble and concern for my Lord that I scarce know what I write [.] my lord came heather yesterday to church [.] thare was 3 dyed the day before of the small pox and that distemper being so much in the town we have not bin thare this 3 weekes [.] we went from hence soone after 7 in the evening desineing [designing] to return to troy [in Monmouthshire] but it pleesed God the horses turning to short the coachman was flung out of the box [.] the horses run a way down a hill and over turned the coach before the postillian could stop them and my Lord apprehending the danger we ware in jumped out of the coach [.] the coach wheel mised him very narrowly [.] he has brused his thigh very much but Dr Tyler who is with him hopes thare is nothing out [.] my Lord is very faint [and] complaines much of a sickness in his stomake and has had yet but an ill night'.[1]

Rebecca's 'Lord' is her husband of some sixteen years, Charles Somerset, Marquess of Worcester, the only son and heir of Henry, first Duke of Beaufort. Rebecca's letter continues with her asking for the duke's doctor to hasten from Badminton House to see Charles at Llanrothal. As was the fashion for the period, Charles had been let blood at midnight by Dr Tyler.

Whether the duke's doctor arrived to see Charles is unknown but he died later that day.

Charles's death is pivotal in the history of the Troy House estate. From this point, Troy largely ceased to be occupied by members of the Somerset family; Badminton House remained the duke's family seat whilst stewards were installed at Troy to manage its various components. The duke had spent generously on aggrandising Troy House to make it reflect his family's status, and Charles and Rebecca had made it their family home. However, it had primarily served as the duke's administrative centre from which Charles oversaw the family's extensive Welsh holdings. The estate became largely frozen in time from Charles's death and it would be another two hundred years before an ancestor of the first duke would reside again for any length of time at Troy. Chapter 2 traces its succession of subsequent owners as well as revealing what went before, but first, a tour of what can be seen today.

Figure 1.1 *Charles Somerset, Marquess of Worcester (1660–98).*
Copyright: National Portrait Gallery, London.

The estate lies 1.6 kilometres south of Monmouth on the border of Monmouthshire with Gloucestershire (OS SO 509 113) in south-east Wales. The river Trothy forms the northern boundary of the estate: this river comes within some ninety metres of the house where it splits into two streams to form two islands, and then resumes as one course before leaving the garden area. The Welsh form of Trothy is *Troddy*, which derives from '*trawdd*', meaning course, and that of this river is very winding. The -dd- is more likely to have disappeared in Welsh from *Troddy* than the -th- from Trothy. Of all the possible reasons for the estate's name, the most plausible is that it derives from the nearby river.[2] In medieval documents the estate is also referred to as 'Little Troye' and 'Troy Parva'.

The influential Welsh Herbert family owned the estate during the fifteenth and sixteenth centuries. This was followed by three hundred years of continuous ownership by the Somersets. Henry Somerset, who occupied Troy House during the late 1660s, was elevated to the title of Duke of Beaufort in 1682. When the ninth Duke of Beaufort put the 675-hectare estate up for auction in 1901, some lots remained unsold, leading to another auction in 1919 and, thereafter, a succession of owner-occupiers of its different parts.[3] Currently, it consists of three main components each under separate ownership: Troy House, together with several buildings from the 1960s, all surrounded by grassed areas extending to the river Trothy; a walled garden of some 1.6 hectares with three modern residential buildings set within its original stone perimeter walls to the west of the house; and, very close to the house, Troy Farm, which is a working dairy farm with the remains of walled gardens, surrounding pasture and extensive woodland.

Current access to the house, farm and the east end of the walled garden is down a track leading off the road (B4293) between Monmouth and Mitchel Troy. Troy cottage lies at the junction of the track with this road. Built in the picturesque *cottage orné* style, the cottage is listed as Grade II.[4] Although now a private residence, during the nineteenth century it was the entrance lodge to Troy House. The track terminates at Troy Farm; at a point some two-thirds along its length it crosses two branches of the river Trothy by two stone bridges some four metres apart, close to a gated entrance to Troy House. Cadw, the Welsh government's historic environment service, list the square gate piers of banded sandstone ashlar and the pair of full-height wrought-iron gates as Grade II and of probable eighteenth-century construction.[5]

Figure 1.2 *Aerial view of Troy House, farm and walled garden, 1994. House, centre right; farm, centre left and very close to the house; walled garden, centre top.* Crown copyright: RCAHMW.

Only part of the house can be seen through these gates and it is that which is most often shown and written about in the few publications that exist for the Troy estate. This section was constructed 1681–4 and, as it faces north, hereafter will be referred to as the north range. It is joined on its south side to other buildings, which are also part of Troy House, but these are very rarely mentioned in any publication. Even the Royal Commission on the Ancient and Historical Monuments of Wales (RCAHMW) on its website, Coflein, focuses on the Carolean part of Troy House when it states that:

Figure 1.3 *View of Troy House from the track that continues to Troy Farm.* Copyright: Ann Benson.

> Troy House [. . .] is a 17th century stone building of 3 storey [*sic*] and dormers. It has a hipped slate roof. The central portion is forward with a pediment. The interior includes fine plaster work and panelling. It was the seat of Dukes of Beaufort.[6]

Similarly, Cadw list the house as a Grade II* building 'constructed in classical style about 1660–70, for the Marquess of Worcester', and in so doing, again refer only to the north range.[7] The house remains substantially unchanged from the seventeenth century but is in a state of disrepair and the surrounding land is somewhat overgrown. Both have been the subject of a planning application for residential development since 2008. The application has not been favourably received by the authorities and as of 2016 remains unresolved, whilst the building continues to decay.[8] A caretaker resides in a small, west portion of the house, which in previous centuries was the abode of the chief steward of the Duke of Beaufort's Welsh estates; otherwise, the house is unoccupied, as it has been since the late 1990s.

Several buildings erected during the 1960s lie close to the house. These were commissioned by an order of nuns, who owned and managed the house as a school for girls from 1904 until 1977, and include a chapel, cloisters, teaching block, theatre, hostel, garage and a covered netball court. They are shown together with the historic house (black) and nearby Troy Farm in a ground plan (Figure 1.4). The historic house

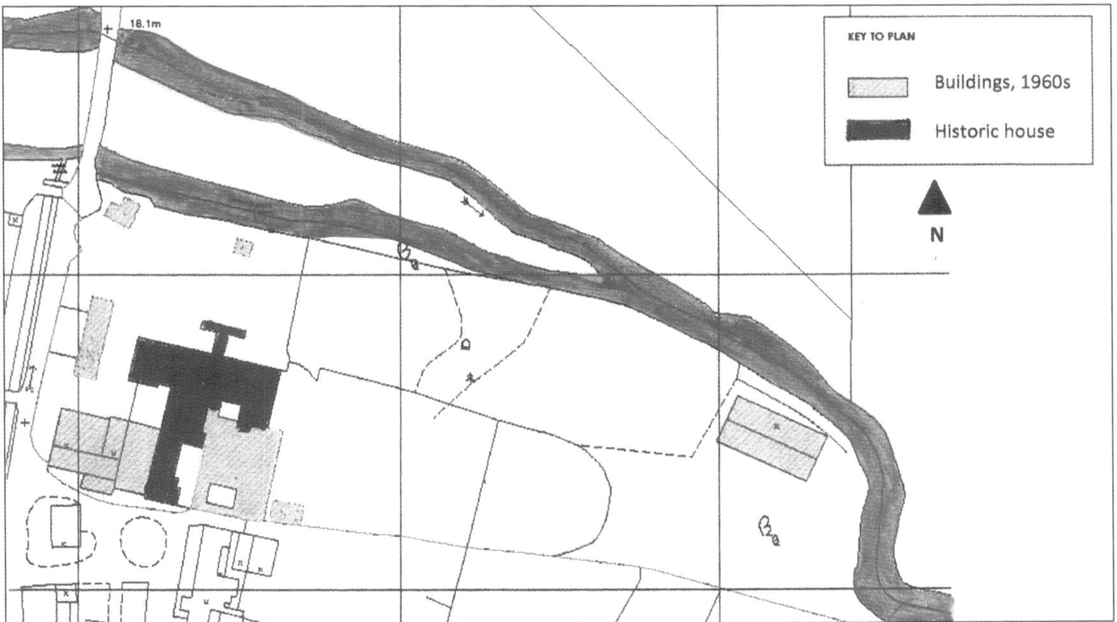

Figure 1.4 *Ground plan of Troy House buildings.* Copyright: Ann Benson.

appears like a capital letter T, where the Carolean north range lies across the top of the T, and, as will be argued below, the house becomes progressively older towards the base of the T. When the nuns sold the house to the current owner in 1977, it was unoccupied for a few years and then leased for use as a special school for boys until 1991, during which time no additional building or landscaping took place.[9]

The track continues past Troy House gates. After some sixty metres, steps can be seen on the right leading up to a small ornamental stone building with a centrally placed door. This opens onto the walled garden, which Cadw date as being from the seventeenth century. They list this garden as II* due to the ornamental entrance and surviving stone walls with bee boles.[10] This garden area is under well-kept pasture with some

Figure 1.5 *Steps leading up to the walled garden's ornamental stone entrance, 1992.* Copyright: Ann Benson.

old fruit trees. The three residential buildings set against the south wall of this garden are each associated with a portion of its land, and that running against the west wall contains a small cemetery, created by the nuns during their ownership.

The track continues past the walled garden's ornamental entrance and after another twenty-three metres it splits into two. One branch continues for a few metres before terminating at farm barns; the other curves to the left immediately behind Troy House to enter the farmyard of Troy Farm (Figure 1.6). The farm is still worked, although the stone and red brick walls of its gardens and orchards are in poor condition. This ground has not been cultivated since the mid-twentieth century.[11] The surrounding pasture and woodland remain largely unchanged since the estate was owned by the eighth Duke of Beaufort in the nineteenth century.[12]

Three connected areas of woodland, shown as Livox Wood, Troypark Wood and Troy Orles on the current OS map, form a long, thin band on top of a ridge that slopes to the east and south of Troy House and the Farm (Figure 1.7).[13] Cadw identify an ice-house and a small ruined building as structures within the farmland. The former is overgrown and damaged

Figure 1.6 *Entrance to Troy farmyard, 2014.*

Copyright: Ann Benson.

Figure 1.7 *Troy Farm and the estate's woodland (Troy House shown as Sch).* Crown copyright (2017) 100057545: detail, OS Explorer Map, Wye Valley and Forest of Dean, OL14.

by a landslide and, due to encroaching ivy, the roof has been lost from the latter. This is speculatively recorded by Cadw's inspector for parks and gardens as a 'game larder', largely due to 'a long-dead sheep inside' being 'mummified at the time of the visit'.[14] However, this is an unlikely purpose for the building, given its considerable distance from the house, and it is shown in chapter 6 to have been a rare conduit house. Although much of the former parkland, now agricultural, has been excluded from the area on Cadw's register, 'the boundaries of this character area have been extended to include the icehouse and "game larder" as they are deemed to be closely associated with the house'.[16]

The history of the Troy House estate is under-researched and under-represented in the literature. The descriptions provided by Cadw, RCAHMW and the Glamorgan-Gwent Archaeological Trust (GGAT), which covers the Troy House estate area, are brief and rely on surveys now decades old (Appendix 1). There are also several anomalies in the descriptions assigned to some of the components of the estate by various agencies. The RCAHMW made a visit to parts of the estate in my company in December 2015, when several photographs were taken. It is hoped that the new insights this provided will eventually find their way into RCAHMW documentation.

A way forward

When the estate was broken up in 1901, lying as it does on the border between Wales and England, archival material was distributed across Welsh and English county record offices. A large amount of material was also sent to the National Library of Wales (NLW), where it is held as the Badminton Special Collection. This scattering of archival material with no overall referencing system may in part account for the dearth of published information on the estate's history. Little use has been made of these primary documentary sources or the Duke of Beaufort's family archives at Badminton House for researching Troy. Also, hardly any map regression or archaeology have been conducted on the estate's components. Consequently, the history of Troy is an enigma, despite its connections to historically significant people and Troy House itself being described as 'one of Wales' finest late seventeenth-century country houses'[17] and 'a very important building within the county [Monmouthshire] and indeed Wales'.[18] A multi-method approach that brings together the existing research but also incorporates a more diverse source of information appears overdue for investigating the history of Troy.

Estate building and landscaping activities are most likely to occur when two conditions exist simultaneously: the owner has sufficient wealth to implement his desired plans, and there is social stability to enable culture and fashion to flourish without the pressures of war and other disruptive forces. If the ownership history of the Troy estate could be established, then it might be possible to know when building and landscaping are most likely to have occurred. Given that few garden features are extant at Troy, the architectural history of the house is also fundamental for a better understanding of how its surrounding landscape has changed over the years. For example, principal reception rooms generally overlook key garden areas; a room known to have existed in the

Tudor period would most likely have overlooked a garden styled in the Tudor fashion. Knowing the location of such rooms across time would support a consideration of how the surrounding land has also been refashioned. Furthermore, given the closeness of the gardens to the east and south of the house to those of the farm (Figure 1.2), they should be considered together, as the boundary between the two may have changed with time.

The publications of Cadw, RCAHMW and GGAT offer their descriptions of the house, farm, gardens and parkland in a discrete manner with few cross-references to features within these different estate components. Adopting a more holistic approach to researching the estate can not only enrich what is understood about its separate parts but, in addition, illuminate how these may be interrelated and were used by those who lived and worked there.

Notes

1 Badminton: FmF 1/4/2.

2 Professor Dafydd Johnston, private communication, 10 November 2016. See also R. J. Thomas, *Enwau Afonydd a Nentydd Cymru* (University of Wales Press, Cardiff, 1938), pp. 169–70.

3 Driver, Jonas and Co., *Troy House Estate Monmouth, To Be Sold on 27th March 1901* (London: Auctioneers Messrs Driver, Jonas & Co., 1901). The auction catalogue is held at Nelson Museum, Monmouth.

4 Cadw listed building reference 2734. There are three types of listed status for buildings in England and Wales: Grade I for buildings of exceptional interest; Grade II* for particularly important buildings of more than special interest; Grade II for buildings that are of special interest, warranting every effort to preserve them.

5 Cadw listed building reference 25791.

6 *www.coflein.gov.uk/en/site/20938*. Accessed October 2014.

7 Cadw, *Gwent, Register of Landscapes, Parks and Gardens of Special Historic Interest in Wales, Part 1: Parks and Gardens* (Cardiff: Cadw Welsh Historic Monuments, 1994), pp. 154–6.

8 Troy House Planning Application, DC/2008/00723, Monmouthshire County Council, Planning Department; *www.monmouthshire.gov.uk.*

9 Private communication during August 2013 with a past student and housemistress of Troy School, Monmouth, 1961–80.

10 Cadw, *Gwent, Register of Landscapes, Parks and Gardens*, p. 155.

11 This fact is reached from triangulating personal communications with: Joan Ryan, who lived at Troy Farm 1920s to 1950s; the current owner of Troy

Farm, Mr Graham Long, who has worked the farm since the 1970s; and Mr Mike Tamplin, who, together with his father before him, worked on the estate during the twentieth century until the late 1970s.

12 Horatia Durant, 'History of Troy House, Four Hundred Years of Splendour', *Monmouthshire Beacon*, 10 August 1956, page unknown.

13 OS Explorer Map, Wye Valley and Forest of Dean, OL14.

14 Cadw, *Troy House, Garden, Monmouth*, NPRN 266097, associated collection of records, catalogue number 834732, Site Dossier. Available at *www.coflein.gov.uk*, accessed July 2015.

15 Ann Benson, 'The Evidence for an Extant Conduit House on the Troy Estate', *The Monmouthshire Antiquary*, XXX (2014), 39–56.

16 Glamorgan-Gwent Archaeological Trust, Lower Wye Valley 038 Troy House. Available at *www.ggat.org.uk/cadw*, accessed July 2015.

17 Michael Tree and Mark Baker, *Forgotten Welsh Houses* (Llanrwst: Hendre House Publishing, 2008), p. 158.

18 Monmouthshire conservation manager, letter of 2 August 2012, filed under planning application DC/2008/00723, Monmouthshire County Council Planning Department.

Two

A History of the Estate's Ownership: Identifying the Key Periods of Estate Development

THE INTENTION here is not to provide a complete line of ownership of Troy across the centuries as one owner handed over to another. Rather, priority is given to identifying the historical significance of those who have owned and lived at Troy within pertaining political and social contexts. Simultaneously, the periods during which the estate is most likely to have undergone building and landscape development due to the nature and circumstances of its owners, are highlighted.

From the eleventh to the early fifteenth century

As Paul Courtney notes, the Norman lords who invaded and conquered Wales assumed the extensive rights previously enjoyed by their predecessors, the Welsh princes.[1] Marcher lords were bound to support the English king during war but reaped the benefit of exemption from royal taxation and had many rights usually held by the Crown. The lordships served as both sources of revenue and independent bases of power, as Marcher law was governed by local custom, not by the royal courts as in England. Consequently, they attracted leading English aristocratic families.

Few documents survive from the eleventh and twelfth centuries to provide an understanding of how individual Marcher lordships functioned. As in England, manors varied in size but commonly consisted of a hall, land worked for the lord's profit (demesne) and tenant land. A distinction was made between 'demesne manors', directly managed for the Marcher lord's profit, and the knights' fees, held by his knightly (or feudal) sub-tenants.[2] Their administration was centred on castles with a variety

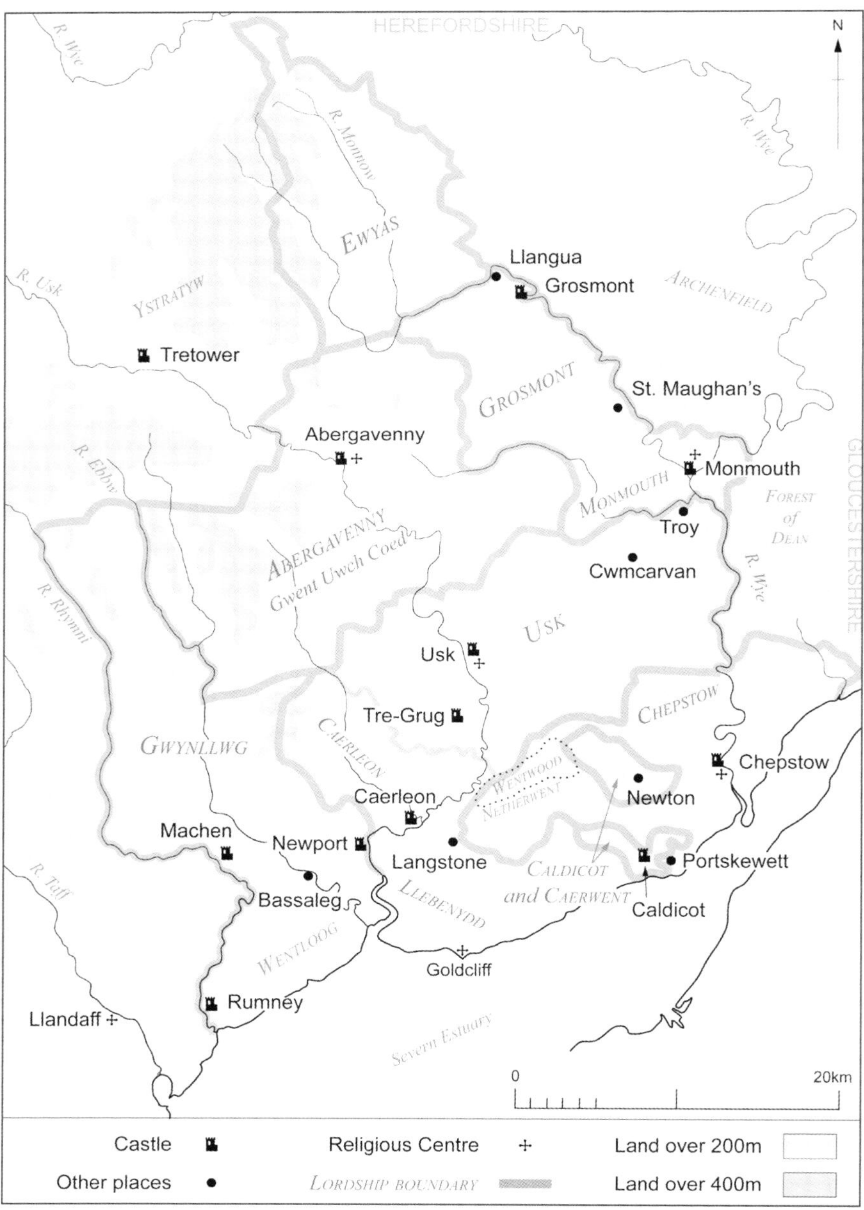

Figure 2.1 *The lordships c.1170.*
By permission of the *Gwent County History.*

of persons responsible for specific types of activities. By the end of the reign of William Rufus (1087–1100) the royal lordship of Netherwent (lower Gwent) covered a vast territory.[3] This was later subdivided into the lordships of Chepstow, Tryleg, Usk and Caerleon.[4] A map of the lordships *c.*1170 shows Troy within the lordship of Usk but very close to the boundary of that of Monmouth, which before 1066 lay within Archenfield, an area held by the Saxons and bounded by the rivers Wye and Monnow.[5] In contrast to the rest of Archenfield, Monmouth shows no sign of the devastation caused by the Welsh raids of 1055.

In his *History of Monmouthshire*, Joseph Bradney notes that 'the manor of Troy Parva was held of the lords of Usk by half a knight's fee, and is first mentioned as having been the seat of Sir Alexander Catchmay'.[6] Catchmay sounds like an English surname and it is tempting to suggest that, like other Englishmen of the time, he was an aristocrat attracted by the power and profit associated with the emerging Marcher lordships as a career opportunity. Bradney also states that he was a companion of Hamelin (Hamelin de Ballon, b. *c.*1060, d.1105/6) who was from the Maine area of France. Hamelin came to England with the Conqueror and was rewarded with lands in Cornwall and south-east Wales. The latter was to become part of the Welsh Marches and Hamelin was charged with its speedy, successful conquest and management.[7] After receiving the lordship of Over Gwent from King William Rufus, he established the castle at Abergavenny about 1075.[8] It is possible that as a companion of Hamelin, Alexander Catchmay was also rewarded with lands and these included the area of Troy; he might also have held these lands by half a knight's fee. Bradney states that Alexander left an only daughter and heir, Jane (b. *c.*1030), married to Sir Alan Scudamore, whose son Sir Titus Scudamore is styled Lord of Troy and Bigsweir.[9]

Bradney's account contains several items that raise doubts about its accuracy, and not just because, so far, Alexander Catchmay or Ketchmey and variations of this name have not been traced in eleventh-century manorial records associated with the area of Troy. Arguably, the earliest known Alexander in the British Isles is King Alexander I of Scotland (r. 1107–24), possibly named after Pope Alexander II (1061–73). However, the popularity of the name from the twelfth century is much more likely due to Old French romances loosely based on the life of Alexander the Great.[10] The Catchmay family were prominent in the seventeenth century in the area that is now east Monmouthshire. Perhaps Alexander Catchmay is an antiquarian reconstruction to fill genealogical gaps or was invented to flatter the family as patrons, to enhance the status of their lineage, or to defend their claims to property in court. Alternatively,

Bradney and his researchers may have made wrong deductions from incomplete evidence.[11]

As Daniel Power notes, Alexander Catchmay sounds like a very unlikely name for the eleventh century, as does Jane, the name of his daughter, although the latter becomes very popular after the middle of the twelfth century.[12] 'Joan' is a version of a name that appears as 'Joanna' in Latin records, but this name, like most of those derived from the Bible, are almost never used by the laity before the mid-twelfth century. 'Jane' is a rendering of the vernacular forms, for example 'Jehanne' and 'Johanne', of Joanna. These do not appear in the records before the thirteenth century simply because vernacular forms of names are hardly ever seen before the end of the twelfth century, as the relevant records are mostly in Latin. On both sides of the English Channel, early modern antiquarians produced far-fetched theories that continue to be reproduced, not least because many have found their way into trusted publications such as *Burke's Peerage*.[13]

Hamelin de Ballon did not conquer Upper Gwent until about 1093 but Monmouth had come under Norman rule as early as the late 1060s. Unlike the Norman conquest of England, the Anglo Norman incursion from the east into Wales was a more gradual affair. In David Crouch's chapter on the transformation of medieval Gwent in the *Gwent County History* series he quotes from evidence that in the time of King William, Earl William FitzOsbern, Walter de Lacy and Ralph de Bernay, a borough (*castellum*) was built at Monmouth (*Mingui*) that controlled entry into the Archenfield region (then a part of upper Gwent).[14] Earl William FitzOsbern was responsible for the building of Monmouth Castle; he granted half of the borough to his three barons, Humphrey, Osbern and William the scribe.[15] Crouch states that a town as much as a castle was built at Monmouth and that the settlement was subcontracted to the earl's followers, who managed the project for a hefty share of the profits.[16] It remains uncertain whether the Monmouth *castellum* expanded westward to include the lands of Troy, 1.6 kilometres south of Monmouth castle, as is whether anyone called Catchmay occupied them.

Certainly by the twelfth century, records of tithes from named settlements to the abbeys of Lyre and Cormeilles in Normandy show claims to the tithes of the district called *Inter Oscham et Waiam* (between the Usk and Wye). Both Lyre and Cormeilles claimed the tithes at Troy between 1067 and 1075.[17] These were most probably given to Lyre by Earl William FitzOsbern (d.1071) or his son, Earl Roger of Hereford, since they were patrons of Lyre, whereas later lords of the region had no connections with the abbey.[18] The claims at Troy indicate an early Norman presence in the northernmost part of Netherwent across the river Trothy from Monmouth in the later lordship of Tryleg (Trelech). When Earl William died in Flanders in 1071 he was succeeded by his son, Roger, who held the earldom until 1075, when he became involved in rebellion and was disgraced.[19] No new earl was appointed and the Norman advance in south Wales came to a temporary halt.

Eventually, a Breton called Gwethenoc from an estate near Dol was appointed; he had been born at a time when the noble families of that part of Brittany were engaged in a far-reaching monastic revival.[20] Gwethenoc founded a Benedictine priory in Monmouth with the help of William of Dol, who had become abbot of St Florent at Saumur in 1070.[21] William sent a prior and monks to inaugurate and serve the new priory and, in return, Monmouth Priory and its endowments were granted to St Florent; this arrangement continued until the fourteenth century.[22]

Grants to Saumur were made by Gwethenoc of several churches along the Trothy and Monnow rivers.[23] A copy of a mid-twelfth-century terrier of this abbey's possessions in Britain shows that it was claiming as old possessions the churches of Dixton and Troy.[24] David Williams identifies the church at Troy as St John of Troia (Troy) in the Llandaff diocese, and that no land was assigned in this church's location.[25] A church of

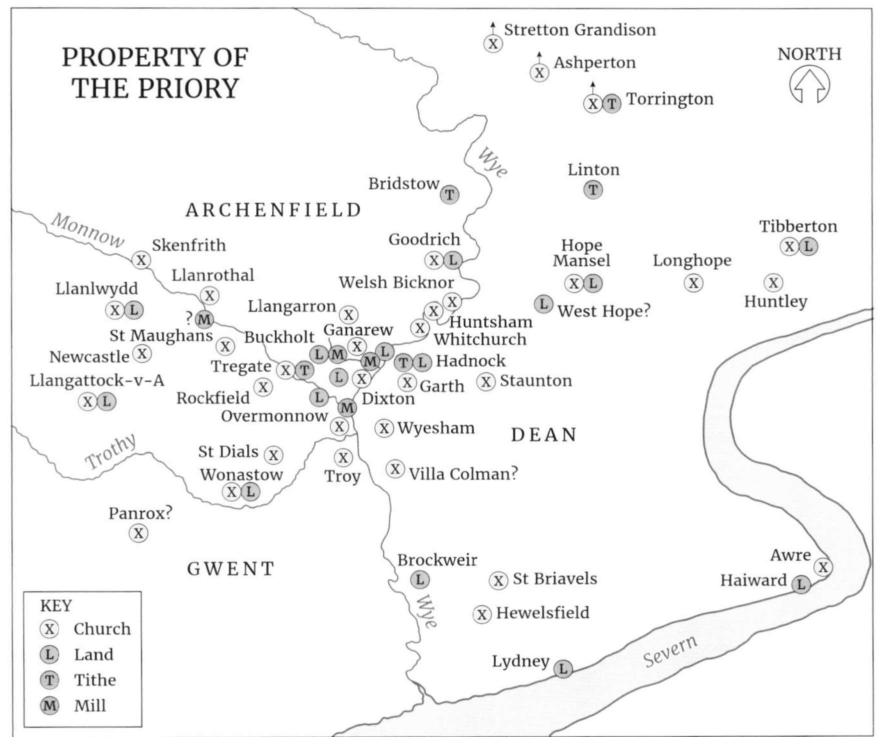

Figure 2.2 *The property of Monmouth Priory in the twelfth century.*

Copyright: University of Wales Press; map based on K. E. Kissack, Medieval Monmouth (Monmouth: The Monmouth Historical and Educational Trust, 1974), p. 20.

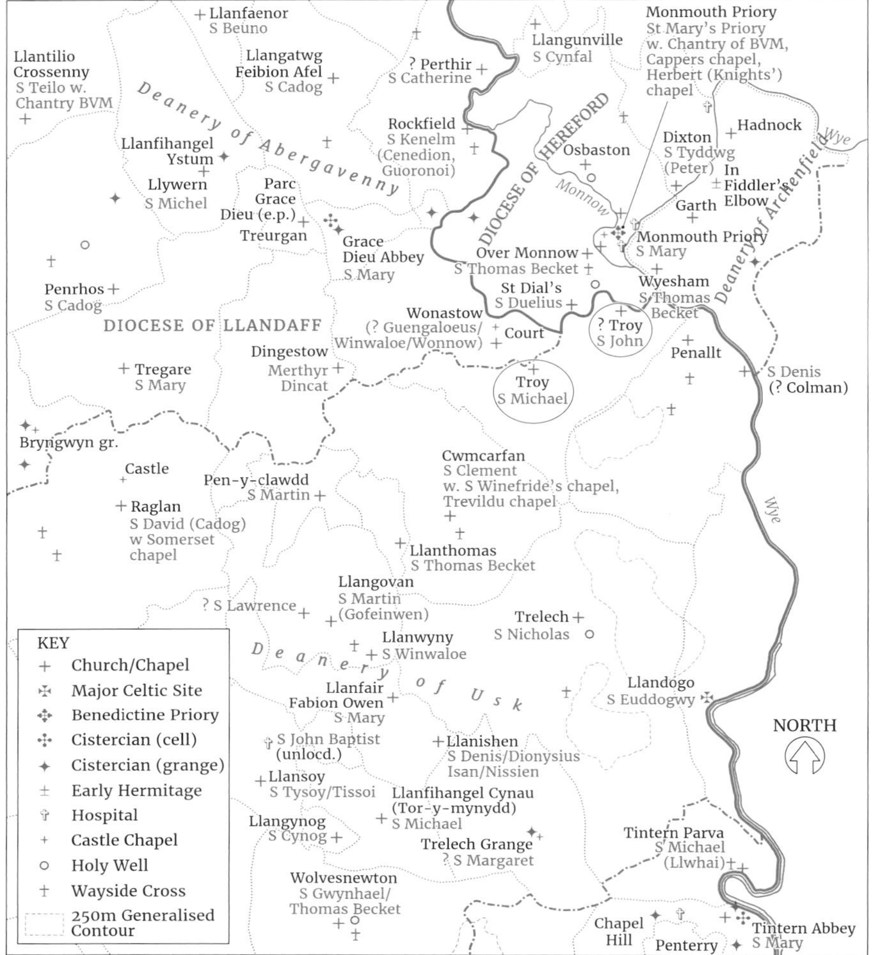

Figure 2.3 *The church in medieval Gwent: Troy St John and Troy St Michael.* Copyright: David Williams.

St Michael is also identified at Mitchel Troy, 1.6 kilometres from Troy (Figure 2.3). This is today's church of St Michael and all Angels. Arguably, this church could be one and the same as the church of St John of Troia, as parish boundaries change across time and records might have been confused. However, a church of Troie is listed in the Taxations of 1254 and the church of Troy cu' capell is in the list for 1291.[26] A 1404 reference to the church also appears in the *Register of Bishop Richard Clifford of Worcester*, where the Troy entry states, '1404: (Rector (Hugh Vaughan) of St John Baptist of Troy'. [27] No such church remains and one can only speculate that it might have been associated with a house and its service buildings at Troy. It is interesting to note that in 1904, some seven centuries later than the terrier of the St Florent abbey (*Abbaye Saint-Florent de Saumur*) listing the church of Troy as a possession, nuns from Saumur came to buy and settle at Troy House and its walled garden.

Adam of Usk mentions Philip Scudamore of Troy, who in 1411, along with others associated with Owain Glyndŵr (Glyndŵr rebellion 1400–10), was taken by the captain of Powis Castle to Shrewsbury, where he was hanged and his head set upon the bridge.[28] If Philip Scudamore really was 'of Troy' by 1411, and, as Bradney claims, in the late eleventh or early twelfth century Alexander Catchmay's only daughter and heir, Jane, married Sir Alan Scudamore, whose son Sir Titus Scudamore was styled Lord of Troy and Bigsweir, there appears to have been a break in the Scudamore occupation of the Troy Parva manor. This is because in 1314 Gilbert de Clare (d.1314), eighth Earl of Gloucester and seventh Earl of Hertford, had the manor and advowson of Troy amongst his possessions; at this time a manor denoted as 'Cwmcarvan with Troy' was also held by the Grey family.[29] Gilbert's possession of the manor of Troy concurs with Bradney's statement:

> In 1314, among the knights' fees in Wales belonging to Gilbert de Clare, earl of Gloucester and Hertford, is a moiety of a knight's fee in Little Troy, held by John Martel, of the annual value of 50s.,[30] and also the manor of Troy, of the annual value of 19l. 1s. 5¼d.[31]

The same Gilbert de Clare (1291–1314) was killed at the Battle of Bannockburn. He left no surviving issue and his death marked the end of the de Clare family.[32] His lands went into royal possession whilst the issue of inheritance was settled.[33] By 1317 his sisters, Eleanor, Margaret and Elizabeth, were all married to favourites of Edward II, respectively Hugh le Despenser, Hugh d'Audley the younger and John de Burgh (Elizabeth afterwards married Theobald de Vernon and, thirdly, Roger d'Amory).[34] The three were granted equal parts of the English possessions, but Despenser received the entire lordship of Glamorgan in Wales and used his relationship with the king to encroach on the lands of other Marcher lords.[35] Certainly, he held the lordship of Chepstow at his death in 1326, and in July 1322 he exchanged the castles of Swansea, Oystermouth and others with his sister-in-law, Elizabeth, for the castles and manors of Usk, Tregrug and Caerleon, and several manors, including that of Troy.[36] After his execution in 1326, the ownership of the manor of Troy goes 'cold' until the start of the fifteenth century.

Bradney states that Sir John Scudamore of Kentchurch, a descendant of Sir Titus Scudamore, son of Jane Catchmay and Sir Alan Scudamore, married the daughter of Owain Glyndŵr and was Lord of Troy Parva in 1425.[37] Whether the possession of the manor of Troy (Troy Parva) was with the Scudamore family in the eleventh and twelfth centuries, then passed to the de Clares and then back to the Scudamores so they held it again by at least 1425 can only be surmised. The name 'de Troy' can be found in Herefordshire records from the thirteenth century, which suggests that a landowning family had a house at Troy.[38] The most substantiated ownership of the manor of Troy during medieval times is to the de Clare family at the beginning of the fourteenth century and that before this the land lay within an area very close to Norman-controlled Monmouth. It is not unreasonable to assume that the manor contained a building or buildings for the lord in at least the early fourteenth century and that what we now know as the site of Troy House and its nearby farmhouse and stone barns may have been the location of that dwelling.

The people associated with Troy from the various historical records are all knighted and of importance at a national level. It is reasonable to suggest that they could have maintained a house and service buildings at Troy. Consequently, the possible survival of medieval features should be a consideration in any examination of Troy's buildings.

William ap Thomas: the foundation of the Herbert dynasty and its association with Troy

Guto'r Glyn (*c.*1412–*c.*1493) was a Welsh-language poet and soldier of the era of the *Beirdd yr Uchelwyr* (Poets of the Nobility) or *Cywyddwyr* (*cywydd*-men), the itinerant professional poets of the later Middle Ages. William ap Thomas (*c.*1380s–1445) became one of Guto'r Glyn's earliest and most prestigious patrons sometime in the late 1430s.[39] Only one poem written by Guto to William has survived; it refers to the courts that are owned by William, and these are Raglan Castle and properties at Abergavenny, Llantilio Crossenny, Tretower in the parish of Llanfihangel Cwm Du in the Usk valley, and Troy, near Monmouth.

> Your enclosure, see here the spotless buildings
> of your fair stone court of Raglan,
> and your whitewashed court in Gefenni
> is this one's daughter, Mary's strength be with you;
> the other is a court in Llantilio,
> Tretower, Troy furthermore.
> There I too received payment
> at your service, O Gwalchmai of Gwent;
> there I was greeted nine times over
> and the respect I enjoyed was better by far.[40]

Although William was merely the fifth son of a Welsh gentleman of only modest importance in north Gwent, he enjoyed a spectacularly successful career at local and national levels. This was largely due to his favourable marriages, as a result of which he had the means to hold many lands, including Troy. In 1406 William married Elizabeth Berkeley, the daughter of Sir John Bluet and widow of Sir James Berkeley.[41] As well as bringing the castle and manor of Raglan to her marriage with William, Elizabeth Berkeley possessed family ties to the influential Beauchamps.[42] When Elizabeth died in 1420, William continued to live in the castle as a tenant of his stepson, James Berkeley. In 1425 there was an agreement that William could hold Raglan for his lifetime. However, in 1432 William purchased the manor of Raglan and its castle outright from James Berkeley for 1,0000 marks.[43] The accumulation of land was one of the mainstays of local power and prestige in the later Middle Ages. The acquisition of the manor and lordship of Raglan was perhaps the most important step by William in laying the foundations of his family dynasty.

William married again, to another widow, Gwladus Gam, daughter of Sir Dafydd Gam of Brecon. Gwladus Gam also strengthened William's connection with the royal court, as Sir Dafydd Gam had served both Henry IV and Henry V in France.[44] Indeed, William, Gwladus Gam's first husband, Sir Roger Vaughan of Bredwardine, Herefordshire, and her father had all been part of the Welsh contingent that fought with Henry V in France, including the Battle of Agincourt.[45] In 1426 William was knighted by Henry VI, becoming known to his compatriots as *Y marchog glas o Went* ('the blue knight of Gwent') because of the colour of his armour.[46]

William is a supreme example of how leaders of regional Welsh society came to acquire wealth and occupy key positions in the governance of mid-fifteenth-century Wales.[47] He assembled substantial lands in south-east Wales during the period 1422–45: these extended from Coety in Glamorgan to Skenfrith on the border with Herefordshire, and he also received a share in lands across England.[48] How he came into the ownership of Troy is not known, as is the case for many of his other lands. It may have been at the time he bought the manor of Raglan; Troy is just eight kilometres from this manor's castle.

As well as running his own estates, William worked as an administrator of other people's lands in his locality. The Marcher lords delegated the job of running their lordships to trustworthy local men like William ap Thomas as they only occasionally visited south Wales. Richard, Duke of York, was Lord of Usk, the lordship in which Raglan itself was situated, and held many other lordships that he had inherited from the Mortimer family. William rose in the Duke's service, becoming first deputy steward of the lordship of Usk, then its chief steward as well as a member of Richard's council by 1440.[49] William was also placed in an influential position due to his first wife being related to the powerful Beauchamp family, who owned the lordship of Glamorgan and that of Abergavenny, where William was a landholder. William was among the influential men chosen to take care of the interests of the under-age heir, Henry Beauchamp, and in particular, to protect Abergavenny until Henry came of age.[50]

By virtue of his title as Duke of Lancaster, the king of England held the lands of the duchy of Lancaster in Wales. In south-east Wales these included: the lordships of Caldicot and Magor, near Chepstow; Ebboth, a manor in the lordship of Newport; and the lordships of Monmouth and the Three Castles (Grosmont, Skenfrith and White Castle). William was appointed steward of Ebboth in 1431, steward of Caldicot for life in 1437, deputy steward of Monmouth by 1441, and possibly full steward of that lordship by 1443.[51] Again, one might speculate that it was whilst serving as steward of Monmouth that he came to hold Troy, just 1.6 kilometres from its castle. He held a number of other offices for the duchy of Lancaster.[52] He also served in the royal shires in south-west Wales, far from his own region and was appointed to several royal commissions between 1420 and 1442.[53]

One couplet in Guto'r Glyn's poem in praise of William ap Thomas arguably substantiates the claim that William is responsible for the building of the great stone tower at Raglan Castle: 'the court is high, high above the others, and your tower higher than other buildings'.[54] William ap Thomas's additions to Raglan Castle demonstrate his willingness to follow contemporary fashion and use buildings as symbols of power. Guto'r Glyn writes that he was greeted and received payment not just at Raglan, but also at other courts owned by William, including Troy. It is reasonable to assume that William made use of his court at Troy when he was fulfilling his duties as steward of Monmouth from 1441. Given William's various positions and influence he certainly had the financial capacity to alter or add to any pre-existing buildings at Troy, although such activity is unproven.

According to Bradney, 'William held Troy with his concubine Cary Ddu (Caroline the Black) who is called "heiress" of Troy'.[55] His illegitimate son, Thomas, is also claimed to have resided at Troy after serving in the French wars under Richard, Duke of York, and Humphrey, Duke of Gloucester.[56] Whether Thomas was William's son by Cary Ddu is unknown: unfortunately, Bradney does not supply references to

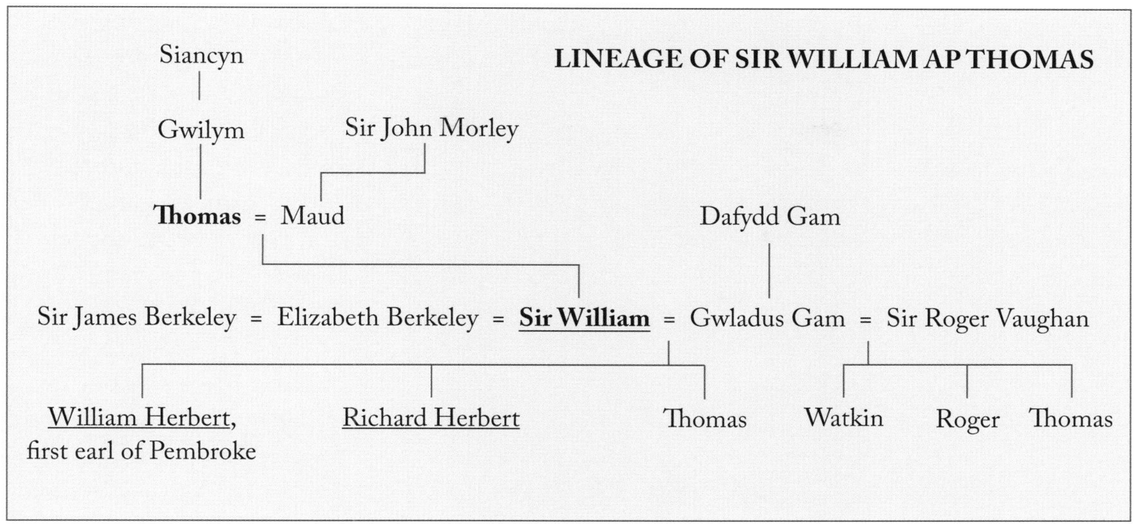

Figure 2.4 *Lineage of Sir William ap Thomas. This genealogical table is based on WG1 'Godwin' 5. Those named in Guto's poem for Sir William ap Thomas are shown in bold print, and the names of his patrons are underlined.*[61]

substantiate or to explore these claims. William held Raglan as his main residence and it is unlikely that he spent significant amounts of time at his court in Troy, but he did pass it on to his oldest legitimate son and heir, also called William (1423–69), by Gwladus, his second wife. His illegitimate son, Thomas, whom Bradney claims occupied Troy, predeceased his half-brother without issue. Another poet of the nobility, Hywel Dafi, allocates the same ownership of courts in his poem of supplication to William, William ap Thomas's son and heir, as did Guto'r Glyn to his father before him.[57]

Like other Welshmen, William ap Thomas had no surname, the ap, or mab, as it should have been, merely denoting that he was William, son of Thomas. However, Edward IV wished William, legitimate son and heir of William ap Thomas, to adopt a surname after the English fashion and a commission was appointed by Edward IV to ascertain the lineage of Herbert.[58] The ensuing report was translated into no less than three languages, Welsh, Latin and French.[59] Why the name Herbert was chosen has not been satisfactorily explained but certainly in an age when noble lineage conferred prestige and status, William would have wished to cultivate a belief that he was descended from the Fitz-Herberts of the eleventh and twelfth centuries. Having an English name would also help to distance himself from the aftermath of the Glyndŵr rebellion.[60]

Figure 2.5 *The alabaster tomb of Sir William ap Thomas (d.1445) and his second wife, Gwladus (d.1454), the Benedictine priory church of St Mary, Abergavenny.*

Sir William ap Thomas died in London in 1445.[62] His body was brought back to Wales. William left numerous children, both legitimate and illegitimate, but, significantly, it was to his legitimate son and heir, William Herbert, who was to become first Earl of Pembroke by the second creation, that Troy then passed.

The Herbert dynasty: power, politics and royal connections

Property at Troy was owned and occupied by various members of the Herbert family from at least 1445 until 1600. The changing political situation in Wales during that period is paramount for understanding the importance of the Herberts and, by association, the status of the Troy estate.

Sir William Herbert (1423–69), first Earl of Pembroke of the second creation, and Thomas Herbert of 'Little Troye'

William Herbert (*c.*1423–69), son and heir of William ap Thomas, was possibly the most influential Welshman of his generation for giving Wales an important role in the turbulent politics of the mid-fifteenth century.[63] He came to hold a position of great power in Wales during the opening years of the reign of Edward IV. Indeed, William's support for the House of York led the poet Lewys Glyn Cothi to hail him as 'King Edward IV's master-lock' in Wales.[64] Throughout his lifetime, Raglan Castle served as his family seat and administrative centre.

William Herbert married Anne, daughter of Sir Walter Devereux, in 1449. By this marriage into the Devereux family Herbert widened his circle of influential connections and secured a substantial dowry. During the 1450s William consolidated his estates and established his trade connections with France and the Low Countries; he owned several ships bringing wine from Gascony to the port of Bristol and across the Severn Channel to the port of Chepstow. Indeed, William is referred to as Herbert 'Chapman', where Chapman is an English occupational surname for a merchant in medieval Britain.[65] William and his illegitimate son, also William (later known as Sir William Herbert of Troy), made a fortune through the very profitable wine trade via Bordeaux, Portugal and Spain, in the success of which the older William's possession of Chepstow Castle with its own landing stage was a key component. William's trading activities certainly brought him wealth, but it was his skills as a soldier and an administrator that led him to attain considerable power throughout Wales.

He secured advancement by serving Richard, Duke of York, Gloucester, the Beauchamps and the Crown in the Marches. In the early years of his service to York he served in France and was there in the last years of English occupation. He was captured and held for ransom at the battle of Formigny in April 1450.[66] The ransom indicates that he was regarded as an important figure by his captors and likely to elicit support from wealthy compatriots; presumably the ransom was paid, but by whom is unknown. At this time Wales was administered by royal office holders, who held office as sheriffs, served as stewards of royal lordships or as constables of royal castles, and by lords who owned lordships or held leases of royal lordships.[67] William became steward of York's lordships of Usk and Caerleon in 1450 and by 1455 he was the Earl of Warwick's sheriff of Glamorgan.[68] With other esquires, including Henry VI's half-brothers, Edmund and Jasper Tudor, he was knighted at Christmas 1452.

The grant of a knighthood by the Lancastrian court was at least partly to gain the allegiance of the Herbert family and their connections in south Wales. William was dominant at Raglan; Richard, Earl of Warwick, was Lord of Glamorgan; the Mortimer estates of the Duke of York lay to the north. All were powerful, potential enemies of the Court in the troubled times leading to civil war. The granting of a knighthood to William was probably an inducement not to attach himself to his powerful neighbours and to remain loyal to the government of Henry VI. Evidence suggests the opposite and that his association with the Duke of York continued.[69] He was involved in several disturbances throughout the 1450s. In 1452 he supported York in his clash with the Duke of Somerset; in 1456 he seized control of the city of Hereford as retribution for the killing of his kinsman, Walter Vaughan.

Together with Sir Walter Devereux he raised a force from York's lands to take back Carmarthen Castle from Edmund Tudor, Earl of Richmond; they also seized Aberystwyth Castle, after which they removed the royal seal for south Wales and gave themselves power to hold a judicial session. They were eventually brought before a great council in Coventry and William was committed to the Tower of London, but he secured bail and escaped back to south Wales. A reward of 500 marks was offered for his recapture, and the serious view which the government took of these events is emphasized by the queen herself intervening to reconcile with William to ensure his loyalty.[70] The government was prepared to overlook his disturbances in order to secure the neutrality of potential enemies in Wales.

The fact that William remained well-behaved under the Lancastrian government for the next three years is a reflection of local considerations and the politics of the time. He was primarily concerned with affairs in the locality where he held lands and offices and which he dominated socially and politically. Extant ministers' accounts and a rental of his lands for 1458–9 show that he was paying great attention to the details of estate administration.[71] Overt action against the government might well have jeopardized his local position. By maintaining a passive loyalty to the government of Henry VI during the last years of its turbulent existence, he secured his personal and local interests. On the collapse of the Lancastrian dynasty in 1461, William became the most important Welshman to attach himself to Edward, Earl of March, son of Richard, Duke of York. William played a leading role in the defeat of the Lancastrian forces at the battle of Mortimer's Cross in Herefordshire (1461). Within a month Edward ascended the throne and William became Chief Justice and Chamberlain of south Wales. Before the end of the same year the new King Edward created William, Baron Herbert of Raglan.

Eventually, William's influence extended to north Wales, when he became responsible for military operations against the Lancastrians in Wales as a whole. In 1461 William captured Pembroke Castle, which Jasper Tudor, Earl of Pembroke, had made the centre of Lancastrian resistance to Edward IV's rule in south Wales. After capturing the castle, William took custody of the 4-year-old Henry Tudor; formal custody of the young heir was granted to William in 1462. Henry was taken to Raglan Castle, where he spent the next seven years in the care of William and his wife, Anne Devereux. Such was the care given to Henry, he retained affection and provided protection for Anne throughout her life.[72] A new Marcher lordship of Raglan was created in 1465; it was independent of the lordship of Usk and the only new lordship to be created after 1285, further demonstrating William's importance to the king. In 1468 William captured Harlech Castle, the last Lancastrian stronghold in Wales and England; his reward was to be created Earl of Pembroke, an honour that made him the first member of the Welsh gentry to enter the ranks of the English peerage.

Political success and the rewards that came in its wake enabled William (now known as the first Earl of Pembroke) to continue his father's work at Raglan with substantial aggrandizement of its buildings and landscape; this building activity continued until his death in 1469.[73] He turned the castle into a palace in terms of appearance and comfort but retained its existing defences; Raglan Castle became the administrative centre of William's activities and it needed to reflect his status and wealth. There is no evidence to show that he lived at or remodelled any of the property at Troy, which he had inherited from his father, William ap Thomas. Indeed, he preferred to reside at Raglan and spent little time even at the royal court.[74] It was William ap Thomas's illegitimate son, Thomas, Earl William Herbert's half-brother, who resided at Troy. He had also taken the surname Herbert, and was called 'Thomas Herbert the elder of Little Troye'.[75] Thomas Herbert the younger, presumably the elder's son, as Earl William had no son, either legitimate or illegitimate, called Thomas, is referred to as a 'gentleman' and also of 'Little Troye'.[76]

There are references to several Thomas Herberts in contemporary records, making identification problematic.[77] However, both Thomas Herbert the elder and Thomas Herbert the younger of Little Troye[78] are clearly recorded as being implicated with Earl William in the disturbances of 1457.[79] Both are also listed alongside William for being pardoned 'of all tresons, felonies, extortions, negligences, trespasses and offences and any consequent outlawries or forfeitures' by the Lancastrian king on 26 June 1460.[80] Consequently, it is reasonable to assume that they were amongst the most important members of William's affinity during the disturbances.[81]

Ties of blood, bonds of kinship and local loyalties were fundamental to Welsh society throughout the medieval period. The events of the fifteenth century in Wales unfolded alongside a strong tradition of local and family loyalties. Earl William garnered that tradition as a buttress to his authority in Wales. He was most ably supported by his brother, Richard Herbert of Coldbrook, and half-brother, Thomas Herbert, who, from the several references contained within the *Herbertorum Prosapia* and other records, is Thomas Herbert the elder of Little Troye.[82]

Thomas Herbert, often in association with his half-brother, Earl William, was given many duties to perform during the first year of the reign of Edward IV. He was given numerous commissions to take into the king's hands the possessions of deceased and rebel persons, including those of Jasper Tudor, Sir William Mulle and James, Earl of Wiltshire; Thomas Herbert was subsequently granted certain of the lands of Sir William Mulle.[83] During the period 1461–9 Thomas became progressively of more use to Earl William and the king. On 23 June 1461 a grant for life was made to Thomas Herbert the elder of the office of constable of the king's castle of Gloucester with a meadow near it called 'kyngesmedewe', with the accustomed fees. One month later he was appointed as one of the esquires of the body, for which he received fifty marks a year from the fee farm of Gloucester town.[84] On 7 November 1461 Thomas was appointed sheriff of Somerset and Dorset[85] and in March 1462 he served with William on the commission to take ships in Bristol to resist the king's enemies.[86] Commissions to enquire into treasons, insurrections and rebellions in south Wales and commissions of the peace in Gloucestershire were held respectively in 1461 and 1464.[87]

Edward IV's foreign policy included discomfiting Louis XI of France. To that end, in September 1462, Thomas was commissioned along with Peter Taster, the Dean of St Severins, and Dr Thomas Kent, a clerk of the council, to go to Spain to treat with Henry the Impotent and his brother-in-law, the King of Spain. The intention was to renew the alliance that had existed between England and Castile and prevent Louis from making alliances south of the Pyrenees. Thomas appears to have had the senior role as he received £124, as opposed to the £112 given to his fellow ambassadors, on top of their twenty shillings a day wages.[88] They stayed for six months: at first they seemed to make progress towards Henry signing an alliance but the commission failed to negotiate a treaty. They returned to the Port of London, bringing with them seventy-six tuns of wine for the king, whilst Thomas had eighteen tuns on his own account.[89] It may be that the closeness with the king that Thomas enjoyed as an esquire of the body played a part in his pardon in 1465 for unsatisfactory discharge of his duties as constable of Gloucester Castle.

Between 1467 and 1469 Thomas continued to hold several commissions, often with his half-brother, Earl William. He was rewarded with substantial grants of land for his services to the House of York. These included lands in Middlesex, Gloucestershire, Herefordshire and the Marches of Wales. With these lands went all woods, mills, fisheries, knights' fees, wards, marriages, reliefs, escheats, courts, views of frankpledge and other appurtenances; he held these lands by fealty only.[90] Several manors were granted to Thomas, many being the forfeited lands of Thomas Cornewaile and Jasper Tudor. With these lands went all franchises, liberties, courts, jurisdictions, leets, views of frankpledge, hundreds, fairs, markets, parks, stews, knights' fees, services, rents, fee farms and advowsons; Thomas was to receive all issues from the first day of the reign.[91] He was also appointed to the office of Chancellor of the Earldom of March in August 1467 and fulfilled the role of collector of customs at the Port of Bristol whilst engaging in trading activities on his own account.[92] Overall, it may be said that due to his support of his half-brother, Earl William, and the House of York, his intimacy with the king as an esquire of the body, and his trading activities, Thomas Herbert the elder of 'Little Troye' had considerable wealth and significant influence.

Earl William had but one year to enjoy this earldom. When Richard Neville, Earl of Warwick ('the Kingmaker') turned against Edward IV, he also became William's enemy. William led an army largely composed of Welshmen against Warwick and the Lancastrians at the battle of Edgecote in July 1469. The Yorkists were defeated and Warwick had William executed the day after the battle. Two of William's brothers, who were considered capable of taking on his political role, were also removed by Warwick; these were Sir Richard Herbert of Coldbrook and Thomas Herbert the elder of 'Little Troye'. Sir Richard was executed alongside William at Northampton and Thomas was put to death at Bristol on Warwick's orders.[93] The fact that Thomas was so removed indicates he was considered to be a man of substance, capable of offering a threat to Warwick and the Lancastrians, at least at a local level.

With Troy as Thomas's main residence, it is reasonable to assume that it would have been a residence of some status for such a person. One can only speculate that Earl William visited and was entertained by Thomas the elder and Thomas the younger at Troy – or that he influenced and finally supported any remodelling of buildings and landscape there. It is inconceivable that Thomas the elder would not have witnessed the aggrandizement of Raglan Castle wrought by William. Perhaps he was influenced by what he saw there and made his own changes to Troy. Certainly, at this time, Troy would have been at least a residence worthy of being occupied by the influential Herbert family.

The rise of the illegitimate line: William Herbert, second Earl of Pembroke (*c.*1451–91); Sir William (*c.*1442–1524) and Sir Charles (*c.*1500–57) Herbert of Troy

Mary Woodville (*c.*1456–81) was a sister of Edward IV's Queen Consort, Elizabeth Woodville. After Edward IV's public recognition of Elizabeth Woodville as his wife, the new queen sought to raise her family's standing by arranging a series of advantageous marriages for her five brothers and seven unwed sisters. In September 1466, Mary was betrothed to William Herbert, the eldest legitimate son and heir of William, first Earl of Pembroke. Mary and William were married on January 1467 at St George's Chapel, Windsor Castle, amid profuse splendour; the bride was about 10 or 11 years old and William was 15. Nothing seems to have aggravated Warwick more than this marriage of the queen's sister to William; it may have influenced, in part, Warwick's decision to execute William's father, the first earl, just a day after the battle of Edgecote.

From this execution in 1469 to the end of the reign of Edward IV in 1483 there was a striking decay in the fortunes of the Herberts; this went hand-in-hand with their usefulness to the Yorkist command. It was inevitable: Earl William's death was both a personal and professional loss to Edward IV and he could find no one with the skills and personality to replace him and control Wales for the Crown. There is controversy about the age of the first Earl of Pembroke's son and heir at the time of his father's death in 1469; he is variously assigned an age of 9, 14 and 15.[94] Certainly, he was too young to take on his father's role in Wales for the Yorkist cause. In 1469 Edward IV made a grant to Anne, Countess of Pembroke, Earl William's widow, of all the possessions held by the late earl, except those of Sir James Luttrell, during the minority of her son. Edward IV also appointed his brother, Richard Duke of Gloucester, as Chief Justice and Chamberlain of south Wales and as steward of all possessions in Cardigan and Carmarthen. Power was slipping away from the Herberts.

When Edward was forced to flee his kingdom in September 1470 as a result of Warwick's conspiracies with the Lancastrians, the Herberts were dealt another blow. Henry VI was re-crowned and Jasper Tudor was given the keeping of all the castles, lordships, commotes, manors, lands and other possessions which the late earl had held.[95] Edward IV landed at Ravenspur on 14 March 1471 and defeated Warwick at the battle of Barnet. With the death of Warwick and success at Tewkesbury and London, Edward retook the throne. William, second Earl of Pembroke was assigned several commissions. Together with Lord Ferrers he was tasked with capturing Jasper Tudor. They failed to do so. Jasper Tudor took Henry Tudor from Raglan Castle, where he had been in the guardianship of the first earl and his wife, and escaped with him to France. Nevertheless, with the removal of Jasper Tudor from Welsh lands, the second Earl of Pembroke was able to take on more offices in Wales and the Marches.

However, as time passed, it appeared that the second earl was ineffectual and did not possess the qualities required to consolidate his father's achievements and keep order.[96] In the winter of 1473–4 there were disturbances in Wales, suggesting that at least some members of the Herbert family, including the second earl's younger brother, Walter, and older half-brother, William, were resentful of not being as influential or under the same protection as they had been during the time of the first earl. A commission was raised to summon, amongst others, William Herbert, clerk (most likely the second earl's half-brother), John Herbert, bastard, two sons of Roger Vaughan of Tretower, and Thomas Herbert, bastard, for divers offences. This is most likely Thomas Herbert the younger of Troy.[97] Another disturbance broke out in 1478, in which the Herberts were again implicated in unlawfully fortifying and victualling Pembroke Castle. Those accused failed to obey when summoned before the council and, taking advantage of his marriage to the queen's sister, the second earl obtained the queen's pardon for his relation's offences.[98]

In 1479 the second earl was replaced as Chief Justice and Chamberlain of south Wales and on 4 July of that year, Edward IV secured the surrender of the earldom of Pembroke by William in exchange for the earldom of Huntingdon. The king conferred the earldom of Pembroke on the Prince of Wales. The king's concern was probably to strengthen the position of the prince and his council in promoting law and order. Arguably, the transfer also reflects Edward IV's low opinion of the second William Herbert's skills and strength of personality. William was the least wealthy of the earls of his time. Mary's death in 1481 also considerably weakened her husband's links with the associates of the Prince of Wales.

It was unfortunate for both the House of Herbert and that of York that Sir Walter Herbert was the second and not the first son of the first Earl of Pembroke: his father's energy and ability appear to have been inherited by Sir Walter rather than his elder brother, the Earl of Huntingdon. Had Sir Walter been vested with the weight of office and the dignities of his elder brother, it is likely that the fortunes of the Herbert family would not have declined so rapidly in the second decade of Edward IV's reign.[99] Described in the *Herbertorum Prosapia* as 'a gentleman of a noble family, and great power in Wales' and by Polydore Vergil as 'a man of ancyent authorytie emong the Welshe men', he was viewed by Henry Tudor during the early 1480s as having such influence that marriage between Henry and one of Walter's sisters would be favourable to the Tudor cause.[100] Nothing came of this plan but it exemplifies the view that Sir Walter had more authority than his official positions might otherwise have indicated.

The decline of the Herbert's influence was reversed early in Richard III's reign after the rebellion and execution of Henry Stafford, Duke of Buckingham at the end of 1483. After the rebellion, William succeeded Buckingham as Chief Justice of the Principality in south Wales and was granted an annuity of 400 marks in recognition of his impending marriage to the king's illegitimate daughter, Katherine Plantagenet.[101] This almost doubled his income. It seems that Richard III did not have as low an opinion as his brother of William. He appears to have remained loyal to Richard III. When Henry Tudor landed in south Wales in 1485 William's and Walter's position forced Henry to take a roundabout route into England.[102] However, neither William nor Walter fought at Bosworth.[103] With the accession of Henry Tudor, the Herbert family ceased to be supporters of the House of York: they bent to prevailing forces to secure their own position. As leading members of the Herbert family adapted to the change of sovereignty, so their relations followed suit. Not unexpectedly, Wales became one of the most loyal parts of the kingdom, largely due to the Tudors' Welsh descent and their rewards to Welshmen. Walter and Henry Tudor had grown up together at Raglan Castle, Walter being the first earl's second son and Henry his ward; Walter was just five years older than Henry. Within a year of the battle of Bosworth, Walter had renewed his friendship with Henry, and several offices and stewardships were awarded to him.

By this time, William, the first Earl of Pembroke's eldest illegitimate son by his mistress, Frond Verch Hoesgyn, was established in his own right as a very influential figure in south Wales. In his will, the first earl left William, variously referred to as 'William Herbert, clerk', 'William Herbert of Pembroke' and 'William Herbert, esquire', a tenement and lands worth ten pounds a year in Penrhos and Clytha; he also directed that this son was to be a priest and was to be granted certain churches.[104] By 1481, the Earl of Huntingdon granted lands at Tal-y-fan worth nearly ten pounds a year to William Herbert and his heirs.[105] Furthermore, in the 1480s the earl granted William 'lately of Pembroke in County Pembroke, esquire', lands in Troy, Wonastow 'Wilston' and St Maughans in Wales, late of Thomas Herbert, William's cousin.[106] This Thomas was Thomas Herbert the younger of Troy, who died without issue. From this time William is known as William Herbert of Troy.[107] He was also granted all the lands that a number of feoffees had held in Abergavenny lordship. In 1490, Sir Walter Herbert, brother of the Earl of Huntingdon, released his rights in the lands of his uncle to William Herbert of Troy, to whom he also refers as his brother.[108]

In short, William, first Earl of Pembroke, had an illegitimate son also called William, who lived at Pembroke before coming to Troy just before 1483.[109] His association with Pembroke began when his father took possession of Pembroke Castle from Jasper Tudor in September 1461. An account for the year ended Michaelmas 1462 describes him as William Herbert esquire, treasurer and steward of Pembroke, which by implication makes him either close to or probably of full age at this time.[110] Although he lost these offices at Pembroke Castle on the death of his father in 1469, he appears to have had a continuing association with Pembroke in the 1470s,[111] and even in 1509 he is confirmed by a grant recorded in the Pardon Rolls as of both places, Pembroke and Troy.[112] When Thomas Herbert the younger of Troy died without issue, the occupation of Troy appears to have passed to William. The first earl's legitimate son, William, Earl of Huntingdon from 1479, occupied Raglan Castle as the main family seat until his death and appears to have relied on his half-brother, William Herbert of Troy, for much of the routine administration of his lands in south Wales and, in particular, the lordship of Monmouth.[113]

Certainly, it was William of Troy who, as William Herbert, esquire, monopolized the most important offices of the earl's western estates in the 1470s and, with his half-brother, Sir Walter Herbert, got into trouble with the government in 1478 and again on several occasions throughout the rest of the century.[114] The troubles were mostly related to exercising authority as stewards of the lordships oppressively and by imposing a collective levy.[115] Richard III granted William the manor of Tockington near Thornbury in 1484 for his service against rebels,[116] and, when William became squire of the king's body, also granted him an annuity of fifty marks to be paid from the lordship of Monmouth.[117] Richard III also appointed him for life as master forester of Wyeswood, Trelech and Penalt,[118] an office subsequently granted to him by Henry VII in October 1495.[119] The earliest evidence of William's tenure of offices in the lordships of Usk, Caerleon and Trelech is from 1502, when he is shown as receiver and accounting for an annual rent of £7 12s. 0d as farmer of the demesne lands of the lordship of Troy.[120] As receiver in 1514–15, he accounted for the same amount of rent and two shillings of new increase for the demesne lands of Troy, and on 16 November 1519, he was granted a twenty-one-year lease of the demesne lands of 'Magna Troy' (Mitchel Troy) at the same amount of rent.[121]

William also had an active and long career in the administration of the duchy of Lancaster: he was steward of Ebboth in 1492, leased the Grosmont demesne and acted as receiver there in 1499, and in 1503 became the receiver of a number of duchy properties in Gloucestershire and Herefordshire. He became an under-steward at Monmouth and in

1509 was appointed as its master-sergeant.[122] William was commissioned on two occasions during the reign of Henry VII, once as justice for some March estates, and acted several times as surety for his neighbours.[123] He served as sheriff of Herefordshire in 1515–16, in which year he was knighted, and thereafter is referred to as Sir William Herbert of Troy.[124] He retained the receivership of Monmouth until his death in 1524.[125] A deed of 1520 provides the earliest evidence of William's tenure of stewardship of Raglan, which he apparently held by successive grants of his half-brother, William, Earl of Huntingdon, Sir Walter Herbert and the latter's widow, Lady Anne Stafford and her second husband, who held Raglan and other lands by jointure.[126] Herbert continued to serve as steward of Raglan after 1520.[127]

When William, Earl of Huntingdon, died prematurely in 1491, his only child, Elizabeth Herbert, was about 15 years old and unmarried. Her claim to inherit her father's lands was disputed by Sir Walter Herbert. The dispute was the subject of an arbitration award made before September 1491, which assigned some of the late earl's lands to Sir Walter.[128] He entered into the castle and lordship of Raglan and received the issues thereof from 1491 until his death in 1507, but not his title. Strangely, the earldom did not pass to Sir Walter, the earl's younger brother.[129] As a feoffee of his half-brother, the Earl of Huntingdon, Sir William Herbert of Troy was closely involved in the temporary partitioning of the Herbert estates between Sir Walter Herbert and Elizabeth in the years 1500–8.[130] The king was also directly concerned with the settlement of the Herbert lands and with Elizabeth's marriage, which occurred on 6 June 1492.[131] Her husband was Sir Charles Somerset, the illegitimate son of Henry Beaufort, third Duke of Somerset, and a second cousin to the king. He was one of the supporters of Henry Tudor and was knighted after landing in Milford Haven in 1485; he retained the king's favour throughout the reign. By approving Elizabeth Herbert's marriage to Charles Somerset, Henry VII ensured that a large part of the Herbert inheritance came into the possession of one of his closest supporters, who was thereby provided with a substantial landed estate.[132] Elizabeth Herbert's marriage to Somerset was to prove of major significance for Gwent, as his descendants, successively earls of Worcester and dukes of Beaufort, occupied a prominent role at local and national levels for four centuries, during which period Troy remained in their ownership.

Sir William Herbert of Troy appears to have been regarded as more like his father, the first Duke of Pembroke, in his abilities and personality than his half-brother, the Earl of Huntingdon.[133] A praise poem to Sir William Herbert of Pembroke and Troy by Guto'r Glyn starts by describing William's role at Pembroke, where he lived before coming to Troy.[134] His activity in continuing to administer the victuals of Pembroke Castle after he had moved to Troy is included. The poem emphasizes William's appearance being like that of his father, and his following in the footsteps of his famous father with military activity, by exerting extensive authority, and, at the poem's end, giving faithful service to his brother, the second earl.

> There is a name up above in blessed Pembroke,
> another William, a second Morien,
> Master William who dispenses osey wine
> to the party of the Herbert earls over there.
> A lord over fortresses is this man,
> following in the father's footsteps where Tewdwr once trod [. . .][135]

William was married twice, first to Margery, before he lived at Troy, and secondly to a widow, Blanche Whitney (née Milbourne), who was born sometime after 1500; Blanche was one of the eleven co-heiresses of Simon Milbourne and Jane (Baskerville) of Burghill, Herefordshire).[136] Both of William's wives are mentioned in his will: he directs that he should be buried on the south side of the new chapel that he has lately built in the parish church of Monmouth in a tomb of marble with images of both of his wives and an epitaph.[137] The building of the chapel and the tomb reflect William's wealth and prominent position, and his capacity to build. His will, dated 15 March 1523 and proved on 13 April 1524 in St Paul's Cathedral in London, also states that his wife Blanche 'shall have the tenement which lately I bilded in Chapstowe [Chepstow]'.[138] It seems reasonable to assume that he would also have been willing to build at Troy to ensure his residence was appropriate for his status.

In August 1502, William's influence in Gwent was acknowledged when Henry VII and Elizabeth, Queen Consort, stayed at his house at Troy during the course of their journey to visit William's half-brother, Sir Walter Herbert, at Raglan Castle.[139] The king even held a meeting of his council at Troy on 15 August.[140] Undoubtedly, William Herbert would have ensured that Troy was a fitting residence to accommodate the king and queen. An inventory of Troy House made in 1557 still recalls this royal visit, with rooms described as the king's little and great chambers, the king's inner chamber, and the queen's little and great chambers.[141] The queen appears to have travelled to Troy separately from the king, with a man being paid three shillings and fourpence to guide her from 'Flexley Abbey [in the Forest of Dean, Gloucestershire] to Troye besides

Monmouth'.[142] She arrived at Troy on 14 August and only continued to Raglan on 19 August.[143] It appears that both king and queen were together at Troy on 15 August when the council meeting took place and, given the names of the chambers in the inventory, they both stayed at Troy. The queen was about five months pregnant at this time and might well have welcomed her rest at Troy before moving to Raglan Castle, some eight kilometres distant, and all the hospitality offered by Sir Walter.

It is unclear whether William was still married to his first wife, Margery, or his second, Blanche, at this time, although Blanche's funeral elegy, composed by the bard Lewys Morgannwg, includes a reference to Henry VII being welcomed at Troy. The elegy also pays tribute to Blanche's royal duties. William predeceased her in 1524 and by the 1530s Lady Herbert of Troy, as she was then known, was in the Royal Household. She held the position of Lady Mistress in charge of the upbringing of the future Edward VI, Mary I and Elizabeth I when she lived with the young Tudor children. She died in 1557, just a few months before Charles, her son and heir by William. Her funeral elegy includes the lines:

> (She was a) Lady (in charge) of Queens,
> A governess she was in her youth.
> She knew in a fitting manner
> The accomplishments of the ladies of the court,
> (And she was the) guardian, before she passed away,
> Of Henry VIII's household and his children yonder.
> To King Edward she was a true
> (And) wise lady of dignity,
> In charge of his fosterage (she was pre-eminent),
> (And) she waited upon his Grace.
> (She, whom) they buried, the Lady of the palace of Troy,
> And her lion (i.e. William), gave hospitality to the old Earls.
> A welcome was given to the King, Henry VII,
> And his Earls; he was great once.
> She gave service all her life,
> To the one who is Queen today [Mary I].[144]

Blanche was responsible for the education of the three royal children until they were 3 years old.[145] She continued as Elizabeth's Lady Mistress for a further ten years, when she appears to have retired. The 1551–2 Household Accounts of the Princess Elizabeth include an item of seventy shillings being 'sent', rather than paid, to Lady Troy, and being especially delivered by the Knight's Marshall's servant, who was paid for this task; the amount appears to be half of what Lady Troy received when Lady Mistress.[146] This sum and its delivery throughout Lady Troy's retirement is indicative of her enduring importance to the princess. On retirement Blanche returned to Troy, where she lived in part of the house whilst Charles, her oldest son by William, occupied the remainder with his second wife, Cicill. This was consistent with the directions in William's will: Blanche inherited William's 'Capitall mese with the appurtenaunc[es] called litill Troy', the manor of nearby Wonastow and the tenement that he had had built in Chepstow.[147] Blanche and Charles had the 'occupying of all' Troy's contents and 'all good[es] and Catall[es] utensilyes and Implement[es] of household [. . .] for term of lyfe of the said Blanche And after her decesse to the said Charlys if he overlyve: having trist that she will kepe hir self sool while she lyvith'.[148]

Sir William Herbert of Troy was an annuitant of Edward Stafford, third Duke of Buckingham, and a frequent visitor with Blanche of Thornbury Castle, Gloucestershire, where their son, Charles, first appears in 1508.[149] Charles is next met with in 1524 when, with George Whitney of Iccomb, Gloucestershire, he stood surety for James Whitney as receiver of Monmouth for the duchy of Lancaster. In July 1533 he became deputy to Henry Somerset, second Earl of Worcester, as duchy steward for Monmouth, and he remained in the duchy's service until he ran into debt towards the end of his life. By the time the *Valor Ecclesiasticus* was compiled, Charles held a number of offices with religious houses. After the Union he was one of the leading figures of the newly formed shire and was its first sheriff in 1540, a position he held again in 1548.[150] In 1544 he went to France for the Boulogne campaign, supplying seven men for the expedition; he was also chosen as the king's standard-bearer, at a wage of ten shillings a day.[151]

Dower and the widow's third entitled a wife to live in her husband's property until her death.[152] Lady Troy's retirement to her own furnished apartments within Troy House whilst her son Charles and his wife also occupied the building was in keeping with this practice. Such arrangements often created a stasis in which little alteration was carried out. Consequently, the inventory of 1557, probably conducted just after the deaths of Blanche and Charles in that year, is likely to show little change from what existed at William's death in 1524. The inventory not only lists the chambers used by Henry VII and his queen in 1502, but reveals rich furnishings. Curtains of green and red silk, wall hangings of rich tapestry fabric, feather bolsters and beds decorated with satin braids filled the king's chambers. The queen's little chamber had a blue and russet theme, and green silk hangings adorned her great chamber. At the time of the inventory the hall at Troy held what amounted to an armoury – fifty-nine glaves, and eighty pikes and spears, whilst a pair of andirons for its fire were valued at six shillings and eight pence, and so were of considerable value for the time. Clearly, Troy was a residence of some status and must have then had at least a pleasant appearance from Thomas Churchyard's stating that 'Neere the towne [Monmouth] Sir Charles Harbert of Troy dwelt in a faire seate called Troy'.[153] Certainly, the surrounding fields of wheat and rye were a considerable asset, as on the 1557 inventory they were valued as 'Total corn in the blade £48 13s 4d'.[154]

During the last years of Sir Charles Herbert's life his fortunes crumbled. Under Edward VI he remained active locally and received a knighthood in 1532, but with the advent of Queen Mary his arrears of payments to the duchy caught up with him and in August 1554, John Phillip Morgan was put in charge of his office.[155] His indebtedness was the main theme of the will that he made on 23 April 1552.[156] As the will was not proved until 22 January 1558, Herbert survived its making by several years, probably dying shortly before his replacement on 20 March 1557 as the duchy's steward for Ebbw. Charles had two daughters by his first wife, Elizabeth ap Rhys, and no children by his second wife, Cicill. Troy, 'with the parke demaynes and all other lands tenement[es] reverc[ions] service[es] and rents belonging to the same house lyinge in the paryshes of Mychell Troy Comcarvan Monmouthe and Pennallte', passed to Charles's eldest daughter, Joan (b. *c.*1526), on his death in 1557.[157] The will shows that at least by 1552 there was a deer park at Troy; its existence is still reflected in the woods above Troy House being called Troypark Wood. Charles directed his executors to sell his manors of Wonastow and St Wogan's to meet his arrears and Wonastow was bought by his younger brother, Thomas, who went on to own considerable property, including the abbey lands of Parc Grace Dieu and the Beaulieu, granted by the king.[158] From this time Wonastow ceased to be attached to Troy and became a separate estate.

Joan married George ap James ap Watkin of Llanddewi Rhydderch,[159] who, in an unknown capacity, served the office of sheriff of the county in 1560, and resided at Troy.[160] The Troy inventory of 1557 refers to a chamber called that of William John ap James, most likely a relation of George. This chamber was certainly comfortably furnished, with two chairs, a tester bed of red and yellow, a feather bolster and blankets, and red and yellow hangings about the walls. In 1584, Joan, George and their son, Charles James, together with others, sold two areas of land at Troy to William Somerset (*c.*1527–89), third Earl of Worcester and of Raglan Castle[161] and it is from this point that the Somerset family become associated with owning Troy.

The Somerset family: owners of Troy for three hundred years

George ap James ap Watkin died in 1585, leaving two sons, but their inheritance was disputed when their aunt laid claim to half of the Troy estate; there followed a long and what would have been an expensive lawsuit.[162] In 1600 Troy was sold by George's son, Charles James, to Edward Somerset (*c*.1550–1628), fourth Earl of Worcester.[163]

The wealth and influence of the Somerset family can be traced back to Charles Somerset (*c*.1460–1526), who was a descendant of the illegitimate Beaufort line of John of Gaunt (1340–99) and Katherine Swynford (1350–1403). Charles's father, Henry Beaufort, third Duke of Somerset

Figure 2.6 *Charles Somerset, first Earl of Worcester.*

(1436–64), was a first cousin of Margaret Beaufort (1443–1509), mother of King Henry VII.[164] As described earlier, he married Elizabeth Herbert (1476–1512) in 1492, the only daughter and heir of William, second Earl of Pembroke (Earl of Huntingdon from 1479).

Elizabeth received the Herbert lands, including Raglan and Chepstow castles, on her father's death in 1491. By his marriage to Elizabeth in 1492, Charles became an exceptionally wealthy man. The combination of this wealth with his personal attributes made him a formidably influential figure. He was made first Earl of Worcester by Henry VIII in 1514, in recognition of his distinguished service abroad in both diplomatic and military roles dating back to the reign of Henry VII. He became Lord Chamberlain during the reign of Henry VIII and was appointed sole commissioner to arrange the Field of the Cloth of Gold. Charles's eldest son, Henry (*c.*1499–1549), succeeded to the title as second earl in 1526. He engaged in diplomacy and his loyalty to the king at the time of the Dissolution was rewarded with grants of church lands and property, including Tintern Abbey in 1537.[165] Henry's eldest son, William (*c.*1527–89), was appointed in 1544 as the king's principal esquire and as a gentleman of the Privy Chamber. He became third Earl of Worcester in 1549. William held positions at the courts of three sovereigns: Edward VI (1547–53), Mary (1553–8) and Elizabeth I (1558–1603), and served with particular distinction during the Elizabethan period.[166] He undertook several missions abroad for the queen and was made Knight of the Garter in 1570. Although residing most often at Chepstow Castle, he transformed Raglan from a fortified castle into a palace, a task continued by his only son, Edward (*c.*1550–1628), who became the fourth Earl of Worcester in 1589.

A previously untranslated praise poem written by Lewys Morgannwg about Edward contains references to him being a bud (line 7), to his nourishing and fostering, all of which suggests that the poem was composed very early in Edward's life, possibly shortly after his birth.[167] The poem makes extensive use of metaphors, which can be difficult for conveying an exact meaning. However, overall the poem looks to the future and sees promises of great things to come from Edward because of his ancestry, his pedigree, his bloodline. Specific reference is made to his father, William, and Raglan Castle being a famed court accommodating an army (line 12). Edward's upbringing is highlighted in terms of the quality of his learning (lines 30–2), horsemanship (line 45), preparedness for battle (lines 45–8) and leadership qualities (lines 27–9, 35–6). If that were not all, he is likened to Absalom, son of the prophet David, who was apparently renowned for his great beauty (lines 53–4).

Gwent is fostering earls
of like honour as the old earls.
I see the form of a lion and its honour
and the heart of an earl [who is] above all.
You are, Edward, Lord Herbert,
[descended] from Earl William, a ruler of noble rank.
We have a bud
as we wait for a Duke of Somerset.
You are a lamb with the golden fleece from this island
and from Raglan, not to be ruled [by any].
There were two earls, there were [two] Williams,
there was a great host [in] a famed court which could accommodate
an army.
Earl William, the father, is from this house,
the earl in due course will be Earl Edward,
a son fostered in the style of Alexander the Great,
nourished on wine and fine feasts.
Salutations, the son of Earl William,
the great Earl of Worcester, greetings, son.
Newly promoted blood [i.e. upstarts] will not approach
[the level of] your blood, let [this new blood] be silent.
Your bud derives from three dukes
and you are the sixth earl from this line.
You are an Edward from father to father,
you are from the house of Edward the Third.
You are a man with [good] blood in his hilt;
from the house of [good] blood you are mighty.
Your fostering completed seek [to lead] men,
seek the ball [i.e. excel/gain renown] during your childhood;
seek the ball as you set out in the world,
seek the book [i.e. authority/learning], excellent earl, likewise.
Courtesy and manners, this is the house where praises are sung,
a hand learned in three languages.
during the life of Earl William you will have the fame
of a second earl, the desire of your mother.
It is well, shepherd [i.e. leader], the way in which you were
fostered,
Gwent is destined [to be led by] you, it was a most famed place,
in the same way as Sir Gwalchmai long ago,
[Gwent was] their breeding ground.
You are, Edward, and always will be of a good mould,

the material of earls, your pedigree is good.
If the trees of Herbert have before now been felled
and uprooted, they were of oak,
in spite of the oak trees that have been cut down,
we have now had a [new] oak tree with your fostering.
Do take up horsemanship, a rider of battle steeds,
making battle on steeds.
Go to battle on a steed, take a spear shortly,
young Hector, shatter those who bear lances.
Take the young in the battle of hearts;
the ball is yours.
A Welshman from Gwent, welcome poets
and the advice of elders.
You are Absalon-like, this offspring and its bosom,
the opinion of all who see you.
There is a prophecy that he will become in time a duke,
the chief of Rhaglan.
The bud of a duke has been born.
Let the Duke Herbert long be with us.[168]

Edward fulfilled the promises expounded in the poem, although not the award of a dukedom. He was a superb scholar, arguably the finest rider and jouster of the day, patron of the arts and a consummate courtier; he proved to be a remarkably astute politician with a gift for being on the right side at the right time.[169] Despite his adherence to the Roman Catholic faith, he became a firm favourite of Elizabeth I. During the Earl of Essex's insurrection, he was briefly detained, but cleared himself of suspicion and later served as one of the peers who tried and condemned Essex. When Essex was executed in February 1601, Edward was on hand to take over Essex's prestigious position as Master of the Horse and was named Privy Councillor. From 1602 until his death in 1628 he was Lord Lieutenant of Glamorgan and Monmouth.

In 1603 Edward's second surviving son, Thomas, along with Sir Charles Percy, was sent by the Privy Council to notify King James of Scotland of the death of Elizabeth I, and of His Majesty's proclamation as her successor. At the coronation of King James I (20–3 July 1603) Edward was prominent at the ceremony as Earl Marshall. He became a favourite of James, and the naming of his sons, Charles and Edward, as Knights of the Bath in 1610 publicly acknowledged the personal intimacy that had developed between his family and that of the king. Edward was particularly active in international affairs during the reign of James I; he encouraged

Figure 2.7 (opposite) *Edward, fourth Earl of Worcester.* By permission of the Duke of Beaufort.

all four of his surviving sons to travel throughout Europe, not just as an essential part of their education but as collectors of intelligence for his own needs and those of the Crown.[170]

Edward had several residences: Raglan Castle was the main Somerset family seat, followed by Chepstow Castle, and, when not at the royal court or his London residence, Worcester House in the Strand, he could also be found at Worcester Lodge at Nonsuch Palace, where he was keeper of the Great Park. So, one might wonder why he purchased the Troy estate south of Monmouth in 1600. Was this purchase driven by the prevailing view that land ownership conveyed power and influence, as well as serving as a potential source of income? Another possible reason, presented here for the first time, is that Edward saw Troy's location as appropriate for his covert religious activities.

Strong Catholic sympathies were rooted in a long Somerset family tradition of recusancy and private adherence to the Church in Rome. Edward's father, William, third Earl of Worcester, and other close family members were suspected of having secret Catholic sympathies. Despite William receiving substantial church lands at the Dissolution, he made a public stand in 1566 against the act, proposing the consecration of archbishops and bishops since 1558 had been 'good, lawful, and perfect'.[171] In 1569 he was suspected of supporting the plot to marry Mary, Queen of Scots, to the Catholic Duke of Norfolk. William's Catholic sister, Anne, was exiled to Paris following the failure of the subsequent Rebellion of the Northern Earls. Nevertheless, William managed to sustain a public, steady loyalty to the Protestant Queen Elizabeth. He refused to visit his sister, Anne, when in Paris and he served as one of the commissioners in the trial of Mary, Queen of Scots.

Edward was even more dextrous than his father in maintaining a balance of loyalties to a Protestant state and the Church in Rome. Indeed, Queen Elizabeth herself is claimed to have remarked that he 'reconciled what she believed irreconcilable, a stiff papist to a good subject'.[172] Publicly, Edward behaved as an impeccably conformist *politique*, and especially during the reign of James I: he took the oath of allegiance to the royal supremacy, attended sermons and sat on the commission for the expulsion of the Jesuits in 1604, whilst in 1605 he was employed in the interrogation of the gunpowder plotters. He even secured the noted Welsh Protestant tutor, Dr Thomas Prichard (*fl.* 1610–*c.*1660), for his children. Edward's appointments, favour at court and behaviour in public masked his clandestine support of the 'old religion' – Catholicism. In essence, he led a double life. Privately, Edward supported the flourishing Jesuit activity in Wales from its very earliest days, and was, in many ways, responsible for its success.[173] This took the form of two key elements: first, his patronage of the Jesuit, Robert Jones (*c.*1564–1615), who arrived in Wales in 1595, and was appointed superior of the entire English and Welsh Jesuit mission from 1609 until his death in 1615; second, he allowed the Jesuits use of his extensive estates as a secure base and headquarters for their very successful Welsh mission, which later became the College of St Francis Xavier.[174]

Initially, Edward gave protection to Jesuits, including Robert Jones, at Raglan Castle.[175] He also granted to the Jesuits in about 1600 some lands and farms, known as the Cwm, near Llanrothal in the secluded Monnow Valley, some nineteen kilometres across land north of Raglan and eight kilometres by river from Troy.[176] The activities of the Jesuit community, and the Catholics whom they served, continued undisturbed from their College headquarters at the Cwm estate until the late 1670s, despite the best efforts of the anti-papists in the county. Moving the Jesuit centre of activity from Raglan to the Cwm provided a far more secluded location that at the time would not have been easy to access by road. Troy House lies just metres from the river Trothy; within a kilometre of the house the Trothy enters the Wye. On turning left at this confluence and travelling

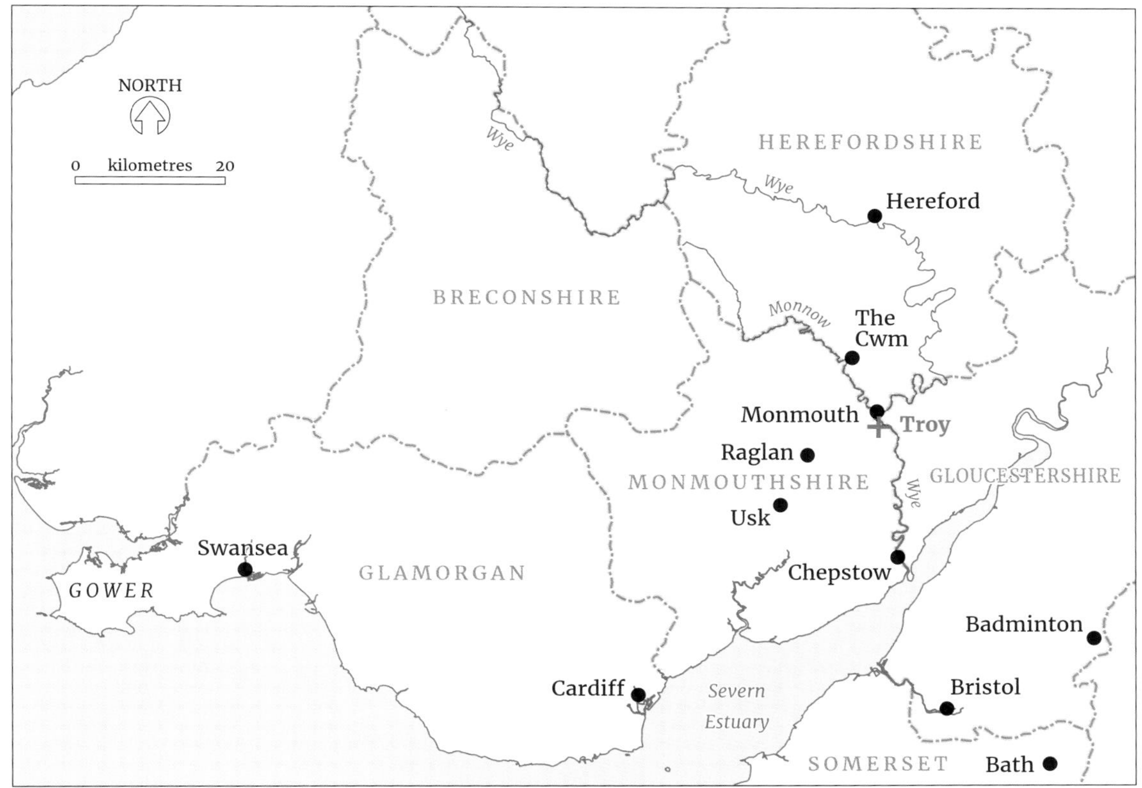

Figure 2.8 *Locations of Raglan Castle, Troy House, Chepstow Castle and the Cwm estate with connecting rivers.*

Copyright: Map by permission of Professor Maurice Whitehead; rivers and Troy added by University of Wales Press.

upstream, the mouth of the Monnow may be reached in less than a kilometre. During the seventeenth century, the Monnow was navigable up to Skenfrith. Consequently, the area of the Cwm could be reached within eight kilometres by river from Troy House. Indeed, the church at Llanrothal actually lies on the Monnow riverbank, and Llanrothal Court, owned and visited by members of the Somerset family during the seventeenth century, is but metres away from this church.

Starting from Troy House, on turning right at the confluence of the Trothy with the Wye, Chepstow Castle, also in the ownership of the earls of Worcester, lies some twenty-two kilometres downstream with its own private landing stage. The Wye enters the river Severn at Chepstow and in turn gives access to the Bristol Channel and continental Europe beyond. Chepstow Castle thus held a strategic location at the entrance to south Wales and enabled links between the Jesuit communities within Europe and those supported by Edward at the Cwm and Raglan Castle, and, as argued here, at Troy House. In 1602, Edward Somerset, fourth Earl of Worcester, became not only Lord Lieutenant of both Monmouthshire and Glamorgan, but also Admiral of the Severn. This latter position conferred complete control over all shipping in the river Severn and further enhanced security for his covert activities.

It is suggested here that Edward's granting of some lands and farms known as the Cwm to the Jesuits in 1600 and his purchase of the Troy estate in the same year is no coincidence. Both were timely for Robert Jones's increasing activity in the Jesuit community. The purchase of Troy not only provided another hiding place for the Jesuits, but it was also ideally located on the route between Chepstow and the Cwm for clandestine river journeys. It is highly probable that Catholic literature was secretly brought into Wales by this relatively easy route. This would have been much more preferable to transportation through Dover or London, where such books would have run grave risk of being discovered and seized, and those conveying them of being imprisoned. Arriving directly at Chepstow Castle, without the normal necessity of passing through a customs point, Roman Catholic books would have passed straight into the custody of the Somerset family ready for onward transportation by river to Troy. From Troy they could be either transported again by river directly to the Cwm, or across land to Raglan Castle just eight kilometres away, rather than the twenty-four kilometres from Chepstow. The Jesuit network would then have enabled the literature to be disseminated to missionary outposts around Wales.

Nicholas Owen SJ (*c.*1562–March 1606) was a Jesuit lay brother who was the principal builder of priest holes during the reigns of Elizabeth I and James I of England. He was arrested in 1594 and was tortured at the Poultry Compter but revealed nothing; Edward secured his release and paid a fine on his behalf.[177] The date of Edward's support in getting Owen released from captivity in 1594 comes within a few years of the arrival of Robert Jones in south Wales, Edward's granting of lands at the Cwm to the Jesuits, and his purchase of Troy. On release, Owen resumed his work and is believed to have masterminded the famous escape of Father John Gerard SJ from the Tower of London in 1597. Whether he was employed by Edward to build priest holes at Troy, and possibly elsewhere during the early seventeenth century, is unknown. However, it is claimed that a priest hole exists at Troy, and this is described in chapter 3.

Edward never lived at Troy. Sir William Powell (d.1611), a wealthy landowner in his own right and described as 'of Llanpill in the parish of Llanfihangel Tor-y-Mynydd', was engaged by Edward as resident steward of the Troy estate.[178] Sir William was the son of David ap Philip of Lanpill and Maud, the base daughter of Sir Thomas Herbert of Wonastow, and was thus related to the Somerset family.[179] Sir William had no issue by his wife and he left his considerable fortune to his adopted, illegitimate daughter, Elizabeth, who married Sir Charles Somerset, fourth surviving son of Edward, fourth Earl of Worcester. The date of the marriage is unknown but it must pre-date 4 October 1611, when Sir William Powell referred to Elizabeth as the wife of Charles in his will. Edward conveyed the use of the manor of Troy to Charles and Elizabeth in their marriage settlement of 1609.[180] Certainly, by early 1611 they were married and living at Troy. However, by April 1611, Charles had commenced a tour of several European countries; this was not uncommon practice amongst newly married young aristocrats.

Sir William Powell died in 1611 and Charles returned from his European travels in May 1612. The young couple's wealth would have been significantly enhanced by Elizabeth's inheritance from her father and, inspired by what he had seen on his European travels, it is likely that Troy would have been enhanced to accommodate the couple in a style to their liking. They are immortalized by the letters C, E and S in a shield over the stone entrance to the walled garden.[181] Charles and Elizabeth were living at Troy in 1625 when he became High Sheriff of Monmouthshire.[182] However, when Edward died in 1628, he left the Troy estate to his second eldest surviving son, Thomas Somerset (1579–*c.*1650). Charles and Elizabeth appear to have then moved to Rogerstone Grange, near Chepstow, where Charles was an active magistrate, mainly on behalf of the Exchequer.[183] Thomas served as Member of Parliament for Monmouthshire in 1601 and 1604–11. He was knighted as Knight of the Bath in 1605 and in December 1626 he was raised to the peerage of Ireland as Viscount Somerset of Cashell, largely by reason of his wife's Irish estates.[184] He travelled extensively through Europe and, indeed, for much of his adult life, lived in Ireland and abroad.[185]

Nineteen days after the pivotal Royalist defeat at Naseby on 14 June 1645, King Charles I arrived at Raglan Castle. He stayed for nearly two weeks and during this time was entertained by the elderly Henry Somerset, fifth Earl of Worcester, who had been made Marquess of Worcester on 2 November 1642 in recognition of his magnanimous support, largely financial, of the king. Evidence of Sir Thomas residing at Troy and his horticultural interests comes from Thomas Bayly, the Somerset's chaplain and chronicler:

> Sir Thomas Somerset, brother to the Marquess, had a house which they called Troy, within 5 miles [8 kilometres] of Raglan Castle: this Sir Thomas Somerset being a neate man, both within, and without his house, as he was a compleat Gentleman of himself, every way delighted very much in fine Gardens, and Orchards, and in replenishing and ordering them with all the varieties of choisest fruits [including apricots], that could be got and in defending his new Plantations from the coldness of the climate, by the benefit of art.[186]

As often quoted, Sir Thomas personally presented a silver dish of apricots grown at Troy to Charles I during his stay at Raglan Castle following Naseby. This act has caused some confusion because Sir Charles Somerset is thought to have occupied Troy from the 1610s to his death in 1665.[187] Did Sir Charles and his brother Sir Thomas occupy Troy with their families at the same time? It seems more likely that Sir Charles and Elizabeth moved to Rogerstone Grange in 1628 when Sir Thomas inherited Troy. However, Sir Thomas spent progressively more time in Ireland and abroad, and he started to take up residence in exile among the English community in Rome from about 1644.[188] Charles and Elizabeth[189] did not go into exile during the Civil War and returned to Troy in the early 1640s.[190]

On 6 October 1644, 'Sir Chas. Somerset, the Earl of Worcester's brother' was denounced by Colonel Edward Massie as a firm opponent of the parliamentary forces in Monmouthshire; Charles was referred to as 'Sir Chas. Somerset of Troy' in March 1650 by the Committee for Advance of Money, who noted he was 'a papist'.[191] The same Committee in December of that year also reported him engaging in detrimental activities throughout 1640s, when 'he maintained at his house [Troy] a garrison of 20 men, armed, and with horses, for the late king, and sent then out scouting, 1643–5, to the great terror of the well-affected; that he harboured the King's officers and soldiers'.[192] Following the execution of Charles I on 30 January 1649, many of the king's supporters fled abroad. Indeed, at about the time of the execution of the king, Sir Charles can be found in Spain, but not because he was seeking greater security.

A scheme, backed by the Prince of Orange, had been proposed for an embassy to go to Spain to seek assistance from Philip IV to support Charles II as the lawful successor to the English throne; Sir Charles was part of that embassy. Letters written by Sir Charles to Charles II in April 1649 place him in Zaragosa (Saragossa) in north-eastern Spain, the regular summer palace of Philip IV.[193] Negotiations dragged on fruitlessly until 1650, the year in which Sir Thomas Somerset died.[194] Sir Charles returned to England about 1651 when Spain formally recognized the Commonwealth, and from then until 1656 he was under constant harassment from the Committee for Compounding.[195] His Catholicism continued to be a ruinously expensive loyalty throughout the 1650s, although after the Restoration he was able to reside quietly on his Troy estate until his death there in 1665.[196] Consequently, the period when he most likely developed Troy's buildings and landscape is from about 1612, when he returned from his European tour, to 1628, when his brother, Thomas, inherited the estate.

On Sir Charles's death in 1665 the estate passed to his great-nephew, Henry Somerset, Lord Herbert (1629–1700). Henry was the only son of the soldier and inventor Edward Somerset, sixth Earl and second Marquess of Worcester (1601–67), who had been immediately imprisoned in 1652 when he returned from exile in Ireland. Henry had been sent to France and Italy with his tutor in 1644.[197] When he returned six years later he found the family's main seat, Raglan Castle, unoccupied and heavily despoiled by parliamentary forces. The family's wealth was ravaged by wartime loans to the king, sequestration and the scientific activities of his father.[198] Family portraits and other contents held at Raglan had been removed to Troy on the orders of the fifth earl before the failed siege of 1646,[199] and it was at Troy that Henry first lived on his return, Worcester House, the Somerset's London home, then being in use by parliamentary officials.[200]

Soon after his return Henry became a Protestant and showed himself loyal to Cromwell's regime. In 1651, when aged 22 years, Henry negotiated a settlement with Cromwell, confirming the latter's ownership of many south Wales properties in return for the right to compound.[201] Edward, fourth Earl of Worcester, had purchased the estates of Great and Little Badminton Gloucestershire from Nicholas Boteler in 1608[202] and on his death both estates passed to his son, Sir Thomas; in turn, on his death, they passed to Thomas's only surviving child, Elizabeth. Elizabeth was a distant cousin of Henry, Lord Herbert, and he inherited the Badminton estates from her in 1655. By this date, Henry had recouped sufficient funds to set about repairing the fabric of Badminton. An impetus to do so came from his marriage to a young, wealthy widow, Mary, Lady Beauchamp (née Capel) on 17 August 1657, when they opted for a 'republican' marriage in front of a Justice of the Peace.

However, the wartime activities of Henry's father and Mary's active royalism led to Henry's being arrested during the Gloucestershire plot and imprisonment in the Tower for two months; he was released on 1 November 1659.[203] After Cromwell's death (d.1658), Henry promptly switched sides to support a Stuart restoration. He sat in the Convention Parliament and in 1660 was one of the twelve commissioners sent to escort Charles II home from Holland. The Restoration in 1660 saw the beginning of a significant increase in Henry's numerous activities, particularly those conducted at Court, so that within twenty years he was the second richest man in England after the king.

The year 1660 also saw the birth of Henry and Mary's eldest surviving son, Charles, on 25 December.[204] By this time Badminton was their main residence and Sir Charles Somerset (1588–1665), Henry's great-uncle, was seeing out his days at Troy; on his death in 1665, Troy House became a secondary residence for the Somerset family. However, for more than 300 years Troy remained an important base from which stewards administered the Somersets' considerable Welsh land-holdings. From 1664 Henry embarked on a major building project at Badminton, whilst Mary focused her attention on creating its magnificent gardens. Henry was MP for Monmouthshire from 1660 until 1667, when he succeeded his father as third Marquess of Worcester. Charles II appointed him constable of St Briavels Castle, warden of the Forest of Dean and Lord Lieutenant of Gloucestershire, Herefordshire and Monmouthshire.

Henry persuaded the king of the importance of maintaining a garrison at the Somersets' Chepstow Castle, describing it as the 'key' to south Wales. Monmouthshire residents claimed that he used it as a private army. Soldiers from the garrison were certainly active in Henry's disputes concerning property rights in Wentwood Forest in 1678, and local MPs accused him of employing them 'to rob the country of its wood'.[205] In 1672 Henry was appointed Lord President of the Council in the Marches of Wales, Privy Councillor and Knight of the Garter. 1672 also saw Henry embark on rebuilding Badminton in the fashionable Palladian style and Mary continue to enlarge the gardens on an unprecedented scale. Henry also built Great Castle House in Monmouth from the ruins of the castle

Figure 2.9 *The first Duke of Beaufort and his family, by S. Browne, 1685.*
By permission of the Duke of Beaufort.

there; the house was to exalt his standing as Lord President. Despite some opposition from the Commons, in December 1682, Charles II advanced Henry to the title of first Duke of Beaufort. The duke and his duchess lived in considerable magnificence at Badminton, although Henry spent most of his time in London, and they rarely visited Troy.

In June 1673, Henry's son and heir, Charles Somerset, Lord Herbert, was admitted as the youngest ever (aged 13 years) Fellow of the Royal Society,[206] and within days departed with his tutor on a tour of France.[207] He attended Christ Church, Oxford, matriculated in 1677 and was awarded

MA in 1682. Charles had oversight of the Somerset holdings in Wales and, on his father's elevation to the title of Duke of Beaufort in 1682, became Marquess of Worcester. On 6 June that year, he married Rebecca Child, daughter of Sir Josiah Child of Wanstead, first Baronet (1630–99), a wealthy merchant who rose to become governor of the powerful East India Company. Charles and Rebecca settled at Troy.

Following the rebuilding of Badminton in the Palladian style in the 1670s, the early years of the next decade witnessed a plethora of building activity by Henry. In 1681 he bought a home in Chelsea, which was remodelled and called Beaufort House, and Mary once again took charge of the gardens. By 1682, Henry turned his attention to Troy, where he added a north-facing range to the existing house and, as discussed in chapter 3, the interior of the existing house was changed to meld the whole together. Given the first Duchess of Beaufort's interest in gardens, an interest which was shared to some extent by her son, Charles, the gardens around the newly modelled house may also have been refashioned.[208] The duke's intention was to make a residence fitting for his son's status as his heir and administrator of the family's Welsh lands. During the building work, Henry required Charles and Rebecca to reside at Monmouth Castle.

Henry played a leading role in the Tory reaction of the 1680s, reforming the county and borough magistracies, remodelling militia commands, and encouraging the surrender of corporate charters in Wales and the border counties.[209] To this end, in 1684 he took a month-long ducal progress through Wales that was chronicled by Thomas Dineley.[210] The progress culminated at Troy, where there were celebrations on a grand scale; the newly extended Troy House would have been shown off as a fitting residence for such an influential family. The year 1684 also saw the birth of Henry, Lord Herbert, the first child and only son of Charles, Marquess of Worcester, and his wife Rebecca. At the duke's insistence, Rebecca gave birth to Henry at Monmouth Castle so as to be associated with the birthplace of Henry V.[211]

Baby Henry suffered ill health and was largely brought up at Badminton by the duchess rather than by Rebecca;[212] his only sister, Henrietta, was born in 1690. Family life continued at Troy, with Charles, Marquess of Worcester, taken up with local political office and military activities.[213] He would rather have spent his time in diplomacy and pursuing his scholarly interests, both scientific and genealogical.[214] He also liaised with his father on matters concerning their Welsh lands, until tragedy struck on 13 July 1698. Charles and Rebecca had visited their cousin at Llanrothal Court in the Monnow valley and, as shown in chapter 1, their return journey to Troy in the early evening ended in a fatal accident for Charles.[215]

Contrary to current popular belief, the accident must have occurred closer to Llanrothal than Troy, otherwise Charles would not have been taken in an injured state back to his cousin's house there.[216] A scholarly, generous and loving son to his mother (see Figure 1.1 for a portrait of Charles), his death marked the end of an era when a member of the Somerset family regularly inhabited Troy.[217]

The Duke of Beaufort's health was already beginning to fail at the time of his son's fatal coaching accident and thereafter he and the duchess spent most of their time at Badminton, where they continued to expand the estate. Occasional visits were made to their house in Chelsea and Tunbridge Wells for the duke to access medical care.[218] Stewards were installed at Troy to take over the administration of the Somerset family's Welsh holdings.[219] Rebecca continued to live periodically at Troy until 1703, when she married John Granville, first and last Baron of Potheridge.[220] On Rebecca's departure in 1703, stewards continued to occupy a few rooms in the west section of Troy House. Henry, Rebecca's son by Charles, remained at Badminton with his grandparents and became second Duke of Beaufort on 21 January 1700; he was just 16 years of age.

The years following the first duke's death were marred by family squabbles, with the first duchess being accused by her children and Rebecca of misappropriating monies.[221] In this respect, the only item relating to Troy amongst her accounts is an entry for paying £700 for goods at Troy House, and these were sold to pay her dead son's debts. Mary took possession of her late husband's personal estate, worth an estimated £92,331; this she used to continue building and expanding the gardens at Badminton, but no such activity is listed for Troy. Ten years after the first duke's death in 1700, his grandson and heir, Henry, together with his mother, Rebecca, filed a bill in Chancery for an account and distribution of his grandfather's estate. Mary died at the Somersets' Chelsea house on 7 January 1715.

Following the death of the first duke, Troy House became only an occasional summer home and a hunting venue for the vast majority of subsequent generations of the Somerset family; paintings and other fittings were largely removed to Badminton. The fourth, fifth and eighth dukes of Beaufort spent more time at Troy than any of their counterparts. Charles Somerset (1709–56) was the younger son of Henry Somerset, second Duke of Beaufort, and his second wife, Rachel Noel. Charles's brother had no issue, so on his older brother's death in February 1746, Charles succeeded him and became the fourth Duke of Beaufort. It was largely when required to fulfil his duties as MP for Monmouthshire (1731–4) and MP for Monmouth (1734–5) that the fourth duke lived at Troy; otherwise, Badminton remained his main residence.

Figure 2.10 *Elizabeth, wife of the fifth Duke of Beaufort.* By permission of the Duke of Beaufort.

Henry Somerset, the fifth Duke of Beaufort (1744–1803), held the office of Grand Master of the Freemasons between 1767 and 1772. From 1768 to 1770, he was Master of the Horse to the Queen Consort. He was appointed Lord Lieutenant of Monmouthshire in 1771 and Lord Lieutenant of Brecknockshire in 1787, holding both offices until his death in 1803, as well as Lord Lieutenant of Leicestershire from 1787 to 1799. He was invested as a Knight of the Order of the Garter on 2 June 1786. It was from 1771 that he split his time between Troy and Badminton. This duke was no courtier or avid politician and his wife was handicapped by lameness, resulting from a coaching accident in 1769. Though much sought after, she was not fond of London society and she preferred life at

Troy during the summer months.[222] They had eight sons and all enjoyed their youth on and around the Troy estate. However, as the fifth duke approached old age he retired to Badminton. Evidence of significant development at Troy, other than repairs to the existing structures, during the time of the fourth and fifth dukes has, as yet, not emerged. By at least 1781, when John Byng, the acid writer of the Torrington Diaries, visited Troy, he related that the rooms were 'so barely furnished that he felt it no breach of manners to go rummaging in odd places'.[223]

The year 1853 saw the beginning of the ownership of the Somerset estates by Henry Somerset, eighth Duke of Beaufort (1824–99), and Troy entering a period of more regular occupation by family members. Although Henry followed the tradition of most previous dukes of Beaufort by combining a political career with soldering, he spent considerable time with his family at Troy whilst fully engaging with local activities, and in particular, sporting events. In conjunction with John Etherington Welch Rolls he established an annual cattle show in Monmouth; this still exists as the Monmouthshire Show. Henry conceived, planned and acted as overseeing editor for the Badminton Library series of sporting books; these were published from 1885 with a volume on *Hunting*.

According to Horatia Durant, historian and Somerset family member, the eighth duke was recklessly extravagant and the inhabitants of Monmouthshire, high and low, enjoyed such entertainment as is recorded as never having been seen before in the county.[224] Examples include: the roasted ox in Monmouth's market-place; the commissions in the Blues; and the new public highway leading out of Monmouth. The eighth duke's proverbial generosity as a landlord resulted in him being fondly called 'Uncle' by local people.[225] A charming picture of life at Troy at this time is revealed in a letter written by the duchess: 'it is after dinner and the young persons are engaged in taking a wasp's nest, all part of the troy programme! There has been cricket and fishing and dabbling and now we wind up with a wasp's nest, a really happy day!'.[226]

During the period of the eighth duke's occupation of Troy, the grounds of the house were the venue for an annual Whit Monday fête for the people of Monmouth: the object of the fêtes was to provide a fund, called the Deficiency Fund, for local parochial finances.[227] Newspaper accounts of these events report that the grounds were in neat and trim condition and a variety of stalls were arranged in a shady area, whilst maypole dancing, bands playing and an exhibition of paintings inside the house added to the entertainment; Wells lights were used to illuminate the grounds, for these events continued into the night.[228] The fête usually culminated at about 9.30 p.m. with 'a very brisk and brilliant pyrotechnic display'.[229]

Figure 2.11 *The eighth Duke of Beaufort, by Ellis Roberts.*

With the increase in the 'coming and going' to Troy House during the second half of the nineteenth century, it is most likely that the approach route to the house from Gibraltar Hill near Troy Lodge, which currently provides vehicular access, was widened and another route was made from near the toll house at the junction of the Raglan and Trelech roads. Certainly, the Gibraltar route pre-dates the eighth duke's time, as it is shown on the Tithe map of 1845, whereas the toll-house route is not. Both routes are shown on the 1881 first edition OS map of Troy House. Henry Somerset became the eighth Duke of Beaufort in 1853 and so it was in his time that the toll-house route was created. Also, the avenue of Wellingtonia trees on the Gibraltar route, some of which remain, must have been added during this duke's time, as this type of tree was first brought to Europe in 1853. They may have been planted to mark Henry's elevation to dukedom at this time. A now-ruined, large, Victorian, brick, compartmented greenhouse in Troy's walled garden west of the house is also from the eighth duke's time. Other trees within the land surrounding the house date from this period, but there is no evidence of significant landscaping or building activity, other than the addition of bathrooms at the southern end of the east wing. Photographs towards the end of the century and the duke's life show a well-tended house and garden (see Figure 4.30).

Although in 1883 the duke's estates in Gloucestershire, Wiltshire, Monmouthshire, Brecon and Glamorgan were computed at 51,000 acres (20,640 hectares) and valued at £56,000 per annum, the passing of the Finance Act in 1894 had a pressing significance for a man of 70.[230] When the eighth duke's son and heir, Henry Somerset, Marquess of Worcester (1847–1924), married in 1895, Badminton was handed over to him and the duke and duchess went to live at Stoke Gifford, near Bristol. Ownership of the Somersets' estates in Monmouthshire, Tidenham and Woolastone were also vested upon the future ninth duke. In 1898, the year before the eighth duke's death, the marquess decided to sell these estates and notices started to appear in the press.[231]

The 10 June 1898 edition of the *Monmouthshire Beacon* listed all of the Beaufort properties, fisheries and sporting rights that were for sale. A tiny advert hidden away with others in the *Monmouthshire Beacon* of 19 August 1898 also publicized: 'the Beaufort estates in Monmouthshire could be purchased *en bloc* for £700,000. Tintern Abbey and Raglan Castle ruins are included and also the Troy House domain'.[232] Eighteen years previously, when Osmond Arthur Wyatt occupied Troy House as the Beaufort's steward, many items of furniture, books, casks and agricultural implements were auctioned at the house; clearly, the house was being wound down long before the 1898 sale notification in the *Monmouthshire Beacon.*

Fleeing French nuns, a special school for boys and, finally, 'at risk'

The Troy estate, complete with its several farms, fishing rights and woodlands was in the first tranche of the 1901 auction of the Beaufort holdings.[233] It was not sold but in 1902 it was purchased by Edward Arnott of The Garth, Monmouth, for nearly £50,000;[234] he appears to have been a lawyer with another address in Reigate.[235] Troy and Longstone farms were leased to Aaron Smith, and Troy House, the walled garden and the property called The Elms, close to and west of Troy's walled garden, were leased to French Endist nuns of the Order of Our Lady of Charity and Refuge.[236] The nuns were from near Saumur, the same area from which centuries before a prior and monks had been sent to inaugurate and serve the new priory at Monmouth. Due to the anti-clerical laws introduced in France towards the end of the nineteenth century, the nuns had experienced religious persecution and they sought a refuge in Britain.

The nuns' lease at Troy was for ten years with an option of purchase in five years, an option which they intended to fulfil.[237] The Reverend Mother Superior, Madame Désirée Clotilde Marie Goullioud, wished to establish a Foundation at Troy House for the 'reclaiming and reforming of erring females'.[238] The house became known as the Convent of Notre Dame de Charité du Refuge.[239] Of Troy's inhabitants at this time, about forty women were Magdalenes; these were converted or reformed women committed to remaining at Troy. Work was taken in as a means of support and for the occupation of the inmates: the nuns ran a commercial laundry from the south part of Troy House and needlework was also offered to the surrounding locality.[240]

Figure 2.12 *Troy Convent Laundry Service.*

Copyright: Ann Benson.

An indenture dated 1906 shows the nuns purchasing Troy House, the walled garden and the house nearby called The Elms.[241] By the 1911 census, Troy was accommodating eleven French nuns aged 21 to 44 years of age, four Irish nuns, two of whom were 'aspirant nuns', one Frenchwoman aged 38 and described as 'worker in laundry', and twenty-three laundry workers aged 15 to 25, all from the United Kingdom; Mother Superior Clotilde Goullioud was then aged 58.[242] The twenty-three laundry workers, none of whom were paid for their work, would have all fallen on hard times before they entered Troy's Convent of Notre Dame de Charité du Refuge. Being orphaned, mentally or physically disabled, unable to find work, or having an illegitimate child were all potentially ruinous conditions in the non-welfare state that existed at this time. How well or harshly these women were treated at Troy is unknown.

By 1935 the financial strain on the Foundation was at breaking point and it was decided to subsume the Order of Our Lady of Charity and Refuge into the Order of the Good Shepherd, as they shared common objectives.[243] Unfortunately, documentary and pictorial archives from the time of the nuns' occupation of Troy are not available. However, from the nuns' graves in the walled garden at Troy, it can be established that the founding Mother Superior Clotilde Goullioud died in 1915, aged 62, and laywoman Marie Charvet, who also signed the 1906 indenture, died in 1957.[244] Several founding nuns are not buried at Troy; many of them moved away from Troy at the time of the merger of the two Orders. Five women who were not nuns and who died between 1945 and 1966 are also buried in the walled garden cemetery at Troy.

After the 1935 merger, life and work at Troy convent continued much as before, but again due to financial difficulties assistance was sought by the nuns. Eventually, the local authority leased Troy House from them, with an agreement that it be run as a reform school for girls; locally, the school was known as St Euphrasia's Convent School for Girls. Land (fishing rights excluded) constituting the large island north of Troy House was purchased by the nuns from Troy Farm owner Mr Williams on 7 July 1950. Land adjoining the house to the east of the farm was also purchased on 12 July 1952. During the 1960s one of the nuns at Troy must have had substantial wealth, as within the memory of the groundsman at Troy, she personally funded the building of a covered netball court in the garden at Troy House.[245] A new chapel, garage, theatre, hostel and teaching block, to accommodate the teaching of science and home economics, were also built during the 1960s, but to what extent the nuns or the local authority paid for this is unknown. All of these structures are extant, although in very poor condition.

By 1977 the nuns decided to close Troy School. The girls were largely relocated to another establishment in Pontypridd and the house, walled garden and The Elms were sold separately. Troy House was purchased for a reputed £72,500 by the current owner, Peter Carroll, a solicitor and property developer who owned several properties in London and lived at Itton Court, Chepstow, Monmouthshire.[246] A planning application to turn Troy House into flats was submitted in 1978 but was unsuccessful. Attempts were then made to lease or resell Troy House. Eventually, in 1983, David Jenkins and Graham Templeman, two special needs teachers from Kingswood School, Bristol, leased Troy House with the intention of turning it into a private residential special school for boys. The building was in a poor state and David Jenkins lived at Troy House whilst substantial repairs and improvements were made. A new boiler and roof repairs were essential as the house was riddled with damp. The school opened with fifty boys in Easter 1984. The school brochure shows the statue of the Virgin Mary still in the pediment over the entrance door; it was put there by the nuns during their occupation to replace an unsafe metal portcullis, the emblem of the Beauforts.

Figure 2.13 *Troy Special School for Boys, 1984–91.*
Copyright: David Jenkins.

No new building or landscape development was conducted during the period of Troy being a special school for boys.[247] Extensive use was made of the house grounds and the ancient woodland for the boys' outdoor activities; a goat and chickens were even housed on the large island north of the house. The ground-floor room containing highly ornamental plaster ceilings was used as a TV room for the boys, and the room next to this, part of the north range, was filled with snooker tables. A second-floor room still has the blackout across the window from when it was a photography darkroom. Even a large table with a model train track remains *in situ*, despite the school going into liquidation in 1991. The monthly costs of maintaining Troy House ran at £1,000; an increase in the rent in 1990 made the school financially untenable. In the summer of 1991 a group of schools in the Warleigh area, near Bath, were invited by David Jenkins and Graham Templeman to run Troy School until the end of the year so that the boys could be assessed and prepared for their move from Troy. The boys were then transferred to Warleigh, and Troy House became unoccupied except for a caretaker, who lived in a few rooms in the west part of the north range, traditionally the area used by stewards from 1600 to 1901.

This arrangement has continued to the present. A planning application for residential development was submitted to the authorities in 2008 but it still requires ecological survey reports for progression to a decision.[248] The grounds around the house are somewhat overgrown and the house is 'at risk', with substantial sections of the early seventeenth-century ornate plaster ceilings having succumbed to damp and crumbled away.

After at least ten centuries of ownership by historically significant figures, the future of Troy House is bleak; that of the farm, currently undergoing husbandry improvements, and the walled garden appears to be substantially more secure.

Notes

1 Paul Courtney, 'The Marcher Lordships, Origins, Descent and Organization', in Ralph A. Griffiths, Tony Hopkins and Ray Howell (eds), *The Gwent County History, Volume 2: The Age of the Marcher Lords, c.1070–1536* (Cardiff: University of Wales Press, 2008), p. 47.

2 Courtney, 'The Marcher Lordships', p. 60.

3 The position of the boundary between Archenfield and Netherwent evokes different opinions, but there is general agreement on its having varied across time.

4 Courtney, 'The Marcher Lordships', p. 48.

5 David Crouch, 'The Transformation of Medieval Gwent', in Ralph A. Griffiths et al. (eds), *The Gwent County History, Volume 2: The Age of the Marcher Lords, c.1070–1536* (Cardiff: University of Wales Press, 2008), p. 28.

6 Joseph Bradney, *A History of Monmouthshire: The Hundred of Trelech*, vol. 2, part 2 (London: Academy Books, 1992), p. 161. Originally published 1913.

7 'Baloun' entry in *The Battle Abbey Roll*, vol. I of three volumes.

8 'Baloun' entry in *The Battle Abbey Roll.*

9 Bradney, *A History of Monmouthshire: The Hundred of Trelech*, p. 161.

10 I am grateful to Professor Daniel Power, Head of Department and Professor of Medieval History, Department of History and Classics, Swansea University for his generously given advice on aspects of antiquarian genealogy and the identification of manorial records.

11 See Canon E. T. Davies, *Bradney's History of Monmouthshire: An Assessment* (Abergavenny: Regional Publications, 1986) for a review of the validity of Bradney's historical observations.

12 Power, personal communication, 21 July 2015.

13 Power, personal communication, 21 July 2015.

14 *Liber de Llan Dâv*, ed. J. Gwenogvryn Evans and J. Rhys, *The text of the book of Llan Dâv, reproduced from the Gwysaney Manuscript* (Oxford, 1893), p. 277.

15 Courtney, 'The Marcher Lordships', p. 51.

16 Crouch, 'The Transformation of Medieval Gwent', p. 5.

17 Crouch, 'The Transformation of Medieval Gwent', p. 5.
18 Power, personal communication, 21 July 2015.
19 K. E. Kissack, *Mediaeval Monmouth* (Monmouth: The Monmouth Historical and Educational Trust, 1974), p. 11.
20 See Rev. S. M. Harris, 'The Kalendar of the Vitae Sanctorum Wallensium', *Journal of the Historical Society of the Church in Wales*, 111/8, 14.
21 Kissack, *Mediaeval Monmouth*, p. 11.
22 Kissack, *Mediaeval Monmouth*, p. 12.
23 Crouch, 'The Transformation of Medieval Gwent', p.16. Crouch offers an extensive list of evidence, most of which is held in France, but also includes TNA, PRO E211/361.
24 Cited in Crouch, 'The Transformation of Medieval Gwent', p. 40, as cartulary of St-Florent-de-Saumur, Archives Départmentales de Maine-et-Loire, H 3713, f.127r.
25 David H. Williams, 'The Church in Medieval Gwent', *The Monmouthshire Antiquary: Millennium Issue*, XVI (2000), 9.
26 Canon E. T. Davies, *Ecclesiastical History of Monmouthshire* (Abergavenny: Regional Publications, 1953), page unidentified.
27 Waldo E. L. Smith, T*he Register of Richard Clifford, Bishop of Worcester, 1401–1407: A Calendar (Subsidia mediaevalia)* (Toronto: Pontifical Institute of Mediaeval Studies, 1976), p. 242. I am grateful to the Rev. Dr David Williams for this reference.
28 *Chronicon Adæ de Usk, 1377–1421* (second edn, 1904), p. 118.
29 See *Calendar of Inquisitions Post Mortem*, vol. 5, pp. 336–7.
30 CCR, Edw. II, 1313–18, p. 137. See Bradney, *A History of Monmouthshire: The Hundred of Trelech*, p. 161.
31 Bradney, *A History of Monmouthshire: The Hundred of Trelech*, p. 161; *Calendar of Inquisitions Post Mortem*, iii, nos. 371 and 538.
32 Michael Altschul, 'Clare, Gilbert de, eighth earl of Gloucester and seventh earl of Hertford (1219–1314)', *Oxford Dictionary of National Biography* (Oxford: Oxford University Press, 2004).
33 Michael Brown, *Bannockburn: The Scottish War and the British Isles, 1307–1323* (Edinburgh: Edinburgh University Press, 2008), pp. 145–6.
34 C. J. O. Evans, *Monmouthshire: Its History and Topography* (Cardiff: William Lewis Ltd, 1953), p. 91.
35 See Michael Prestwick, *Plantagenet England: 1225-1360* (new edn; Oxford: Oxford University Press, 2007), pp. 197–200, for an account of the rebellion that followed involving Hereford and Roger Mortimer.
36 Courtney, 'The Marcher Lordships', p. 46.
37 Bradney, *A History of Monmouthshire: The Hundred of Trelech*, p. 161.
38 *A Descriptive Catalogue of Ancient Deeds*, iii, B.4099.
39 See the Welsh and English versions of information about Guto'r Glyn and his patrons with translations of his poems on *www.gutorglyn.net*, the work of the Centre for Advanced Welsh and Celtic Studies, Aberystwyth.

40 Taken from poem 19 at *www.gutorglyn.net/gutorglyn/poem*. Accessed 25 July 2015.

41 D. H. Thomas, *The Herberts of Raglan and the Battle of Edgecote 1469* (Enfield: Freezywater Publications, 1994), p. 11. Thomas draws on the *Herbertorum Prosapia*, a seventeenth-century manuscript detailing the genealogy of the different branches of the Herbert family. A copy of this manuscript is held at Cardiff Library under MS 5.7.

42 R. A. Griffiths, 'Lordship and Society in the Fifteenth Century', in R. A. Griffiths et al. (eds), *The Gwent County History, 2: The Age of the Marcher Lords, c.1070–1536* (Cardiff: University of Wales Press, 2008), p. 262.

43 Thomas, *The Herberts of Raglan*, pp. 4–5.

44 Thomas, *The Herberts of Raglan*, p. 4.

45 T. Nicholas, *Annals and Antiquities of the Counties and County Families of Wales: containing a record of all ranks of the gentry with many ancient pedigrees and memorials of old and extinct families* (1872; facs. edn Baltimore, MD: Genealogical Publishing.com, 2000), p. 777.

46 Arthur Clark, *The Story of Monmouthshire*, vol. 1 (Llandybïe: Christopher Davies Ltd, 1962), p. 122.

47 John Kenyon, *Raglan Castle* (Cardiff: Cadw, 1988), p. 4.

48 Thomas, *The Herberts of Raglan*, pp. 6–7.

49 For more details of William's work for the duchy of Lancaster see Thomas, *The Herberts of Raglan*, p. 8, and R. Somerville, *History of the Duchy of Lancaster*, Vol. 1: 1265–1603 (London: Chancellor and Council of the Duchy of Lancaster, 1953), pp. 653–4.

50 Thomas, *The Herberts of Raglan*, pp. 9–10.

51 Thomas, *The Herberts of Raglan*, pp. 7–8; Somerville, *History of the Duchy of Lancaster*, Vol. 1, pp. 646–7.

52 A detailed account of the career of William ap Thomas is given in Thomas, *The Herberts of Raglan*, pp. 4–12.

53 Thomas, *The Herberts of Raglan*, pp. 8–9.

54 Thomas, *The Herberts of Raglan*, p. 10.

55 Bradney, *A History of Monmouthshire: The Hundred of Trelech*, p. 162.

56 Bradney, *A History of Monmouthshire: The Hundred of Trelech*, p. 162.

57 W. G. Lewis, 'Astudiaeth o Ganu'r Beirdd i'r Herbertiaid hyd Ddechrau'r Unfed Ganrif ar Bymtheg' (unpublished PhD thesis, University of Wales, Bangor, 1982), section 2.5–8; A. Cynfael Lake (ed.), *Gwaith Hywel Dafi* (Aberystwyth: University of Wales, Centre for Advanced Welsh and Celtic Studies, 2015), poem 69.

58 See H. Durant, *Raglan Castle* (Pontypool: Griffin Press, 1966), p. 27, Thomas, *The Herberts of Raglan*, p.13, and H. T. Evans, *Wales and the Wars of the Roses* (Stroud: Sutton Publishing Ltd, 1995) for differing accounts of how the name Herbert was chosen.

59 Kenyon, *Raglan Castle*, p. 9.

60 Thomas, *The Herberts of Raglan*, p. 13.

61 *www.gutorglyn.net/gutorglyn/poem*. Accessed 25 July 2015.
62 Thomas, *The Herberts of Raglan*, p. 11.
63 Kenyon, *Raglan Castle*, p. 9.
64 *Gwaith Lewys Glyn Cothi*, ed. D. Johnston (Cardiff: University of Wales Press, 1995), no. 112.
65 'Chapman' is the cognate of the German *Kaufmann*.
66 R. Griffiths, 'Herbert, William, first earl of Pembroke', *Oxford Dictionary of National Biography* (Oxford: Oxford University Press, 2004), available at *http://www.oxforddnb.com/index/13/101013053/*. Accessed July 2015.
67 John Sleigh, *Monmouth and the Somersets* (Monmouth: Monmouth Field and Antiquarian Society, 1987), p. 9.
68 Thomas, *The Herberts of Raglan*, p. 14.
69 Thomas, *The Herberts of Raglan*, p. 16.
70 Thomas, *The Herberts of Raglan*, p. 17.
71 Thomas, *The Herberts of Raglan*, p. 19.
72 CPR, 1485–94. See R. A. Griffiths and R. S. Thomas, *The Making of the Tudor Dynasty* (Gloucester: The History Press, 1985), pp. 57–60, for a discussion of Henry's early years at Raglan.
73 Kenyon, *Raglan Castle*, p. 10.
74 Thomas, *The Herberts of Raglan*, pp. 13–53.
75 Thomas, *The Herberts of Raglan*, p. 87.
76 Thomas, *The Herberts of Raglan*, p. 17.
77 Thomas, *The Herberts of Raglan*, p. 87.
78 CPR, 1441–46. CFR, 1452–61.
79 Thomas, *The Herberts of Raglan*, p. 88.
80 Thomas, *The Herberts of Raglan*, p. 88.
81 Thomas, *The Herberts of Raglan*, p. 17.
82 Thomas, *The Herberts of Raglan*, pp. 87–8.
83 Thomas, *The Herberts of Raglan*, p. 89.
84 Thomas, *The Herberts of Raglan*.
85 CPR, 1461–67.
86 Thomas, *The Herberts of Raglan*, p. 89.
87 Thomas, *The Herberts of Raglan*, p. 89.
88 Thomas, *The Herberts of Raglan*, p. 90.
89 The tun (Old English: *tunne*, Latin: *tunellus*, Middle Latin: *tunna*) is an English unit of liquid volume (not weight), used for measuring wine, oil or honey.
90 Thomas, *The Herberts of Raglan*, p. 91.
91 Thomas, *The Herberts of Raglan*, p. 93.
92 Thomas, *The Herberts of Raglan*, p. 90.
93 See C. L. Scofield, *The Life and Reign of Edward the Fourth* (London and New York: Longman, Green and Co., 1923), vol. 2.
94 The *Herbertorum Prosapia* states that the young earl was 9 in 1469, but in another section that he was 14. The inquisitions 'post mortem' indicate he was either 14 or 15 at the time of his father's death (PRO C140/32; PRO E149/222/10).

95 Thomas, *The Herberts of Raglan*, p. 75.
96 See Thomas, *The Herberts of Raglan*, pp. 73–83, for a discussion of the possible reasons for the ineffectiveness in the political arena of William, second Earl of Pembroke.
97 CPR, 1467–77, p. 429.
98 CPR, 1476–85, pp. 128 and 182; Thomas, *The Herberts of Raglan*, p. 78.
99 See Thomas, *The Herberts of Raglan*, pp. 98–102, for arguments to substantiate this assertion.
100 Quoted in Thomas, *The Herberts of Raglan*, p. 98.
101 These grants were of brief duration, as he lost the chief justiceship and annuity as a consequence of the general annulment of Richard III's grants following Henry VII's accession.
102 Charles Ross, *Richard III* (University of California Press, 1981), p. 158.
103 Ross, *Richard III*, p. 211.
104 *Herbertorum Prosapia*, pp. 55–8.
105 NLW Badminton M. R., 1589 and 1590.
106 CPR, 1467–77, pp. 488 and 454; NLW Badminton Deed, 347; *Herbertorum Prosapia*, pp. 76 and 80.
107 G. H. R. Kent, 'The Estates of the Herbert Family in the Mid Fifteenth Century', (unpublished PhD thesis, University of Keele, 1973). Accessed through Ethos, No. 528432, August 2015.
108 NLW Badminton Deeds, 798 and 347.
109 W. R. B. Robinson, 'The Administration of the Lordship of Monmouth', in *The Monmouthshire Antiquary* (2002), XVII, p. 37.
110 NLW Badminton Manorial no. 1564.
111 R. A. Griffiths and R. S. Thomas, *The Principality of Wales in the Later Middle Ages: The Structure and Personnel of Government I, South Wales, 1277–1536* (Cardiff: University of Wales Press, 1971), p. 186.
112 'Henry VIII: Pardon Roll, Part 1', in *Letters and Papers, Foreign and Domestic, Henry VIII, Volume 1, 1509–1514*, ed. J. S. Brewer (London, 1920), pp. 203–16.
113 W. R. B. Robinson, *Early Tudor Gwent 1485 –1547* (Welshpool: W. R. B. Robinson, 2002), p. 16.
114 Kent, *The Estates of the Herbert Family in the Mid Fifteenth Century*, p. 58; Robinson, *Early Tudor Gwent 1485–1547*, pp. 16–20.
115 Robinson, *Early Tudor Gwent 1485–1547*, p. 17–8.
116 CPR, 1476–85 No. 470.
117 PRO DL 42/20 f.17.
118 BL, H MS 433 95, cited in Robinson, 'The Administration of the Lordship of Monmouth', p. 38.
119 Robinson, 'The Administration of the Lordship of Monmouth', p. 38.
120 PRO E 315/83 f.24, cited in Robinson, 'The Administration of the Lordship of Monmouth', p. 38.
121 Robinson, 'The Administration of the Lordship of Monmouth', p. 39. PRO C 54/387 No. 29.

122 R. Somerville, *History of the Duchy of Lancaster* (London: Phillimore, 1953), vol. 1, pp. 648, 638 and 652.
123 CCR, 1485–1500, Nos 129, 1064. CPR, 1494–1509, pp. 288 and 599. CCR, 1500–09, No. 453.
124 Somerville, *History of the Duchy of Lancaster*, p. 648.
125 Robinson, *Early Tudor Gwent 1485–1547,* p. 5.
126 Robinson, 'The Administration of the Lordship of Monmouth', p. 39.
127 Badminton Deeds and Documents No. 1781.
128 CCR, 1485–1500, no. 617.
129 The earldom was granted again to the Herbert family in 1551 as the tenth creation to Sir Walter's nephew, Sir William Herbert. Today, the Herbert family still retains the earldom of Pembroke, among others.
130 CCR, 1500–09, Nos. 522, 496, 509 and 860.
131 BL, Add. MS 7099, f.5.
132 Robinson, *Early Tudor Gwent 1485–1547*, pp. 3, 21–32.
133 Kent, *The Estates of the Herbert Family in the Mid Fifteenth Century*. Also see endnote references in Robinson, *Early Tudor Gwent 1485–1547*, p. 2.
134 Taken from the translation of poem 28 at *www.gutorglyn.net/gutorglyn/poem*, Centre of Advanced Welsh and Celtic Studies (CAWCS), ed. Barry Lewis. Accessed September 2015.
135 Part of poem 28, 'In Praise to William Herbert of Pembroke and Troy' (CAWCS), ed. Barry Lewis.
136 Robinson, 'The Administration of the Lordship of Monmouth', p. 38. I have not found any further information about Margery, William's first wife.
137 TNA PRO 11/21/327, 15 March 1523.
138 TNA PRO 11/21/327, 15 March 1523.
139 Robinson, 'The Administration of the Lordship of Monmouth', p. 30.
140 L. M. Hill (ed.), The Ancient State Authoritie, and the Proceedings of the Court of Requests by Sir Julius Caesar (Cambridge: 1975), p. 67.
141 PRO DL 3/69 R3f.
142 N. H. Nicolas (ed.), *Privy Purse Expenses of Elizabeth of York* (London: William Pickering, 1830), p. 47.
143 Nicolas, *Privy Purse Expenses of Elizabeth of York*, p. xcii.
144 Quoted from 'Elegy to the Lady Blanche', in Ruth Elizabeth Richardson, *Mistress Blanche, Queen Elizabeth I's Confidante* (Woonton: Logaston Press, 2007), p. 40. See Lewys Morgannwg, Llansteffan MS 164, 118, in National Library of Wales, for the original elegy, which was first translated and published in A. Cynfael Lake (ed.), *Gwaith Lewys Morgannwg*, vol. 1 (Aberystwyth: University of Wales, 2005).
145 Richardson, *Mistress Blanche*, p. 42.
146 Richardson, *Mistress Blanche*, p. 45.
147 TNA PRO 11/21/327, 15 March 1523.
148 TNA PRO 11/21/327, 15 March 1523.
149 *www.tudorplace.com.ar/HERBERT3.htm*. Accessed October 2015.

150 Richard Hanbury-Tenison, *The High Sheriffs of Monmouthshire and Gwent* (R. Hanbury-Tenison, 2008), p. 1.
151 *www.tudorplace.com.ar/HERBERT3.htm*. Accessed October 2015.
152 The law and customs protecting the property rights of widows were abolished by parliamentary statue for Wales in 1696 and everywhere in the UK by 1725. See Amy Erickson, *Women and Property* (London and New York: Routledge, 1993).
153 Thomas Churchyard, *The Worthiness of Wales a Poem* (London: Thomas Evans, 1776), p. 5. Reprinted from the edition of 1587.
154 PRO DL 3/69 R3f.
155 *www.tudorplace.com.ar/HERBERT3.htm*. Accessed October 2015.
156 Sir William Herbert's will, TNA PRO 11/40/29.
157 Bradney, *A History of Monmouthshire: The Hundred of Trelech*, p. 162.
158 Sir Charles Herbert's will, TNA PRO 11/40/29. See also *www.tudorplace.com.ar/HERBERT3.htm*. Accessed October 2015.
159 *Vide*, vol. 1, p. 284. Cited in Joseph Bradney, *A History of Monmouthshire: The Hundred of Trelech*, vol. 2, Part 2 (1913; London: Academy Books, 1992), p. 163.
160 Hanbury-Tenison, *The High Sheriffs of Monmouthshire and Gwent*, p. 6.
161 Bradney, *A History of Monmouthshire: The Hundred of Trelech*, p. 163.
162 Hanbury-Tenison, *The High Sheriffs of Monmouthshire and Gwent*, p. 7.
163 Bradney, *A History of Monmouthshire: The Hundred of Trelech*, p. 163.
164 See Jonathan Hughes, 'Somerset , Charles, first earl of Worcester (*c*.1460–1526)', *ODNB*. Online edition accessed February 2015.
165 Michael G. Brennan (ed.), *The Travel Diary (1611–1612) of an English Catholic Sir Charles Somerset* (Leeds: Leeds Philosophical and Literary Society Ltd, 1993), p. 4.
166 Kenyon, *Raglan Castle*, p. 14.
167 I am most grateful to Cynfael Lake for his translation and interpretations of Lewys Morgannwg's poem to Edward.
168 Copyright of this translation lies with Cynfael Lake.
169 Brennan, *The Travel Diary (1611–1612)*, p. 4.
170 John Nichols, *The progresses and public processions of Queen Elizabeth: among which are interspersed other solemnities, public expenditures, and remarkable events during the reign of that illustrious princess* (London: printed by and for John Nichols and Son, 1823) vol. 1, pp. 317–18. See Brennan, *The Travel Diary (1611–1612)*, p. 7, for additional information.
171 Brennan, *The Travel Diary (1611–1612)*, p. 7.
172 David Lloyd, S*tate-worthies, or, The states-men and favourites of England since the reformation their prudence and policies, successes and miscarriages, advancements and falls* (London: printed by Thomas Milbourne for Samuel Speed, 1670), p. 582.
173 See Hannah Thomas, 'A great number of popish books: a study of the Welsh Jesuit missionary library of the College of St Francis Xavier, c. 1600–1679'

(unpublished PhD thesis, Swansea University, 2014) for a full account of Jesuit activity in Wales.

174 See Thomas, 'A great number of popish books', ch. 3, for an account of the development of the College of St Francis Xavier.

175 Maurice Whitehead, 'Piety and Patronage: the English College, Rome, the earls of Worcester and links with Wales 1578–1679', in *The Venerable* (Rome: Venerabile Collegio Inglese, 2014), pp. 18–22.

176 Brennan, *The Travel Diary (1611–1612)*, p. 8.

177 William Sterrell is the agent who paid (on behalf of Edward Somerset) to have Nicholas Owen released in 1594/5; see J. M. Finnis and Patrick Martin, 'Thomas Thorpe, "W.S", and the Catholic Intelligencers', *English Literary Renaissance* (2003), 38/3, 23, quoting *Hatfield Papers*, 111, 112: William Sterrell to William Wade (October 15 [1594]), seeking warrant for the release of Nicolas Owen.

178 Horatia Durant, 'History of Troy House, Four Hundred Years of Splendour', in *Monmouthshire Beacon*, 10 August 1956, page not shown on this reference copy. Sir William Powell is shown as Elizabeth's adopted father on the 1609 document, *Settlement before marriage of Charles Somerset Esq., son of Edward, Earl of Worcester, and Elizabeth Powell* (Badminton: D2700/0C/1). See also Bradney, *A History of Monmouthshire, The Hundred of Trelech*, pp. 230–1.

179 Bradney, *A History of Monmouthshire, The Hundred of Trelech*, p. 232.

180 Badminton: FmD3.

181 This feature is discussed in detail in chapter 5.

182 Hanbury-Tension, *The High Sheriffs of Monmouthshire and Gwent 1540–2000*, p. 30.

183 Hanbury-Tension, *The High Sheriffs of Monmouthshire and Gwent 1540–2000*, p. 30.

184 Charles Mayes, 'The Early Stuart and the Irish Peerage', *The English Historical Review* 73/287 (April 1958), 227–51.

185 Brennan, *The Travel Diary (1611–1612)*, p. 8.

186 Thomas Bayly, *Worcester's Apophthegmes or Witty Sayings of the Right Honourable Henry (late) Marquess and Earl of Worcester, by T. B. (1650)*, Apophthegm 9.

187 Bradney, *A History of Monmouthshire: The Hundred of Trelech*, p. 163.

188 *Calendar of the Proceedings of the Committee for Advance of Money, 1642–1656*, part III, p. 1218, cited in Brennan, *The Travel Diary (1611–1612)*, p. 36.

189 The date of Elizabeth's death is unknown.

190 Brennan, *The Travel Diary (1611–1612)*, p. 38.

191 CSP Domestic, 1644–1645, p. 18, cited in Brennan, *The Travel Diary (1611–1612)*, p. 36.

192 Brennan, *The Travel Diary (1611–1612)*, p. 36.

193 Brennan, *The Travel Diary (1611–1612)*, p. 37.

194 *Calendar of the Proceedings of the Committee for Compounding, &c., 1643–1660*, part IV, pp. 2887–8.

195 Brennan, *The Travel Diary (1611–1612)*, p. 37.

196 Bradney, *A History of Monmouthshire: The Hundred of Trelech*, p. 163.
197 Maurice Whitehead, of the Venerable English College, Rome, places Henry in Rome and at the College during this period.
198 Badminton: P4/3.
199 Horatia Durant, *The Somerset Sequence* (London: Newman Neane, 1951), p. 102.
200 Durant, *The Somerset Sequence*, p. 112.
201 Molly McClain, 'Somerset, Henry, first duke of Beaufort (1629–1700)', *ODNB* (Oxford University Press, 2004; online edn, September 2013). Accessed 20 March 2015.
202 Durant, *The Somerset Sequence*, p. 113.
203 Molly McClain, 'Somerset, Henry, first duke of Beaufort (1629–1700)', *ODNB* (Oxford University Press, 2004; online edn, September 2013). Available at *www.oxforddnb.com/view/article/26009*. Accessed 20 March 2015. Brennan, *The Travel Diary (1611–1612)*, p. 38.
204 Henry Somerset, Lord Herbert, was born before 1660 but died in infancy.
205 Molly McClain, 'Somerset, Henry, first duke of Beaufort (1629–1700)', *ODNB*.
206 Ann Benson, 'Charles Somerset, Marquess of Worcester', *Library and Archive*, Royal Society, London.
207 Ann Benson, *A briefe memorial of my voyage into France 1673–1674 Charles, Lord Herbert*, transcription of the travel diary for His Grace, the Duke of Beaufort, Badminton, 2014.
208 Steward's Troy 'house book', 1687–1690, Badminton: RF/1. Letter from Charles, Marquess of Worcester to his mother, first Duchess of Beaufort, 13 January 1696/7, Badminton: FmF 1/3/2.
209 Molly McClain, 'Somerset, Henry, first duke of Beaufort (1629–1700)', *ODNB*.
210 Thomas Dineley, *The Account of the official progress of His Grace Henry the first Duke of Beaufort . . . through Wales in 1684*, by photolithography from the original MS of Thomas Dineley, 1888. Anna Tribe's personal copy accessed at Raglan, July 2012.
211 Durant, *The Somerset Sequence*, p. 125.
212 Guardianship of their grandson, Henry, by the first Duke and Duchess of Beaufort dated 1685, Badminton: FmE 5 5/1/1. Letters between Charles and his mother, the Duchess of Beaufort, show that even before his fatal accident in 1698, his son, Henry, spent much time at Badminton. Badminton: FmF 1/3/2.
213 Benson, 'Charles Somerset, Marquis of Worcester', Royal Society.
214 Durant, *The Somerset Sequence*, p. 145; Benson, *A briefe memorial*, 2014.
215 Durant, *The Somerset Sequence*, p. 145.
216 Durant, 'History of Troy House, Four Hundred Years of Splendour', in *Monmouthshire Beacon*, 10 August 1956, page unknown.
217 Letters from Charles to his mother are in a tender tone and evidence a shared interest in horticulture. Badminton: FmF 1/3/2.
218 McCain, *Beaufort*, p. 198.

219 John Curre (d.1685) was steward at Troy before and for three years after Henry was elevated to the title of first Duke of Beaufort. He was followed by Charles Price (d.1703). See Bradney, *A History of Monmouthshire: The Hundred of Trelech*, p. 164.
220 CSP Domestic, 1698, p. 353; Beaufort MS, *Case of . . . Dowager Duchess of Beaufort.*
221 Wilts. RO 1300/716, 728; 1300/324B.
222 Durant, *The Somerset Sequence*, p. 145.
223 John Byng, *Tour to the West (31 May–14 July 1781)*, held at Oxford, Bodleian Library.
224 Durant, *The Somerset Sequence*, p. 198.
225 Durant, *The Somerset Sequence*, p. 194.
226 Horatia Durant, 'Four Hundred Years of Splendour', unpublished paper held by Durant's niece, Anna Tribe, August 1974.
227 *Monmouthshire Beacon*, 8 June 1900. Accessed December 2015, Nelson Museum, Monmouth.
228 A Wells light was a large paraffin-fuelled (kerosene) blowlamp used for engineering work, particularly for illumination, in Victorian times.
229 *Monmouthshire Beacon*, 8 June 1900. Accessed December 2015, Nelson Museum, Monmouth.
230 Durant, *The Somerset Sequence*, p. 203.
231 *Monmouthshire Beacon*, 10 June 1898. Accessed December 2015, Nelson Museum, Monmouth.
232 *Monmouthshire Beacon*, 19 August 1898. Accessed December 2015, Nelson Museum, Monmouth.
233 Messrs Driver, Jonas & Co. (Pall Mall), auction catalogue for *Troy House Estate Monmouth*, 27 March 1901. Accessed August 2012, Nelson Museum, Monmouth.
234 Bradney, *A History of Monmouthshire: The Hundred of Trelech*, p. 164.
235 I am very grateful to Dr Nicola Bradbear of The Elms, Mitchel Troy, for providing me with access to her house deeds that also refer to Edward Arnold as the purchaser of The Elms in the early 1900s.
236 *Monmouthshire Beacon*, 4 September 1903. Accessed December 2015, Nelson Museum, Monmouth.
237 Letter from Sister A. R. Kelly, Good Shepherd Convent, Blackley, Manchester to author, 4 January 2012.
238 'Troy House', in *Monmouthshire Beacon*, 4 September 1903. Accessed December 2015, Nelson Museum, Monmouth.
239 C. J. Evans, *Monmouthshire: Its History and Topography* (Cardiff: William Lewis Ltd, 1953), p. 418.
240 *Monmouthshire Beacon*, 1 September 1905. Accessed December 2015, Nelson Museum, Monmouth.
241 Indenture dated 9 March 1906 signed by Edward Arnott of The Garth, Monmouth and three nuns from Troy House. Information provided by Nicola Bradbear.

242 1911 Census accessed through *Ancestry.com* on 8 August 2012.
243 Letter from Sister A. R. Kelly, Good Shepherd Convent, Blackley, Manchester to author, 4 January 2012.
244 Letter from Sister Jenny, The Priory, Northfield, Birmingham to author, 18 September 2012. One Troy Convent logbook from the 1950s is kept at Nelson Museum, Monmouth; other material was destroyed on the nuns' orders when they left Troy in 1977. People who worked at Troy during the nun's occupation were not required to sign any information-gagging order.
245 Michael Tamplin, groundsman at Troy during the 1960s, personal communication, 20 August 2012.
246 Michael Tamplin, from his archive.
247 David Jenkins, personal communication, 5 December 2015.
248 Monmouthshire Planning Department, application DC/2008/00723.

Three

Troy House: a Building History

FROM ITS OWNERSHIP HISTORY, Troy House has the potential to be a complex mix of building phases from the medieval period to the 1960s. It warrants a scholarly detailed architectural investigation, but this is not possible, due to unresolved long-term access difficulties. Nevertheless, by combining a consideration of how the approach to Troy has changed across time with map regression, documentary searches and some of the extant features of the house, farmstead and ancillary built structures, it is still possible to illuminate Troy's building history.

The approach: an ancient access route and the identification of reception courtyards

The first Duke of Beaufort's Carolean north range of Troy House has a central doorway above a double flight of steps. From the time of its construction in the early 1680s to the present day, it has served as the main procedural entrance to the house and is accessed from the north.[1] However, as Joseph Bradney states, 'The most ancient approach to Troy was by a roadway which still exists on the south side of the kitchen garden [walled garden], leading from the main road to Trellech'.[2] Indeed, John Aram's and Joseph Gillmore's estate maps of respectively 1765 and 1712 record an access route from the west to the pre-Carolean parts of the house and what is now known as Troy Farm.[3] The Aram map shows this route ending at one of the three buildings which, together with the south side of Troy

Figure 3.1 (right) *Detail, John Aram's map of 1765 showing the access route to a courtyard.*

Map by permission of Llyfrgell Genedlaethol Cymru/The National Library of Wales; annotations: Ann Benson.

Figure 3.2 (below) *Detail, Joseph Gillmore's map of 1712 showing the access route to a courtyard.*

Map by permission of Llyfrgell Genedlaethol Cymru/The National Library of Wales; annotations: Ann Benson.

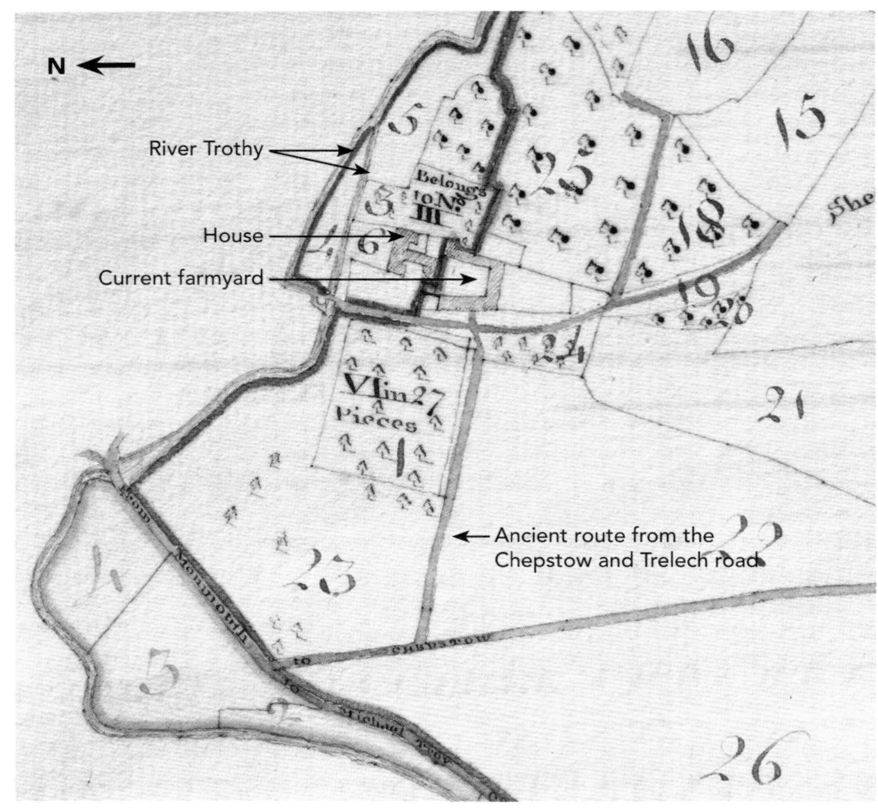

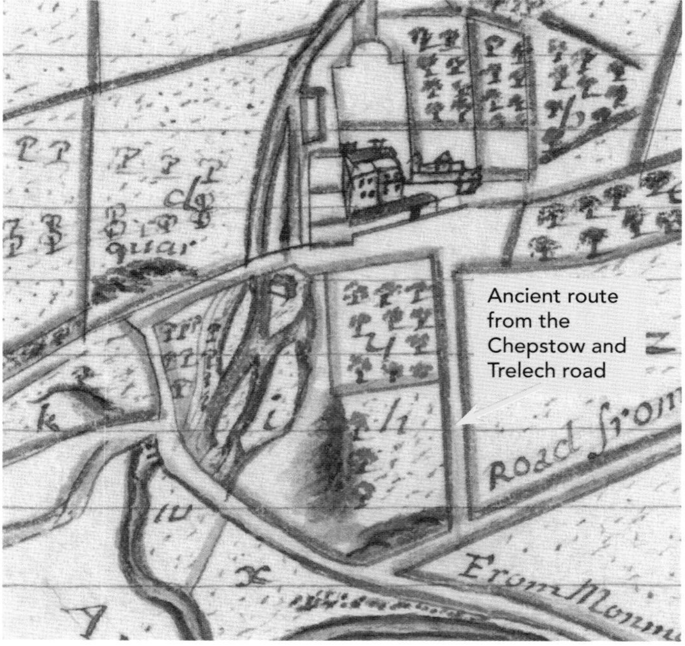

House, form a courtyard currently used as a farmyard.[4] Aram's layout of buildings is still visible today, although the building on the west of the yard where his route terminates was largely demolished by the current farmer some decades ago.

Overall, the Gillmore map lacks detail but, as already shown on that of Aram, it also records the route from the Trellech road and a courtyard to the south of the house. In addition, there is what could be a gateway through a wall to the west of the house.

The layout of the farmstead is of a complex of three ancient linear buildings set at right angles to each other around a central square yard that, on its fourth side, is completed by the south wing of Troy House and its stone-pillared entrance. The row of cottages on the east side of the yard, now the farmhouse, appears to be the converted remains of an earlier building, which John Newman believes is possibly of medieval date.[5] Access to the interior of the farmhouse to confirm this claim has not been granted. Photographs from the 1930s show the whole building harled and whitewashed; only the majority of the northern end, which is closest to Troy House, and the extreme southern end of the farmhouse have retained this cladding. The size and alignment of the revealed stones forming the exterior walls of the rest of the farmhouse substantiate Newman's medieval attribution.

Figure 3.3 *Troy Farmhouse: during the 1930s (above); in 2015 (below).*

Copyright: Ann Benson, 1930s photograph; Crown copyright: RCAHMW, 2015 photograph.

However, the northern section of this building has clearly been extended at a later date. The northern end of the farmhouse contains the remains of a very large masonry black oven inside the gable wall. Although now solely used as a residence, the farmhouse would have previously provided several service functions, such as a brewery and a wash house for the estate. Indeed, it is listed as including a wash house and dairy on both the 1901 and 1919 Troy Farm auction catalogues.[6]

Figure 3.4 *Troy barn (above) and detail of its corner post (inset), 2015.*

Crown copyright: RCAHMW; detail, Ann Benson.

A Grade II listed barn lies on an east–west axis at right angles to the farmhouse on the south side of the yard; Newman writes that it is 'a seven-bay BARN, probably of the C18'.[7] According to the RCAHMW, it is 'probably a late C18 or early C19 rebuild of an earlier timber-framed structure' where the eastern end of the structure consists of 'a lofted stable/coach-house' that has been rebuilt in red brick and with a slate and corrugated asbestos sheet roof.[8] The barn is built of random sandstone rubble of five bays; the stable portion to the east is of two bays. The barn has opposed wagon doorways that on the north elevation are very tall and break through the eaves. To the left and right of these doorways the walls have plinths that are just over one metre tall; they are constructed from large, chunky stones. A heavy, very weathered oak sill sits on each of these plinths, and on each of these are four oak wall-posts recessed into the masonry. These are as weathered as the oak sills and appear to be contemporary, indicating that they are all part of an original wooden structure. The remains of tenants on the north-west corner post show that the original barn structure had most likely three tiers of timber framing.[9] Each bay of the north front of the barn has two slit breathers in the lower half of the wall and one in the upper in a triangular arrangement. The south front has one slit breather per bay and these are only on one level. All slit breathers have been blocked internally.

The large size and chunkiness of the plinth stones imply an early date, and support Newman's medieval ascription for the barn. Arguably, at a later date, the original medieval wooden structure was infilled with rubble sandstone and then, at an even later date, the slit breathers were blocked and the east gable end bricked up to create a separate section. The 1901 and 1919 auction catalogues for Troy Farm state that the barn has cellars underneath and that the brick section was used as a stable.

Figure 3.5 *The interior of Troy barn with the triangular arrangement of its blocked slit breathers, 2015.* Crown copyright: RCAHMW.

The barn is joined at its south-west corner to a stone wall that returns northwards to terminate at a small stone building with a low roof, currently used as a store. The west corner of this small building has the remains of an archway constructed from large cut stones with a recessed moulding on their east-facing sides (facing the farmhouse). The recess would have accommodated a door. The keystone lies abandoned nearby (Figure 3.6). Some decades ago, the farmer demolished the archway and most of its attached building lying to the north and facing the farmhouse. A Monmouth resident who lived at Troy Farm for some twenty years before the Second World War

Figure 3.6 *The original archway in line with the oldest route to Troy House (left) (1930s) and (below) the remains of the arch with the keystone on the floor (2015).*
Copyright: Ann Benson, 1930s photograph; Crown copyright: RCAHMW, 2015 photograph.

Figure 3.7 *St John the Baptist Church of Troy? The building left of centre has a large gable window and what appears to be a bell-tower. Detail,* A Panorama of Monmouth, with Troy House, *c.*1672, *by Hendrik Danckerts.*

By permission of Nelson Museum, Monmouth.

recalls the archway and this building. Her photographs from the 1930s show an intact Gothic arch matching the remains already described. It is significant that this archway is in line with the oldest approach to Troy House, as shown on the Aram and Gillmore maps.

Another 1930s photograph shows this archway joined to an un-coursed stone building on the west side of the farmyard, the one largely demolished by the farmer some decades ago. During the period, 1900–30, it housed stables and carriages.[10] The current farmer also recalls this building containing a small chapel at its southern end; he describes it as having 'ancient' wooden doors that he sold when the building was largely demolished. Perhaps this was the location of the St John the Baptist Church of Troy in the 1404 *Register of Bishop Richard Clifford of Worcester*, as identified in chapter 2.[11] Tantalisingly, Hendrik Danckerts's painting of Troy from 1672 shows a building that looks remarkably like a church in a similar location (Figure 3.7).

The 1930s photograph of the building (Figure 3.8) shows the roof has clearly been renewed but the remains of a rectangular window, mullioned to give two- or possibly three-centred arched heads, is visible on the left side of the photograph. Also, this window appears to have been partially sealed with stonework. The old photograph does not facilitate clear enlargement but Figure 3.9 shows its appearance. The occupier of Troy Farm at this time recalls the window being covered by internal hinged metal shutters.

It is not inconceivable that this window and its internal metal shutters – and the building as a whole, particularly given the chunkiness of the stones in the attached archway – dates from the late medieval period,

Figure 3.8 *The building lying on the western side of the farmyard as it looked during the 1930s, now largely demolished.*
Copyright: Ann Benson.

although this style of window continued at the vernacular levels almost until the eighteenth century. Within living memory, the northern end of this building terminated close to the un-coursed stone wall encircling the southern end of Troy House and was separated from it by an opening of less than three metres.

The fourth and northern side of the farmyard consists of a wing of Troy House, which has been identified by John Harris and the architect responsible for Troy's planning application, Graham Frecknall, as the oldest part of the house.[12] It is separated from the farmyard by the un-coursed stone wall that contains a pillared entrance. The entrance gives access to a small paved yard and is in line with an ancient doorway to this section of the house. Before the nuns built their cloisters and chapel to the side of this yard in the 1960s, the space was much larger and was also completely enclosed by the house and the un-coursed stone wall. In short, it was a large courtyard. There

Figure 3.9 *The remains of an ancient window in the building lying on the western side of the farmyard (1930s).*
Copyright: Ann Benson.

Figure 3.10 *Entrance to the south wing of Troy House from the farmyard.*
Copyright: Ann Benson.

are just metres between this part of Troy House and the farmhouse: close proximity between main residence and farm buildings is characteristic of medieval dwellings.

In 1913 Bradney reported that there were 'three ancient archways to the [farm] yards'.[13] Certainly, one would be the Gothic archway shown in the 1930s photograph (Figure 3.6). The other two 'ancient archways' are most likely one extant, joining the farmhouse to the un-coursed stone wall (arch 1) and one joining the same stone wall with the now lost stable building (arch 2). The relative positions of the arches and how they relate to Aram's map is shown in Figure 3.11.[14]

Bradney's claim that the oldest approach to Troy is from the ancient road connecting Trelech with Monmouth is supported by this route being shown on both the Aram and Gillmore estate maps as running down the western side of the walled garden and being in line with the Gothic archway leading to what is now Troy's farmyard. The buildings surrounding this yard appear to be of medieval origin and would have formed an outer reception courtyard or base court (from the French *bas*). This court gives direct access through the extant stone gateway on its northern side

1 Extant archway into gardens east of the current farmhouse.

2 View from where second archway existed.

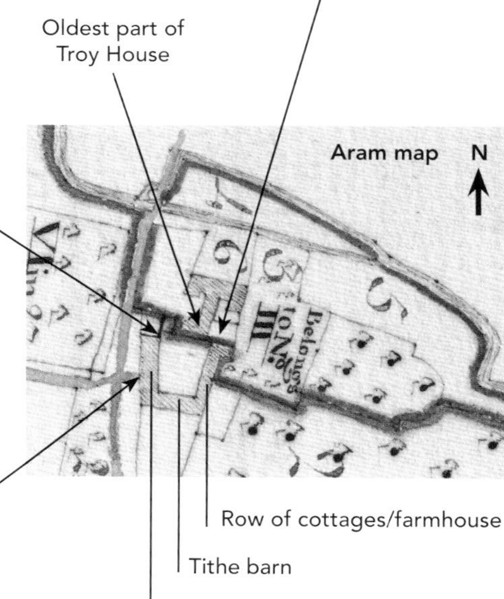

3 Archway in stable building that no longer exists.

Figure 3.11 *Three archway entrances to the current farmyard/outer reception courtyard (photographs taken during the 1930s).*

to an inner reception court – the now paved area – that adjoins the oldest section of Troy House, argued here as being from the medieval period. Other evidence for a residence of some status existing at Troy in the medieval period comes – although tenuously – from pottery found in the 1950s during field walking plough soil at Troy Meadow, a field adjoining the house.[15] Two pieces of a much-abraded medieval Malvern encaustic floor tile in Malvern, rather than Monmouth, fabric were found at this time. During 1991 a tile kiln of the Malvern School was discovered at Cadogan House just inside the medieval town defences north of Monmouth's Priory Church. Remains found here include tile wasters decorated with the designs that can be seen in Monmouth's Priory Church and another tile dated AD 1456. The tile found in Troy Meadow is the only Malvern tile in the Malvern fabric known for Monmouth.[16] Its presence indicates the possible existence of a nearby medieval residence of some status, with owners who had knowledge of the Malvern School and were able to purchase directly from Malvern-based kilns.

Few examples of complete estates from the fifteenth to seventeenth centuries survive for comparison with Troy. Those that do, for example Hardwick Hall, Derbyshire, show that the house was encompassed by walled enclosures. As noted by Paula Henderson, no Tudor or early Stuart member of a household or visitor would have been able to separate the house from its surrounding courts and gardens.[17] Outer, or base courts, consisted of offices, stables, and barns serving several functions, for example servants' lodgings, and it is here that visitors would most likely dismount from a horse or exit a coach.[18] Arguably, Troy's current farmyard served this purpose in at least the late medieval and early Tudor periods, and perhaps even later. It would have been used thus during the estate's occupation by Thomas Herbert the elder and Sir William Herbert of Troy in the mid- to late fifteenth century, and in the early sixteenth century when William welcomed Henry VII and Elizabeth, his pregnant Queen Consort. Sir William Powell and his daughter and

Figure 3.12 *Medieval floor tiles: left, Malvern fabric sample; right, two Malvern fabric finds at Troy.*
Copyright: Ann Benson.

Figure 3.13
Detail, Prospect of Llannerch Park from the East, *English School, 1662.*
Copyright: Sotheby's, London.

son-in-law, Elizabeth and Sir Charles Somerset, would have been familiar with it in the early years of the seventeenth century. In this period it was not uncommon for such a *bas* court to lead on to an inner reception courtyard that, with geometric areas of grass and topiary, served as a more aesthetically pleasing, formal entrance to the house.[19]

It is reasonable to suggest that this inner reception courtyard might well have been that which is now paved leading to the door of the oldest part of Troy House. A seventeenth-century painting of Llannerch, Denbighshire, shows such an arrangement of outer and inner courtyards: in the first of these there is a service building and a stepped block for mounting a horse or entering a coach; this space opens on to a formally planted inner reception courtyard close to the house. Even the stone pillars between the two courtyards are topped with balls as at Troy.

Troy House: different building phases

A ground-floor plan of Troy House taken from line drawings held by RCAHMW is useful for indicating different building phases. The plan is adapted to show external door and window positions and does not include any of the nuns' additions of attached theatre, chapel and cloisters from the 1960s. This footprint of the historic house resembles a capital letter T, with the north range, which is from the time of the first Duke of Beaufort in the 1680s, running along the top of the letter; the south wing, facing the current farmyard, lies at the base of the letter.

So what of the history of Troy's south wing other than its being claimed by Frecknall and Harris as the oldest part of the house? It was re-roofed and stuccoed during the time of the nun's building activity in

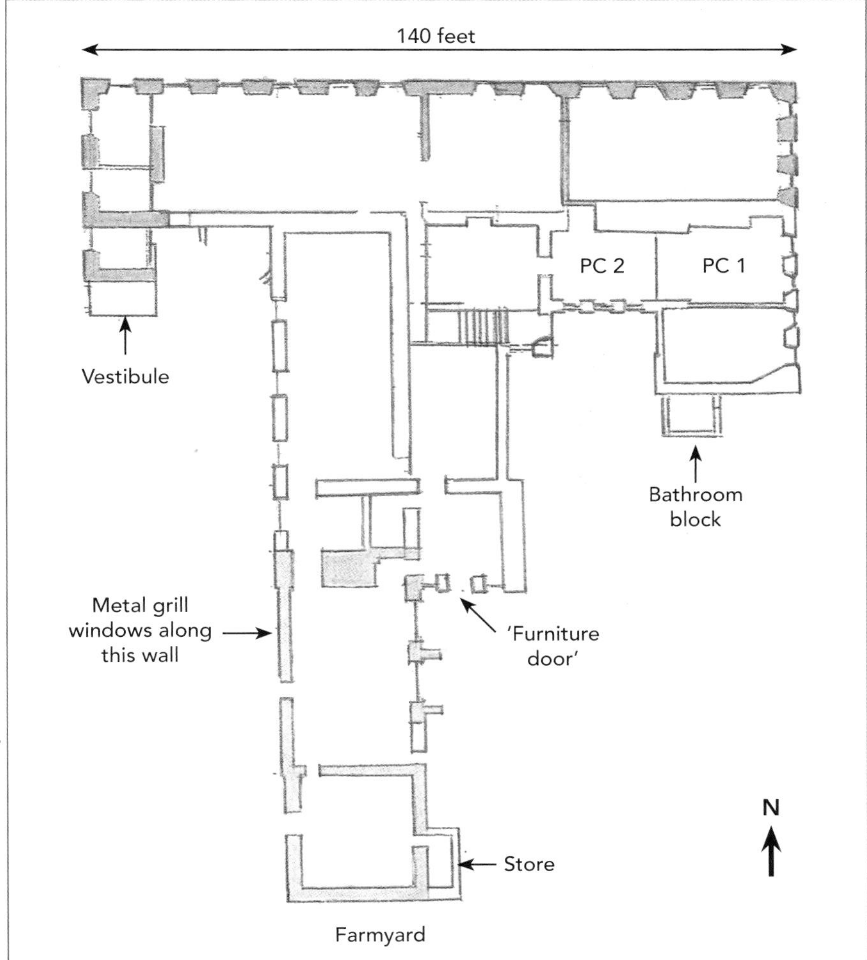

Figure 3.14 *Footprint of historic Troy House: south wing (pale blue), north range (red) and rooms with ornate plaster ceilings (PC 1 and PC 2).* Copyright: Ann Benson.

the 1960s, when it was the location of their commercial laundry. The wing has false ceilings on both the ground and first floors. However, holes in the first-floor ceiling reveal the higher section of the south wing's north wall, on which stone corbels can be seen. These corbels are oriented to support beams running above the south wing on a north–south axis. This suggests that the roof height of at least this end of the south wing was once higher than it is now.

The remains of a square lead clock-face can be seen on this wing's gable end that overlooks the current farmyard. The clock's workings were removed by the nuns when they installed a new boiler for the laundry in this wing (the boiler's metal chimney stacks remain). In 1913 Bradney wrote: 'On the south wing is a clock turret containing an ancient clock, which strikes on a bell, on which is the date 1607.'[20] The clock carries the inscription, 'Sir William Powell of Troye in the Countie of Monmothe Knight caused this bell to be made the XXIII Of Marche Anno Domini 1607' (Old Style).[21] As the steward of Edward, the fourth Earl of Worcester, William resided at Troy until his death in 1611. He was made a knight on 7 January 1608 (New Style); perhaps this event was marked by the erection of the clock-bell. It is possible that the clock-face was originally in another location and was moved here before Bradney's comments of 1913 but from its appearance, this is unlikely.

Figure 3.15 *Detail, lead clock-face of Sir William Powell's 1607 clock-bell on the gable end of the south wing.*
Crown copyright: RCAHMW.

Other evidence suggests that this south wing may pre-date 1607. The wing now consists of one very large and one much smaller room on the ground floor, and one large room on the first floor accessed by a modern staircase at the southern end. There are two opposing exterior doorways positioned approximately halfway along the wing's length; they both give access to the one large room that forms two-thirds of the wing's ground floor. The door on the wing's west wall is said to be the oldest door in the house;[22] since 1962 it has opened, not on to surrounding garden, but directly into the attached theatre built at this time. What would have been the exterior of the west wall is hidden behind a wall of the attached theatre, which has sections of brick and others of just plasterboard panels. The doorway on the east wall that opens on to the paved yard was enlarged and a wide modern doorway inserted by the nuns; this was the main door through which their laundry service operated. All of the window openings on this wall have also been enlarged and modern metal casements inserted.

The dimensions of the ground floor, opposing positions of the two external doorways, and evidence from extant corbels suggest the south wing may have been a hall house of two storeys, although Frecknall and Harris believe this wing may also have developed from an earlier Welsh longhouse.[23] There is no evidence of any pre-existing wooden structure having been infilled with stone, as in the case of the farm barn; this may indicate that the south wing was intended to provide accommodation for those of some status. The walls appear to be at least half a metre thick of rough-cast sandstone, which is hidden on the house side (east) by plasterboard. The theatre wall lies some sixty centimetres from the wing's original exterior west wall and the gap thus formed contains large metal water pipes, most likely inserted by the nuns during the wing's conversion to a laundry. Inside this gap can also be seen the remains of at least three stone mullion windows complete with iron grilles set into the original wall.[24] One window has three lights and no transoms. Some of these grilles and windows have been damaged by the insertion of the large water pipes and the brick wall of the theatre. The style of both the mullioned windows and the iron grilles on the west wall of the south wing resembles that of the medieval period (Figure 3.16).[25]

The plan of a hall house usually comprised four bays, with the two central ones forming the main hall open to the roof with the hearth in the middle, and two doors to the outside at one end forming a cross passage. Such a cross passage is at least evidenced by the opposing doorways of the south wing. Beyond the cross passage the outer bay at the lower end of the hall contained one or two rooms devoted to service functions, such as storing and serving food and drink (rooms commonly called buttery

Figure 3.16 *Sketch of one of the south wing's windows with a metal grille, the latter broken on one side to accommodate a brick wall.*
Copyright: Ann Benson.

and pantry), while the room in the bay at the other end, the upper end, was a reception room (the parlour). The open hearth found in a hall house created heat and smoke. A high ceiling drew the smoke upwards, leaving a relatively smoke-free void beneath. Later hall houses were built with chimneys and flues. In earlier ones, these were added as alterations and additional flooring was often installed. This, and the need for staircases to reach each of the upper storeys, led to much innovation and variety in floor plans.

The end bays each had an upper floor containing rooms (solars) used by the occupants as their private living and sleeping quarters. Are the corbels seen at first-floor level on the south wing's north wall evidence of beams forming a solar at this end of the hall? Solars did not communicate with each other because the hall rose to the rafters between them and smoke from a central open hearth on the ground floor would have risen into this space. Developments over time saw the open hearth being moved to the end of the hall and a chimney built to channel the smoke away from the building. The remains of a chimney opening for a hearth is extant on the inside of the north wall of the south wing. Was an original, central open hearth changed to a hearth and chimney on this north wall at some time – and did the south wing exist as a Welsh longhouse before being altered to a hall house, which was then altered again to create solars?

Frustratingly, more questions than answers are raised by the south wing, while the nuns' alterations to the roof, window and door openings certainly add to the puzzle. Unaltered hall houses are almost unknown: having started in the medieval period as a home for a lord and his community of retainers, the hall house changed in its structure across time.

The most substantiated ownership of the manor of Troy (Troy Parva/Little Troy) during the medieval period is to the de Clare family at the beginning of the fourteenth century. Among the knight's fees belonging to Gilbert de Clare, Earl of Gloucester and Hertford, was a moiety of a knight's fee in Little Troy, held by John Martel, of the annual value of 50s., and also the manor of Troy, of the annual value of 19*l.* 1*s.* 5¼*d.*[26] It is most likely that the south wing and the farmyard/outer reception courtyard buildings constituted the Troy residence at that time. The property then passed to Sir Philip Scudamore of Troy. The current farmhouse may well have provided accommodation for his retainers during the time he was associated with the Glyndŵr rebellion.

In 1411, Sir Philip, along with others associated with Owain Glyndŵr, was taken by the captain of Powis Castle to Shrewsbury where he was hanged. Troy was then owned and periodically occupied by William ap Thomas with his concubine Cary Ddu (Caroline the Black), who was called 'heiress' of Troy, until his death in 1445. With William's penchant for building, manifested in the great stone tower at Raglan Castle, perhaps he had a mind to build or change the south wing and infill the wooden structure of Troy's barn with stone. His stewardship of Monmouth from 1441 would certainly have been a stimulus to have a comfortable residence nearby. His illegitimate son, Thomas, known as 'Thomas Herbert the elder of Little Troy', is also claimed to have resided at Troy after serving in the French wars under Richard, Duke of York, and Humphrey, Duke of Gloucester. Given Thomas's joint activities with his half-brother, Sir William Herbert, the first Earl of Pembroke, his numerous commissions from Edward IV during the 1460s and intimacy with him as esquire of the body, Troy would have been a residence of some status. If the south wing had been a Welsh longhouse, it would have most likely been changed into a hall house before 1460.

A consideration of how the south wing relates to the rest of Troy House should help to reveal Troy's building history. On the other side of the north wall of the south wing at ground-floor level there is a suite of three rooms on a west–east axis that extends further east than the south wing itself, hereafter called the cross wing. Its walls are of un-coursed stone and are not similar in appearance to the original walls of the south wing, indicating that they were not built at the same time. The east section of the cross wing contains a doorway in direct line with the stone-pillared entrance from the farmyard. The door was called the 'furniture door' during the nuns' occupation, largely because it was used as a service entrance for goods being carried in and out of the house. It has since been blocked with a false wall on its reverse; the date of this is unknown. The wooden door has patched sections on either side at its head so it fits in the arch of the stone surround. This door looks contemporary with that in the west wall of the south wing. Anecdotes imply that this is the door removed by the nuns from the east wall of the south wing to make a larger doorway for their laundry.[27]

When the 'furniture' stone doorway was seen by the senior architectural historian at RCAHMW he commented: 'we came across quite a few dressed-stone doorways like this with "segmental" or three-centred heads in Glamorgan and considered them mid- or second-half of C16th in date'. Allowing for reasonable leeway, this would place the doorway in the period of the illegitimate son of Sir William Herbert, Earl of Pembroke, namely, Sir William Herbert of Troy (1442–1524). He is shown in Troy's history of ownership to have been a very wealthy and influential man, and a builder of at least a substantial part of Monmouth church. He also entertained Henry VII and Elizabeth of York (Queen Consort) at Troy in 1502 and would have ensured that Troy was a fitting venue for a royal visit. If this part of the house was built during Sir William Herbert of Troy's time, there is yet another puzzle. The room that would have been entered from the 'furniture door', hereafter called the 'furniture room' for ease of reference, has two ceiling beams with end stops. The RCAHMW architectural historian assigns them as being roll-moulded beams (not ovolo-moulded beams) of a date consistent with the doorway, so mid- to late sixteenth century. However, others assign them to the seventeenth century, long after Sir William's time.[28] When RCAHMW photographed this room for the main object of their interest, a smoke jack, they also included the two ceiling beams.

Figure 3.17 *The 'furniture door' in the east section of the cross wing, 1950s.* Crown copyright: RCAHMW.

The cross wing appears to have been built after and on to the south wing. From the ownership history of Troy it is highly unlikely that Williams's son, Sir Charles Herbert, developed Troy House after his

Figure 3.18 *Roll-moulded beams in the room entered from the 'furniture door' (below), and detail of an end stop (left).* Crown copyright: RCAHMW; detailed image: Ann Benson.

father's death in 1524. The inventory of 1557, made in the same year as the deaths of Sir Charles and his mother, Lady Blanche Herbert, William's wife, can be taken to be what largely existed in William's time, including the rooms called the king's and queen's chambers from the royal visit in 1502.[29] The inventory lists a 'Hawle' (hall) that was large enough to contain a substantial number and variety of arms as well as a cupboard and, confirming the presence of a hearth, a pair of 'Aundyrons', which were horizontal iron bars upon which logs were laid for burning in an open fireplace.

Apart from the hall, nine chambers are named: three for the king, of which two had chimneys; two for the queen, of which one had a chimney; a white chamber; an 'oulde' closet; a chamber for William John ap Jennes (James); and one for 'my lady Elizabeth', who may have been the first wife of Sir Charles Herbert. All of these chambers cannot be accounted for by the space offered by the south wing and the adjoining cross wing, even if both had two storeys.[30] No service rooms are listed in the inventory, nor any chambers for Sir William or Sir Charles. The inventory is brief and appears to concentrate on the revenue garnered from the surrounding land and what was of value within the chambers. Perhaps it only listed those chambers that were the most luxuriously furnished. Furthermore, when the widowed Lady Troy retired from her royal duties in about 1546, she moved back to Troy House and occupied a suite of her own rooms until her death in 1557 whilst her son, Sir Charles, and his wife occupied the rest of the house.[31] This implies that even more rooms than those listed in the 1557 inventory existed at Troy before 1552. So what does further examination of the house reveal to explain this discrepancy?

A photograph taken by RCAHMW in the 1950s shows the east wall of the cross wing before it had the nuns' cloisters and chapel built against it in the 1960s. The wall appears to show the remains of a floor joist at first-floor level and a door or window lintel at ground-floor level. The implication is that another section of building extended further east from the room containing the 'furniture door'. If this were part of Sir William Herbert of Troy's house, then it might account for the number of rooms in the 1552 inventory. Close inspection of the photograph reveals the chimney stack above this east wall has quoins that match those of the 1680s north range, raising

Figure 3.19 *Visual evidence of a demolished section of building east of the 'furniture door'? Note the floor joist and ground-floor lintel in this 1950s photograph.*
Crown copyright: RCAHMW.

the question, was this section or wing of the Tudor building demolished by the first duke and the chimney stack made good in the style of the rest of the new north range building? Interestingly, where the lintel of a window or door can be seen in the east wall on the photograph, the nuns knocked through a doorway to give access to their cloisters in the 1960s.

As Newman states, the first Duke of Beaufort's north range is 'what was in the 1680s the approved modern pattern of a hipped roof over a regularly fenestrated block, the central portion brought slightly forward under a pediment'.[32] It is of a single pile, three bays deep and thirteen bays wide, the central five being under the pediment, and of three tall storeys with a wave-moulded plinth; there is also wave moulding to the pediment. The walls are of old red sandstone with thin ashlar dressings; the quoins are raised and grey. The walls are known to have been harled (roughcast rendered) from the light-coloured appearance of the house in Thomas Smith's painting of 1702, an etching of 1793 and a watercolour of 1801.[33] The harling is not present on the north range in a photograph of unknown date from the late nineteenth century.[34] So, between 1801 and the time of this image, the harling was removed and the quoins took on a raised appearance. The remains of limestone, which would be used for the harling, and old red sandstone quarries are both present within the estate's Troy Orles Wood, less than two kilometres from the house.[35]

Letters written by Henry, the first Duke of Beaufort, to his wife, Mary, show that he engaged Robert Warren to begin designing the additions to Troy House in 1678, whilst also providing the duke with architectural advice on changes to his house in Chelsea.[36] Warren is not included in Howard Colvin's biographical dictionary of architects, and, to date, has not been identified as a mason, carpenter or surveyor, or as being engaged by other persons for design and building work.[37] Payment for Warren's work at Troy appears to begin in January 1679 with the entry in the first Duchess of Beaufort's accounts, 'given Ro. Warren for drafts of Troy . . . 15s'; the building work began in 1681 and the last payment for it was made in 1684, giving a total building cost of £2,413 5s. 8d.[38] The duke had initially wished to convert Chepstow Castle into a residence for his son

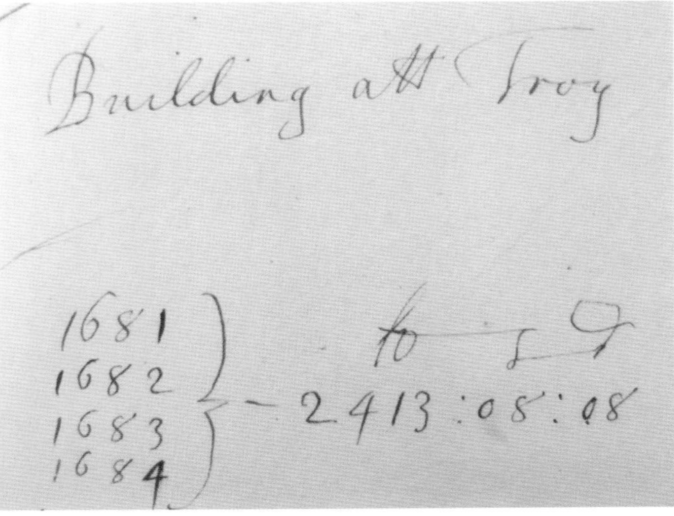

Building att Troy

1681
1682
1683
1684 — 2413 : 05 : 08

Figure 3.20 *Troy building costs, 1681–4.* By permission of the Duke of Beaufort.

and heir, Charles, a plan that was abhorrent to locals who had experienced their civil liberties being invaded by the duke in nearby Wentwood forest; the duchess and Charles persuaded the duke otherwise.[39] The building work at Troy was started before Charles's wife had even been chosen (m.1682) but it was clear that the duke and duchess wished Charles to make Troy his home. As the duchess writes underneath the Troy building costs in her account book:

> This building was done w[th]out any manner of promise upon my Sonnes marriage but purely my Lords goodness to my Sonne to have him have a house without his charge suitable to his quality, when the house was that farr built my Sonne so'th his whole were invited to live here that the money hee must have spent in housekeeping might be laid out in finishing the house to his mind.[40]

The windows of the north range have red sandstone raised surrounds, including those on the three bays of both the west and east returns of

Figure 3.21 *The west elevation of Troy House in the 1950s showing the raised red sandstone window surrounds of the 1680s build.* Crown copyright: RCAHMW.

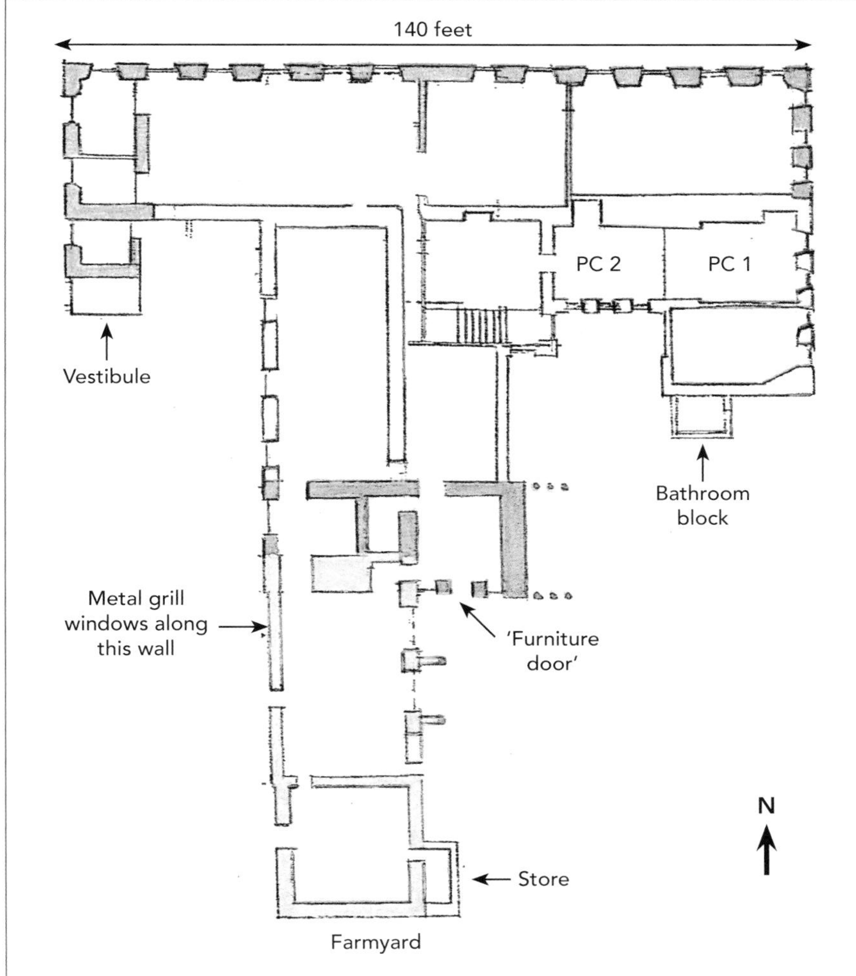

Figure 3.22 *Footprint of historic Troy House: south wing (pale blue), cross wing and its conjectural projection (dark blue), 1680s build (red), and ground-floor rooms with ornate plaster ceilings, PC 1 and PC 2.*

the range. Similar windows are also seen on the part of Troy House that adjoins the north range on the west and extends to where the 1960s theatre joins the south wing (Figure 3.21). Consequently, this west wall of the house is most likely to have been built, or adapted, at the same time as the north range was added in the 1680s; no major building work, other than the building of the bathroom block on the south of the eastern section of the house, took place at Troy House after 1698, as discussed in chapter 2.

When the positions of this style of window are shown on the floor plan (red) together with the south wing (pale blue) and its cross wing (dark blue), it reveals the extent of other building works of an unknown date adjoining the north range (Figure 3.22). These works include three rooms with extant fine plaster ceilings, rooms PC 1 and PC 2 on the ground floor, and on the first floor above PC 2, room PC 3. No other plaster ceilings appear to exist at Troy than those described here. The interior of the south-eastern corner of the building shows a strange curved wall on each storey. There does not seem to be any satisfactory explanation for this wall unless it is part of an unidentified priest hole (an identified one is described later) or is part of a pre-existing tower (perhaps that shown in Hendrik Danckerts's painting of Troy) that has been incorporated within the present building.

The east elevation of the house clearly shows the return of the three-storey north range joined to a four-bay, four-storey block with segment-headed sash windows, which Newman states are of an eighteenth-century type, and a facing of grey ashlar blocks (Figure 3.23).[41] Having examined Troy's roof space, Frecknall suggests that the east elevation, which contains the rooms with the ornate plaster ceilings, has been refaced with an applied layer approximately thirty centimetres thick, perhaps as a

Figure 3.23 *East elevation of Troy House showing the attached 1680s north range.* Crown copyright: RCAHMW.

Figure 3.24 *Troy's main staircase of 1681–4 and, on the far left, the extra steps for accessing the older four-storey east section of the house.* Crown copyright: RCAHMW.

means of grafting the north range to an older structure.[42] The east elevation of the house shows the first duke's clumsy north range addition with different stone composition. In his memoirs, the tenth Duke of Beaufort describes the first duke as a compulsive builder with sketchy knowledge of architecture 'as is evidenced to this day, for there are many inexplicable little gaps in the house [Badminton] that have either been filled in or covered over'.[43] According to the tenth duke, first-class master builders saw that the work was professionally sound, even though they were not allowed to alter the plans and remedy the defects. All of which prompts the question, when we view the east elevation of Troy House today, are we seeing the thinking of the first duke or that of his designer of the 1681–4 changes to Troy, namely Robert Warren?

The juxtaposition of the three storeys of the north range and the four storeys of the older section of the house is also clearly visible internally in a very spacious open-well staircase (Figure 3.24). This is in its own pavilion, contemporary with and projecting from the south of the north range; the pavilion's windows have red sandstone dressings in the same style as those of the north range. The oak staircase rises from the ground floor to the third floor of the north range. Three of the four storeys of the eastern section of the house are accessed by a few extra steps at each of the main staircase's landings. Newman describes the magnificent staircase as having 'thick twisted balusters, which are formed into newels in groups of four, and a ramped handrail'.[44] It is suggested here that the staircase is contemporary with the north range and dates, therefore, from 1681 to 1684.

A twentieth-century wooden partition now partly divides the ground-floor rooms, PC 1 and PC 2, in the east section of the house, but they were originally two separate rooms: their ceilings differ in style and their cornices are at different heights. Clare Gapper, an expert on plaster ceiling design, states that as a style, the enriched-rib ceilings of room PC1 do not appear much before the 1590s, and ceilings as elaborate as this are more common around 1600; by the 1620s this decoration would have gone out of fashion.[45] The elements that seem inspired by Renaissance sources, especially grotesques derived from classical Rome via Raphael and da Udine's Vatican loggia of about 1515, are the sphinxes and the putti in the floral sprays of the cornice. Cartouches also emerged in Renaissance Italy and were then popularized by the decorative plasterwork by Rosso and Primaticcio for Francis I at Fontainebleau in the 1530s and 1540s. All these features were spread throughout Europe by the engravings of decorative ornament that were increasingly being printed. Sir Charles Somerset would have seen these decorations at first hand when he visited France and Italy during 1611–12 before he settled at Troy with his new wife, Elizabeth Powell, daughter of his father's steward.[46]

The dramatic basket pendant of room PC 1 ceased to be fashionable by 1620, again supporting the view that this room's interior dates from the early seventeenth century when, as reasoned here, Sir Charles was enhancing the estate on returning from his European tour in 1612. The plaster ceiling of the first-floor room, PC 3, has narrow ribs with their intersections containing oak leaves, small faces and a flower that resembles a marigold. Whether the oak leaf represents England is uncertain and the significance of the faces has not been found. However, the marigold was adopted by James I on his accession in 1603. As discussed in Troy's ownership history, the Somersets were royal favourites of James 1 at this time, again lending credence to the ceiling's having been created by Sir Charles soon after 1612. Only important reception rooms would have had such elaborate plaster ceilings. Matching the plaster ceiling design and the chimney and window placements with those in an 1890s photograph of what was then known as the oak room in Troy House shows that this

Figure 3.25 *Plaster ceiling details in order of: ground-floor rooms, PC 1 and PC 2; first-floor room, PC 3 above PC 2 (1950s).* Crown copyright: RCAHMW.

Figure 3.26 *The oak room at Troy House c.1895.*

Crown copyright: Historic England.

was room PC 2. The early seventeenth-century oak panelling was removed from Raglan Castle for installation at Troy House at an unknown date, and then in 1895, before the Troy estate was put up for auction by the ninth Duke of Beaufort, it was removed again to Badminton, where it remains.[47]

Once this panelling had been taken away from Troy, a doorway was knocked through to the main 1680s central stairwell and another to a room in the adjoining north range. The latter room had a cellar beneath it during the nuns' occupation. It was entered via a flight of steps in the garden. When the nuns needed to replace the floor in this room they discovered the cellar and a doorway leading to a tunnel containing some artefacts, mostly cards and books. The tunnel was not explored and on their orders, the cellar and steps were sealed.[48]

The plaster ceiling of the first-floor room, PC 3, is clumsily bisected by a wall on its eastern side to provide space to accommodate a narrow corridor. It links rooms in the north range with this part of the eastern section of the house and with a small extension, containing bathrooms, built on the south of the east elevation in the nineteenth century. From the consistent thickness of the north wall of rooms PC 1, PC 2 and PC 3, this wall appears to be an earlier exterior wall of Troy House before the north range was grafted on to it. Whether this east section of the house was built in the early seventeenth century, the time of Sir Charles and Elizabeth

Somerset's occupation, or even earlier and was merely aggrandized with ornate plaster ceilings between 1612 and 1620, cannot be deduced from the available evidence.

What we do know from an inventory of the contents of Troy House conducted by Sir Charles Somerset in 1620, is that the house contained the following rooms deemed worthy of listing for their contents:

> new parler . . . lower chamber in the tower . . . middle towre chamber . . . drawing chamber . . . upper tower chamber . . . greate chamber . . . outer parler . . . Hugh Williams chamber . . . pantrie .. . chamber over the olde kitchen . . . hall . . . room by the new kitchen . . . new kitchen . . . larder . . . skullerie . . . day house . . . dairie hall . . . entrie . . . dairie kitchen . . . storehouse.[49]

The use of the terms 'new' and 'olde' in the 1620 inventory implies that building work may have taken place about the time of Charles and Elizabeth's early seventeenth-century occupation, but also that additions to an existing house rather than a completely new house are most likely being referred to by Charles. On the death of Charles's father, Edward Somerset, fourth Earl of Worcester, in 1628, the young couple moved to Rogerstone Grange and Charles's older brother, Thomas, who had then inherited Troy, was interesting himself in Troy's gardens.[50] Consequently, it appears that a larger house than can be accounted for by the south wing, the cross wing, and rooms PC 1, PC 2 and PC 3 existed at Troy in the first twenty years of the seventeenth century and that during this period, some alterations were made to increase the kitchen facilities, add a new parlour, and adorn at least three of the rooms with plaster ceilings. As will be shown in succeeding chapters, Charles also improved other components of the estate.

The painter Hendrik Danckerts (1630–79) visited England briefly in 1650, but returned to work for Charles II in 1666 to paint harbours and the royal palaces. He is known to have worked in Wales in the early 1670s from a drawing of the river Taff in Glamorgan.[51] He is recorded from 1669–75 as receiving small payments from Henry, the Marquess of Worcester (the future first Duke of Beaufort),[52] for painting several pictures of Badminton House and one of Troy House (Figure 3.27).[53] Given these payment dates and Danckerts's leaving England in 1679, it is likely his painting of Troy was completed in about 1672, as usually attributed.[54] The owner of Troy House from 1628, Thomas Somerset, Viscount Somerset of Cashell, died in 1651 and at least by that time his younger brother, Sir Charles Somerset, had moved back to Troy and lived there quietly until his death in 1665.

Figure 3.27
A Panorama of Monmouth, with Troy House, *c.*1672, *by Hendrik Danckerts.*

By permission of Nelson Museum, Monmouth.

It is not known who occupied the house, other than a steward, between 1665 and the time of Charles, Lord Herbert's occupation of Troy following his marriage in 1682. Certainly, it is unlikely that significant new building would have been conducted at Troy in the years leading up to the Civil War or immediately afterwards, when Henry, the future first Duke of Beaufort, was working hard to re-acquire the Somersets' compounded estates. It seems reasonable to assume that the house, line of trees stretching towards Monmouth, and part of the garden shown in the painting, were extant during Sir Charles Somerset's occupation from 1612 until 1628, when Thomas inherited the house.

However, the mountain in the painting's background is shown much larger than in reality. Monmouth town with a church spire and a tower are shown in the distance; the only tower in this location is that of Monmouth Castle, but this was at least partly demolished in 1647 by 'townsmen and soldiers'.[55] The painting offers a romanticized view, and doubt remains about how accurately it represents the house and garden. The existence of a tower at Troy House has also been questioned but, as described above, Sir Charles Somerset's inventory of 1620 lists a tower with three storeys, each apparently containing one chamber. The tower may have been an extrusion tower; these were not uncommon in late Tudor and early Stuart periods.[56] The future first duke personally employed Danckerts in the 1670s and it is unlikely that the painting was done by an assistant free to embellish at will. The painting of Troy was probably commissioned to record its appearance before Henry embarked on its aggrandizement in the 1680s.

The house is painted from the south-east. An enlarged view shows a complex set of buildings, lying close to and south of a much grander building. This is three storeys high, and in addition, has an attic with windows that are substantially smaller than those in the rest of the house; a tower is also present. No tower survives at Troy and the current east elevation shows the three storeys of the return of the north range joined to an older section of four storeys, where the fourth storey has windows that are only slightly smaller than the rest. Could it be that the house occupied by Sir Charles Somerset in the first half of the seventeenth century was of lower height than that of the intended north range with its ducal proportions? On proceeding with the addition of the north range in 1681–4 it may have been necessary to turn the attic level of the old house into a more substantial fourth storey with larger windows to create continuity in roof lines. In so doing, was it also necessary to push out the wall of the east elevation of the old building to match again the dimensions of the north range? Certainly, as Frecknall notes after inspecting the existing roof space, the eastern elevation of the older building has been 'refaced with an applied layer approximately 1 foot [thirty centimetres] thick'.[57]

Figure 3.28 *Detail, A Panorama of Monmouth, with Troy House, c.1672, by Hendrik Danckerts.*

By permission of Nelson Museum, Monmouth.

Frecknall has conducted an analysis of Danckert's painting, a measured survey and a reassessment of the buildings at the house from wall thicknesses and their disposition, especially at ground and basement levels. He is of the opinion that 'there are the remains of an earlier house', which he speculates 'is a modified H-plan of Elizabethan style, part of which was demolished after 1672, with surviving parts contained within the south return of the present eastern section of the existing house'.[58] So far, we can agree on parts of a house pre-dating the north range being extant in the south return of the eastern section of the existing house. Frecknall believes Danckerts's painting shows a gap between the northern gable of the south wing and the southern return of the main pile and that this was filled by a cross wing – what has also been identified here as a cross wing – in the seventeenth century. However, this does not account for the earlier date attributed to the door of this cross wing, the 'furniture door'. Indeed, even Frecknall states that he would expect this part of the building to be earlier than 1672.

Based on a consideration of Troy's ownership history together with its architectural features, Troy House appears to have developed through nine centuries; ecclesiastical records certainly indicate a human presence at Troy's location from the 1100s. The south wing is the oldest part of Troy House: it may have evolved from a medieval Welsh longhouse but was established as a hall house by the early Tudor period, when Sir William Herbert of Troy was in residence. By the beginning of the sixteenth century other rooms had been added by the addition of a cross wing on a west–east axis; this was at least two storeys in height and extended further eastwards than what now remains. The main door to the whole dwelling thus formed was the 'furniture door'. This is most likely the house that was occupied by Sir William Herbert of Troy when he welcomed Henry VII in 1502. To account for the number of rooms in Sir Charles Somerset's inventory of 1620, and the location of the rooms with plaster ceilings from 1612–20, further building work must have taken place during the sixteenth century or within the first years of the seventeenth century. Whether this took the form of another building to produce two separate houses cannot be deduced without a more detailed and invasive investigation of Troy's walls at basement level. However, the thickness of the walls of the west elevation and its parallel internal wall indicate that they pre-date those of the 1681–4 north range.

The 1681–4 stairwell containing an oak staircase appears to have been inserted in a void surrounded by earlier walls on three of its sides. It is possible that the most eastern part of the cross wing was demolished at this time to enable more light to flood the stairwell; equally plausible is the possibility that it was demolished at an earlier date to provide a garden, as this area would have been very close to and in direct view from the house's principal rooms containing the 1620s plaster ceilings. The presence of the attached 1960s buildings, namely the chapel and cloisters on the eastern elevation and the theatre and teaching block on the western elevation, prevent archaeological investigation during which the presence of old foundations could be explored. If Troy's planning application, which includes

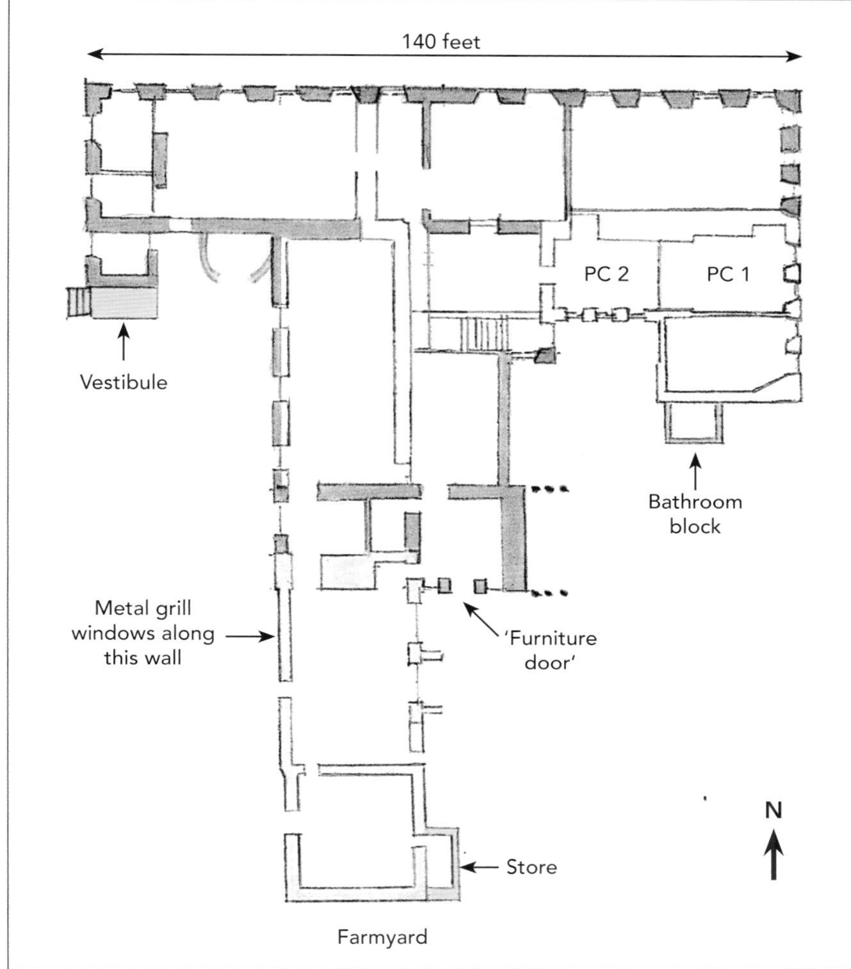

Figure 3.29 *Troy House: a suggested building phase plan: Medieval to early Tudor south wing (pale blue); early Tudor cross wing (dark blue) and its conjectural projection (dotted dark blue); Tudor and early Jacobean build, and Jacobean (1612–20) plaster ceilings in rooms PC 1 and PC 2 (white); late Carolean (1681–4) build (red); Nineteenth-century bathroom block, store-room attached to south wing and vestibule (yellow).*
Copyright: Ann Benson.

the removal of these 1960s buildings, is successful, extensive archaeological investigation of these areas would be justified.

In the centre of the north range is a large T-plan external stone staircase with nosings to the steps. These rise in two parallel flights to a half-landing and then bridge across in a long flight at right angles to the house towards a large square-headed doorway at the *piano nobile* level. The stone walls beneath this staircase have been used to create a small room that is accessed by a doorway at ground-floor level on the north wall. This room connects via a passage to the interior of the north range and would have been used by servants to transfer luggage from coaches arriving at the north range entrance from the 1680s. Blocked doors on the west and east faces of the staircase indicate that its plan was initially different from that which now exists; most likely it did not extend so far north and presented a much steeper flight of steps. The extant doorway on the north wall has a bolection moulding surround similar in design to that seen for the doors of Swangrove on the Badminton estate, home of the dukes of Beaufort. This lodge was designed by William Killigrew around 1703. Whether he was involved in amending what Robert Warren had designed for Troy in 1681–4 is unknown.

Figure 3.30 *View of Troy's stone staircase (above) and the detail of its ground-floor doorway bolection moulding (inset).* Crown copyright: RCAHMW.

There is a final puzzle about the built structure of Troy House: a priest hole. At the very top of the narrow staircase that runs from the south of room PC 1 in the east section of the house there is a narrow door on the left. This gives access to one of the attics; this has no windows. On entering this attic there is a chasm on the left, which appears to run almost vertically down behind some panelling. In its appearance it is similar to the priest hole at Oxburgh Hall, Norfolk, thought to have been built by Nicholas Owen. This structure in the attic at Troy was still visible during the nuns' occupation of the house; they showed it to their handyman as a priest hole in the 1950s. By the time David Jenkins was running Troy House as a school for boys in the 1980s it had been filled in with rubble, when and by whom is unknown. Is this where Edward, fourth Earl of Worcester enabled the Jesuits to hide during their persecution in the early years of the seventeenth century? And where does it emerge, within – or without – the house?

Notes

1 Badminton: FmF 3/7 and FmF 1/2/20.
2 Joseph Bradney, *A History of Monmouthshire: The Hundred of Trelech*, vol. 2, part 2 (London: Academy Books, 1992), pp. 165. Originally published 1913.
3 Joseph Gillmore, *Troy in Monmouth-shire, from The Mannor of Troy. Cophill Farme and Whitterns Farme in an[d] about Piercefield all in Monmouthshire Surveyed Anno MDCCXII*, National Library of Wales, WIAbNL002846217; John Aram, *A Plan of His Grace the Duke of Beaufort's Estates in the Manor and County of Monmouth surveyed by Robt. Whiteley and copy'd by Jn° Aram 1765*, National Library of Wales, WlAbNL004581355.
4 John Aram, *A Plan of the Duke of Beaufort's Estates*, 1765.
5 See John Newman, *The Buildings of Wales: Gwent/Monmouthshire* (London: Penguin Books, 2000), p. 392, for a brief description of Troy House and Troy Farm.
6 Driver, Jonas and Co., *Troy House Estate Monmouth, To Be Sold on 27th March 1901*, (London: Auctioneers Messrs Driver, Jonas and Co., 1901); Stephenson and Alexander, *Troy Estate Plan of Freehold Farms & Lands to be Offered for Public Auction at the Beaufort Arms Hotel, Monmouth* (Cardiff: Messrs Stephenson and Alexander, 1919). Both original copies of sales particulars are at Nelson Museum, Monmouth.
7 Newman, *The Buildings of Wales*, p. 392.
8 RCAHMW, ID 2088. Report available at *historicwales.gov.uk*, accessed June 2015.
9 Further investigation is required to rule out the presence of a fourth tier, as some of the tenants are not clearly visible.
10 See the two auction catalogues for Troy Farm, n.6.
11 See chapter 2, n.27.
12 See architectural reports in the Troy House planning application: Monmouthshire Planning Department, application DC/2008/00723, which is duplicated with DC/2008/00724.
13 Bradney, *A History of Monmouthshire: The Hundred of Trelech*, p. 165.
14 All photographs are from the early 1930s and were kindly provided by Mrs Joan Ryan (d.2014), whose father, Alfred Edwin Jones, occupied Troy Farm following the previous owner's death (Aaron Smith) in 1905, and owned the farm until the late 1930s.
15 The exact location of the find is unknown; the pottery is deposited at Monmouth Archaeology. I am grateful to Stephen Clarke, professional archaeologist at Monmouth Archaeology, Monmouth, Monmouthshire, for access to the tiles.
16 Stephen Clarke, *Down the Dig: Monmouth – An Adventure in Archaeology* (Monmouth: Monmouth Archaeological Society, 2008), p. 88.
17 Paula Henderson, *The Tudor House and Garden* (New Haven and London: Yale University Press, 2005), p. 1.

18 Henderson, *The Tudor House and Garden*, p. 1.
19 Henderson, *The Tudor House and Garden*, p. 1.
20 Bradney, *A History of Monmouthshire: The Hundred of Trelech*, p. 165.
21 C. J. Evans, *Monmouthshire: Its History and Topography* (Cardiff: William Lewis Ltd, 1953), p. 418.
22 Personal communications: Peter Carroll, owner of Troy; Mike Tamplin, groundsman at Troy; Graham Frecknall, architect.
23 Graham Frecknall, John Harris: supporting statement to appendices dated 22 December 2008, planning application DC/2008/00723, Monmouthshire Planning Department.
24 The retired groundsman of Troy is still able to recall this wall's appearance before the nuns' building of the attached theatre.
25 See Ronald Brunskill, *Handbook of Vernacular Architecture* (London: Faber and Faber, 2000), pp. 117 and 123, for comparative examples from the medieval phase.
26 Bradney, *A History of Monmouthshire: The Hundred of Trelech*, p. 161; *Calendar of Inquisitions Post Mortem*, iii, nos. 371 and 538.
27 Conversations with ex-workers on the Troy estate during the nuns' occupation of the house.
28 Monmouthshire Conservation Officer's comments during a tour of Troy House, May 2015.
29 PRO DL 3/69 R3f.
30 See chapter 2 for an account of the Herberts' occupation of Troy during the sixteenth century.
31 The 1546 household list for Lady Elizabeth (future Queen Elizabeth I) does not mention Lady Herbert of Troy, indicating that she retired from her position in late 1545 or early 1546.
32 Newman, *The Buildings of Wales: Gwent/Monmouthshire*, p. 391.
33 *Troy House (View from the Wye Bridge)*, Thomas Smith *c.*1720s; the etching is the *Front View of Troy House* by J. Gardnor, engraved by J. Gardnor and J. Hill, 1793; the unsigned watercolour of 1801 is owned by Mrs Gillian Davey of Mitchel Troy, Monmouthshire.
34 RIBA, London: this photograph is shown in Figure 4.30.
35 See geological mapping of the ridge to the east and south-east of Troy House at *http://mapapps.bgs.ac.uk/geologyofbritain/home.html.*
36 Badminton: FmF 1/2/79.
37 H. M. Colvin, *A Biographical Dictionary of British Architects 1600–1840* (New Haven and London: Yale University Press, 2008). Ann Benson is currently researching what appears to be other work conducted by Robert Warren.
38 Badminton: FmF 3/7, FmF 1/2/20.
39 Badminton: FmE 4/1/13.
40 Badminton: account extract, FmF 3/7; FmF 1/2/20.
41 Newman, *The Buildings of Wales: Gwent/Monmouthshire*, p. 391.
42 Monmouthshire Planning Department, application DC/2008/00723, Appendix A, Architectural Analysis, Graham Frecknall.

43 The tenth Duke of Beaufort, *The Duke of Beaufort: Memoirs* (Richmond upon Thames: Country Life Books, 1981), p. 66.

44 Newman, *The Buildings of Wales: Gwent/Monmouthshire*, p. 391.

45 Private communications during September 2012 with Dr Claire Gapper, author of *www.claregapper.com*, providing information about the history of decorative ceilings.

46 See chapter 1's section on Sir Charles Somerset, son of Edward, fourth Earl of Worcester, and *The Travel Diary (1611–1612) of an English Catholic Sir Charles Somerset*, ed. Michael G. Brennan (Leeds: Leeds Philosophical and Literary Society Ltd, 1993).

47 The oak panelling was removed before 1901 but the exact date has not been discovered.

48 Housemistress of Troy Approved School for Girls; Mike Tamplin, groundsman at Troy at this time of the nuns sealing the cellar.

49 Sir Charles Somerset, *An inventorie of what is mouvable awe left at Troy the 20th of Octob. 1620.* Badminton: OC/2; RF/1. The inventory is confirmed as being in Charles's hand.

50 See chapter 2, the Somerset family members.

51 This painting of the river Taff is now in the British Museum (1957-7-13-1), formerly in the collection of the sixth Earl of Malmesbury.

52 Childs Bank Accounts. Badminton Muniments: RC 2/1: £4 12s. 0d; £6 10s. (1672), £33 (1674), £6 10s. (1675).

53 Letter from Henry, later first Duke of Beaufort, to his wife, Mary, 27 February 1675: Badminton: FmF 1/32. Letter from William to his mother Mary, Marchioness of Worcester: Badminton: FmF 1/8/24. The British Museum holds Danckerts's drawings of the north front and another of the east front of Badminton House; the paintings are lost.

54 Danckerts, a Roman Catholic, was obliged to leave England at the time of the 'Popish Plot' (1679).

55 A. J. Taylor, *Monmouth Castle and Great Castle House*, Gwent (London: HMSO, 1951), p.10. See also Keith Kissack, *The Making of a County Town* (London: Phillimore, 1975), p. 42.

56 See Nathaniel Lloyd, *A History of the English Country House* (London: Architectural Press, 1975) for a description of the history of extrusion towers.

57 Graham Frecknall, personal communication, May 2015.

58 Graham Frecknall, Appendix A, Planning application DC/2008/00723, which is duplicated with DC/2008/00724, Monmouthshire Planning Department. Frecknall's building phase plan includes the position of his speculative H-plan Elizabethan house. Troy's owner has not permitted reproduction of the plan but it may be viewed on the planning department's website, *www.monmouthshire.gov.uk/planning.* Accessed 12 August 2016.

Four

Troy House Gardens: Location and Nature Across Time

GIVEN THE CLOSENESS of the land to the east of the house to the farm's gardens, they are considered together here, as the boundary between the two may have changed over time. Information about Troy House gardens is sparse, including any relating to the nuns' horticultural activities as recently as the twentieth century.[1] This investigation of the history of the gardens is based on the premise that a building's principal reception rooms generally look on to key, aesthetically pleasing garden areas.[2] With these rooms at the house now largely identified across time from chapter 3, gardens may be located and then their nature deduced – with some supposition – from maps, paintings, documents and archaeological surveys alongside reference to major garden history texts. The house is considered in stages from its oldest to its newest parts, each part being extrapolated to its garden area. Consequently, the south part comes first and then, in an anticlockwise direction, the sequence is east, north and, finally, west.

Gardens to the south of the house

An aerial view of Troy helps to show the relationship between the *bas* court (the current farmyard) and the garden area south of the house. This area is now traversed by cloisters and the chapel, but immediately before their construction in the 1960s, it was an L-shaped garden space

Figure 4.1 *Aerial view of Troy's 'yard'.* Crown copyright: RCAHMW; annotations, Ann Benson.

for the nuns' private use (see Figure 3.19). The garden was enclosed by an un-coursed stone wall with a gateway on its east section. This part of the wall was demolished during the nuns' building work of the 1960s and its foundations now lie under the chapel. This area is shown as an enclosed garden with a perimeter path on the 1881 OS map. Of all the maps and documents that exist for the Troy estate, only the tithe map of 1845 offers a name or use for this L-shaped area, and this is simply, 'yard'.[4]

This L-shaped courtyard area corresponds to that shown as two sections on Aram's map of 1765 (Figure 4.2). Both of these sections are separated from the gardens to the east, perhaps by the old stone wall demolished during the nuns' occupation. The map implies that these sections were also separated from each other by some means. As argued in chapter 3, the section shown closest to the *bas* court (current farmyard) was most likely a reception courtyard. The other section would have been a garden in the early Jacobean period, as it lies next to and is overlooked by the principal reception rooms with the 1612–20 plaster ceilings. This garden area was presumably enjoyed by Sir Charles Somerset during his occupation and enhancement of the Troy estate from 1612 to 1628. As the area lies close to the south wing, which was most likely a hall house in the Tudor period, it may also have been used as a garden by Sir William Herbert of Troy and his son, Sir Charles, during the reigns of

Henry VII and Henry VIII. Such enclosed gardens next to the house were particularly fashionable in both Tudor and Jacobean times. The area may have been a 'privy garden', designed for sole use by the master of the house and favoured guests. This type of garden evolved from the medieval *hortus conclusus*, when they were a common setting for images of the Virgin Mary in artwork. It is fitting that in the twentieth century this enclosed area was used by the nuns and contained a statue of the Virgin Mary holding baby Jesus (see Figure 3.19).

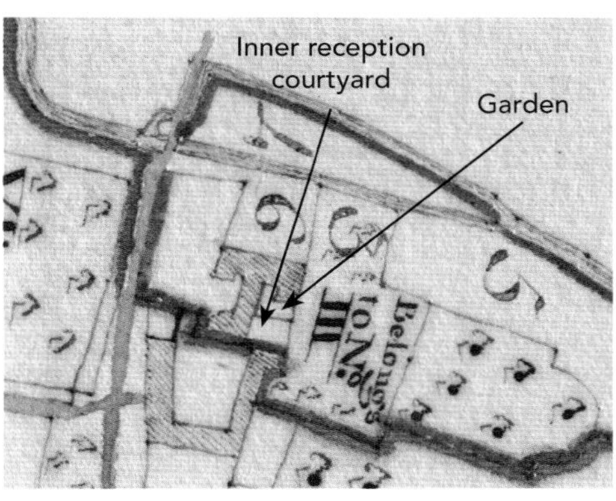

Figure 4.2 *Detail of Aram's 1765 map showing two enclosed areas and their probable uses.*

Map by permission of Llyfrgell Genedlaethol Cymru/The National Library of Wales; annotations, Ann Benson.

So what might this garden area have looked like during the sixteenth and the seventeenth centuries, when the powerful Herbert and then the Somerset families respectively occupied Troy House? In about 1558 the first horticultural manual written in English and solely dedicated to the 'Arte' of gardening was published by Thomas Hill. This work, *A most briefe and pleasaunte treatise, teaching how to dresse, sowe, and set a garden*, was aimed at owners of small manor houses, and proved to be so popular that it was reprinted in seven subsequent editions under the title, *The profitable arte of gardening*. First published in 1577, *The Gardener's Labyrinth* was also by Hill and a bestseller. Before Hill's books, classical Greek and Roman husbandry manuals, which were imported along with other Renaissance humanist ideas and texts at the beginning of the century, were being translated into English and formed the basis of such works as Fitzherbert's *Boke of Husbandrie* (1523).[5] Ovid's Metamorphoses, Pliny the Younger, Vitruvius, Alberti and Francesco Colonna's *Hypnerotomachia Poliphili* were all sources of ideas for iconographical programmes, entertainment, and horticultural and architectural features.[6] The Somersets were exceptionally cultured, well-travelled and moved in royal circles; they would have been familiar with these influences.

Herbals listed and described plants with their medicinal benefits, but did not address gardening itself. Hill's books were the first to popularise gardening as a pleasurable activity, and during Elizabeth 1's reign (1558–1603) gardening became a national passion.[7] Hill did not claim to be original: his gardening advice was 'gathered oute of all the principallest aucthors' or 'gathered out of the best approved writers'.[8] His publications had the major advantage of providing copious illustrations. The picture in Figure 4.3 is from his chapter describing the 'forme of the disposing the quarters into beddes, and apt borders about, with the sowing, choice and defence of the seedes, and weeding of the beddes'; a wooden, shaded arbour for playing bowls is also shown.

Figure 4.3 *Thomas Hill,* The Gardener's Labyrinth.
By permission of Oxford University Press.

Most sixteenth-century garden design constrained flowers and herbs within rigid geometric patterns.[9] Gardening literature and practice reflected contemporary society's passion for order and symmetry, 'gardening manuals did more than just describe gardens, they also mirrored wider social concerns'.[10] In his 1613 practical guide to husbandry, *The English Husbandman*, Gervase Markham also wrote, 'it [good husbandry] is most necessary for keeping the earth in good order, which else would grow wilde [. . .] and nothing remained but a Chaos of confusednesse'.[11] His view was that the creation of order on a rural estate or within a small garden was essential for maintaining harmony, but also that the imposition of that order contributed to the physical and moral well-being of the nation.[12] The well-tended, geometric garden patterns continued to dominate publications produced during Jacobean and Caroline times. In his publication of 1618, *The New Orchard and Garden*, William Lawson observed that 'The forme that men like in general is square',[13] and John Parkinson agreed in his 1629 publication, *Paradisi in sole paradisus*, with 'The foure square forme is the most usually accepted with all'.[14] Such forms could have existed within the garden area south of the house, as shown on Aram's map, and have been viewed by Sir

Charles Somerset from the rooms with ornate plaster ceilings on both the ground and first floors.

Tudor and early Stuart courtyard gardens frequently contained intricate knot gardens of evergreen plants, such as rosemary and hyssop, the designs of which could best be viewed from above, as would be the case from room PC 3 at Troy; they would be filled with herbs and flowers such as carnations and gillyflowers.[15] Elisabeth Woodhouse argues that the knot as representative of Elizabethan gardens has been 'blown out of all proportion' in its importance, largely due to the Arts and Craft movement focusing on recreating some of the features of Elizabethan gardens through the activities of Reginald Blomfield, Inigo Thomas, H. Inigo Triggs, Edwin Lutyens and Gertrude Jekyll.[16] Woodhouse argues for a far richer eclectic model with more complex iconography than is seen in any recreation. Glass and gilt were used to create a theatrical brightness; Sir Francis Bacon endorsed their use in his *Essay on Gardens* (first published in 1597) with 'over every space between the arches some other little figure, with broad plates of round coloured glass gilt, for the sun to play upon'.[17] Aviaries introduced the movement and pleasant sounds of birds; statuary would have classical and mythical references, and mazes would represent life's journey. All were common features of sixteenth- and seventeenth-century gardens.

Knot gardens often framed a fountain, which could be embellished with coloured glass, and were interspersed with areas of lawn, topiary, wooden tunnel-like arbours planted with roses, providing shaded scented walks, and carved heraldic beasts. However, by early Stuart times, when Sir Charles Somerset occupied Troy House, the heraldry had given way to a greater emphasis on patterns created by plant arrangements and coloured gravels. Similarly, the native plants of cornflowers and heartsease typical of Tudor gardens, and as would be known by Sir William Herbert of Troy, were later supplemented by more unusual species such as gentians and cyclamen, as the quest for the more exotic was fed by explorations of the far reaches of Europe and the New World. Such courtyard gardens would usually be situated on the south side of the house in order to get the full benefit of the sun, as is the case with the location of this proposed courtyard garden at Troy.[18] Small walks traversed the different sections of the garden; broader, straight walks connected the parts of the garden to the house and to other garden areas. So what lay beyond Troy's south-facing courtyard garden? Certainly other enclosed garden spaces, but where were these located across time, and what were their designs?

Danckerts's painting and land to the east of the house and farmhouse

A search for images of Troy's landscape that pre-date Gillmore's estate map of 1712 and show Troy during the time of Sir Charles Somerset, before the addition of the 1680s north range, produced only the painting of about 1672 by Hendrik Danckerts (1630–79). As shown in chapter 3, the painting's accuracy in portraying Troy House is disputed, although the contentious points mainly relate to the mountain and Monmouth Castle's tower in the background.

Tantalizingly, part of a walled garden of quadripartite structure is shown to the south-east of the house. This design was typical of Tudor and Stuart times and may date from when Sir Charles Herbert owned the house or even his father, Sir William Herbert, who was arguably responsible for extending Troy's medieval house during the late fifteenth century. The four quadrants appear to be of greensward and they are separated by pale-coloured pathways. Close examination of the painting shows that the wall forming one side of this area and extending southwards is actually joined to the house. The lie of the land and trees prevent the identification of where this wall terminates and what it encloses. This wall appears taller than the other two walls bordering the four greenswards. The fourth side of this garden has a shrub by the house, but no other wall is present to completely enclose the greenswards. The painting looks down on the house, and the location from where it was painted was found. However, modern farm buildings and tall trees prevent the taking of photographs from the same situation for pinpointing the possible position of the walls of the quadripartite garden.

Figure 4.4 *Detail of the quadripartite garden,* A Panorama of Monmouth, with Troy House, *c.*1672, *by Hendrik Danckerts.*

By permission of Nelson Museum, Monmouth.

Figure 4.5 *Garden area to the east of Troy House and its attached chapel.*

Crown copyright: RCAHMW.

The appearance of the current house from the east shows the incongruous addition of the north range completed in the 1680s by the first duke; this is joined to the older four-storey section occupied by Sir Charles Somerset; this in turn is joined to the 1960s chapel and, finally, a castellated stone archway in a Tudor style joins this to the north end of the farmhouse. The nuns' designed landscape shown in the aerial photograph (Figure 4.5) is no longer visible except for a few scattered trees.[19]

From considering the current structures, the quadripartite walled garden in Danckerts's painting would lie approximately in line with the 1960s chapel or, perhaps due to the oblique angle taken in the painting, closer to the farmhouse. The land to the east of the farmhouse contains walls some two metres high that look similar in their arrangement to those in Danckerts's quadripartite garden, and it is tempting to suggest that they are the same. However, they might also have formed enclosures for the growing of food, close to the service buildings, of which the farmhouse would have been a component at some time. These walls are shown as A and B in Figure 4.6, which also shows walls C, half a metre high, D, the same height as A and B, and E, which is some three metres high and attached to the farmhouse. All of these walls are made of stone except for B. This has one side entirely of brick and its other side has sections that have a stone base with brick additions, as if these were for repairing the wall.

The structure of wall B (Figure 4.7) suggests English bond but this is haphazard along the wall's length. The original wall appears to have been entirely of stone, rather than with merely a stone plinth. It is not possible to put a firm date on any section, although chemically dating the creation date of the bricks would give an estimate. There is no evidence of cavities for any heating system, as might be used to help raise fruit, if this were a kitchen garden area at some time. It is only from the eighteenth to the mid-nineteenth century that heated walls (also known as 'hot walls') became common; the first recorded hot wall was at Belvoir Castle in 1718.[20]

Figure 4.6 (right) *Garden area containing several old stone walls (A, B, C, D, E) to the east of Troy's farmhouse.*

Crown copyright: RCAHMW; annotations, Ann Benson.

Figure 4.7 (below) *Garden wall B of brick and stone.*

Copyright: Ann Benson.

The stone walls A–E in this whole area could be from the Jacobean period or earlier and form part of the original walled enclosures; walls A and B could even be those of the quadripartite garden shown in Danckerts's painting. However, stone wall A terminates with the remains of the gable end of a single-storey stone building, which appears to have been built on to wall A at a later date. Stone remains lying on the ground in line with this gable end suggest a building, possibly divided into compartments, of some six metres in length. Given the height of its simple gable end, it is most likely this building was not one used for the family's entertainment, such as a Tudor or Stuart banqueting house, but rather a service building, possibly used for growing mushrooms, from the eighteenth century, storing fruit, vegetables or tools, or even as kennels. Certainly, during the twentieth century, when the nuns occupied the house, it was used as occasional accommodation for 'gentlemen of the road'.[21]

Close by and further to the east, there are the ruined remains of a smaller, separate building that is shown on the coloured 1881 OS map; this building is remembered by a past housemistress of Troy School (1964–76) as Hermitage Cottage, and it was occupied by a gardener.[22] Pigsties were also present here in the twentieth century (Figure 4.9).[23]

Figure 4.8 *Gable end of wall A.* Copyright: Ann Benson.

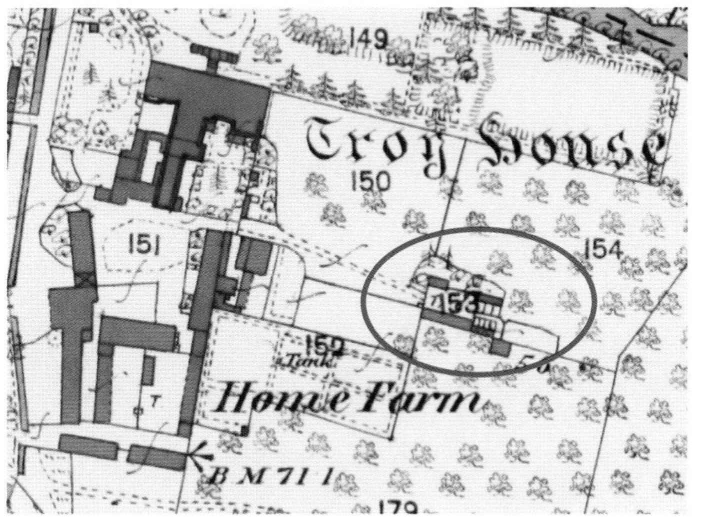

Figure 4.9 *Buildings at the end of wall A. Hermitage Cottage is far right, next to a double row of pigsties.* By permission of the British Library Board; Mitchel Troy Parish, 1881 OS map.

Given the status of the sixteenth- and seventeenth-century owner-occupiers of Troy, one would expect a banqueting house to be present within a stroll from the house. These became a common feature of Elizabethan and Jacobean country houses. They were used as places for indulging in the dessert course of sugared treats, which were taken in a separate place from the main meal.[24] They were often positioned on a roof or raised terrace to overlook the gardens.[25] It is possible that the ruins at the end of wall A were indeed part of a banqueting house complex that over time and with depredation became more useful as service buildings.

In 2012 I conducted a resistivity survey within the area bound by walls B, C and D to 'see' beneath the soil's surface.[26] A grid of twenty by twenty metres was marked out with string and divided into one-metre strips with tapes. Readings at one-metre intervals, following the guiding tapes, were taken using a resistivity meter. The captured data was then transferred to a computer to produce a plot in greyscale tones; light tones imply low resistance and dark tones indicate greater resistance, as might be offered by the buried foundations of a stone building. The survey results show no obvious underlying structures, such as extant pathways. However, they do show very slightly darker grey areas sitting approximately where crossing pathways are recorded on the 1881 OS map (see the area labelled as '150 Tank' in Figure 4.9). Although these pathways are long since gone, the compaction of the underlying soil that they created has been identified here as areas of slightly greater resistance. At the head of this quadripartite arrangement of pathways, and next to the farmhouse, there is a square enclosure with a perimeter path. Within living memory this area was used as a tennis court until the 1940s and has not been cultivated since. A resistivity survey of the land bound by walls A and B could not be conducted, due to the amount of rubble and extraneous matter dispersed over the entire area.

Only the 1845 tithe and 1901 Troy auction catalogue maps illuminate the use of the area immediately east of the farmhouse, but then only as 'garden'. The tithe map shows a round feature very close to the farmhouse. It is shaded in the same way as the curvilinear structure near the river Trothy and the river itself, indicating the presence of water. This was most likely a dipping pond for the garden in 1845 rather than an ornamental feature, but it might also have been the site of an earlier fish pond. There is no indication of an area of water in this location on any other map relating to Troy.

Overall, the 1765 Aram map lacks detail, its main purpose being to record tenants' names against areas of estate land. Other than the house and farmhouse, which are crudely drawn, there are no other buildings, and the area under discussion is shown as just one enclosed space with surrounding orchard. However, the 1712 Gillmore map is more detailed in this respect: it shows two enclosures in the area east of the current farmhouse, beyond which there are several named orchards. This is similar to the 1845 tithe map, indicating this area has a long history of being composed of enclosures and orchards.

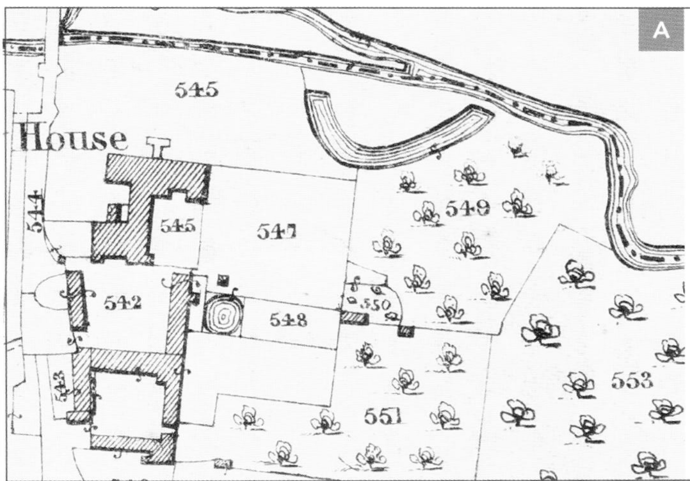

542 = Troy Farm and premises
543 = Yard
545 = Troy House and premises
548 = Garden
549 = Pasture and orchard
550 = Shed yard and plantation
553 = Pasture and orchard
551 = Description missing from map

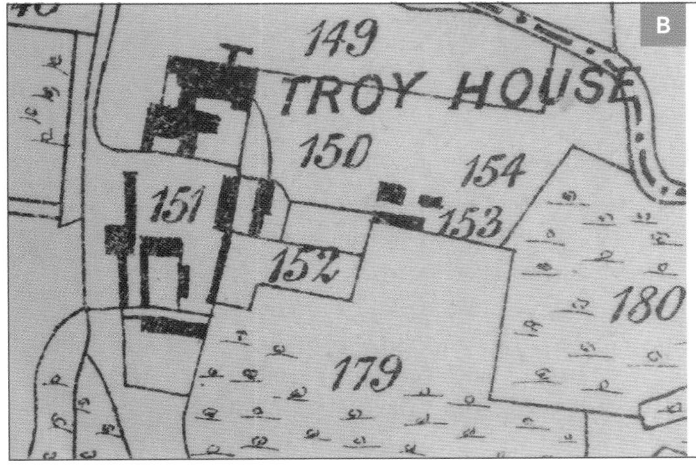

149 = Grounds of House
150 = Orchard
151 = Yard shared between House and Farm
152 = Garden
153 = Pigsties
154 = Orchard
179 = Orchard
180 = Orchard

Figure 4.10 *Uses of land east of the farmhouse across time. A: Detail of tithe map, 1845, showing apportionments. B: Uses of lots in Troy's 1901 auction catalogue.*

Map A by permission of Gwent Archives; map B by permission of Nelson Museum, Monmouth; images copyright, Ann Benson.

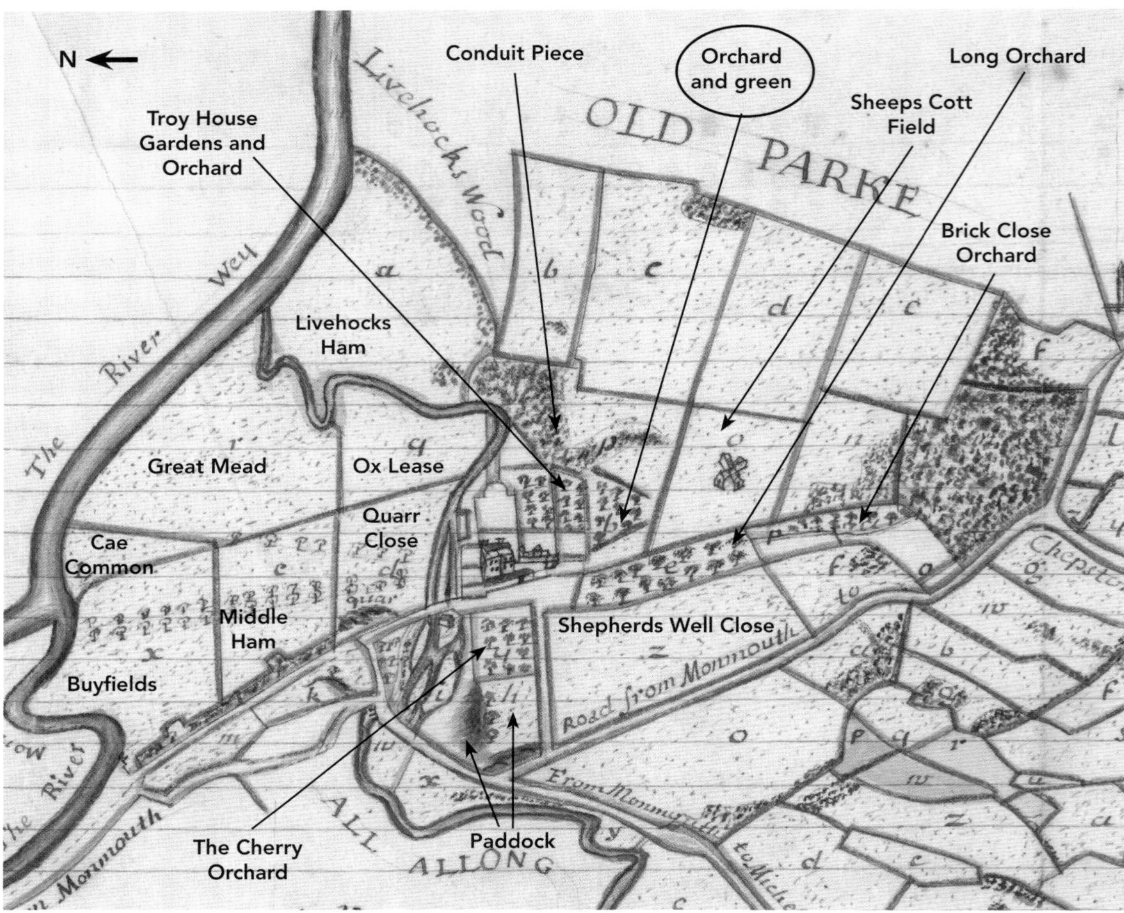

Figure 4.11
Gillmore's 1712 map with its named areas. Names derived from attached records.
Map by permission of Llyfrgell Genedlaethol Cymru/The National Library of Wales; image copyright, Ann Benson.

The Gillmore map lists an area to the south-east of the current farmhouse as 'Orchard and Green' (Figure 4.11). The area is shown with trees, and one can only assume that the land between this and the 'Long Orchard' is the 'Green'. A search of Troy estate accounts lists payment during 1685–98 for the 'hand mowed and grassed cutting' of 'The Bowling Green and Orchard'.[27] Given the status of the estate's owners, one would expect a bowling green to exist even before 1685, as bowling was particularly popular during the reigns of Elizabeth I (1533–1603) and James I (1566–1625) for people of quality.[28] If the green was in this location, it strengthens the case for the areas of land associated with the house extending to the east and south of the current farmhouse. This is further supported by Gillmore's assigning the area of orchard to the east of the farm as 'Troy House Gardens and Orchard' (Figure 4.11). Whether this area was for kitchen crops or pleasure remains unknown, but certainly Charles, Marquess of Worcester, showed a strong interest in horticulture and agriculture in the diary he kept during his European tour, May 1673 to April 1674.[29] When married and living at Troy he wrote to his mother requesting some seeds for his garden, especially 'kitchen garden things'.[30] Perhaps Charles melded pleasure and profit by taking an interest in kitchen gardening within the walled enclosures south-east of the house.

Gardens to the east of the house

A search for gardens close to the east elevation of the house revealed a striking feature of an exedra-shaped (semi-circular) area in the same location on both the Gillmore and Aram maps (Figures 4.12–13); this is not shown on either of the 1845 tithe or 1881 OS maps. The exedra tops a rectangle of land at the base of which there is a separate area, approximately square in shape, that adjoins the house. No trees are shown in either of these areas on Gillmore's 1712 map, but on that of Aram in 1765 they are in the style used for an orchard. The absence of trees is not due to Gillmore's omitting the use of this motif, as he uses it in the area closer to the farm. Although the exedra shape is not shown on the 1845 tithe map, the same area is apportioned as orchard/pasture, as it is on the 1881 OS map. Consequently, between 1712 (Gillmore) and 1765 (Aram), the area of the exedra appears to have become an orchard, or at least full of trees. This could be explained by the house being unoccupied by Somerset family members following the fatal accident of the first duke's heir in 1698. Thereafter, with only a steward in permanent residence, there would be no

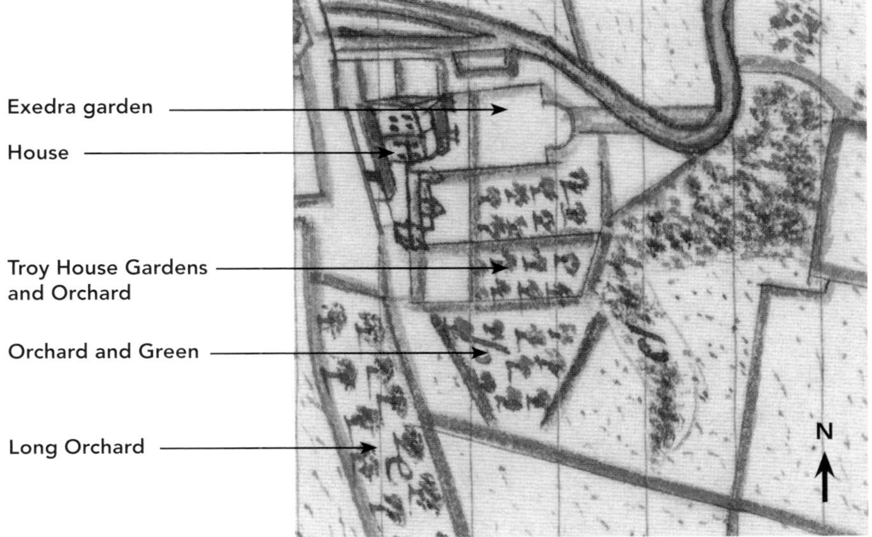

Figure 4.12
Annotated detail of Gillmore's 1712 map showing gardens east of the house.
Map by permission of Llyfrgell Genedlaethol Cymru/The National Library of Wales; image copyright, Ann Benson.

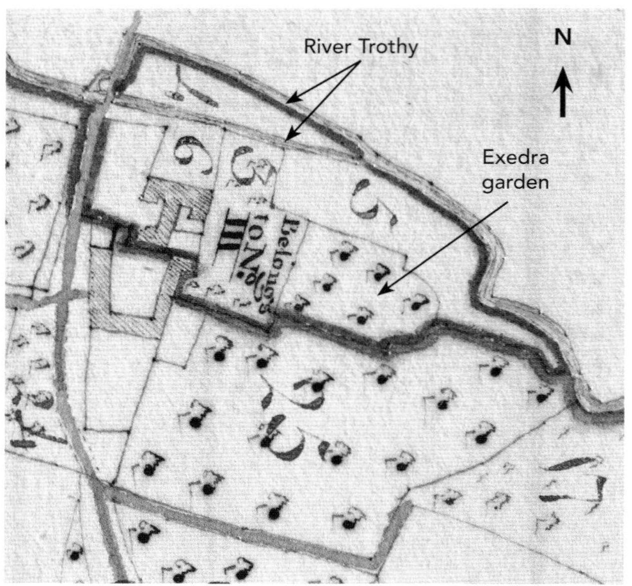

Figure 4.13
Annotated detail of Aram's 1765 map showing gardens east of the house (3=Gardens; 4=Pleck meadow; 5=D^o^ [ditto]; 6=House; 25=Home Orchard).
Map by permission of Llyfrgell Genedlaethol Cymru/The National Library of Wales; image copyright, Ann Benson.

reason to maintain expensive formal gardens overlooked by key reception rooms previously used by the family.

An exedra-shaped (semi-circular) area of garden east of the house is also shown in the aerial map of 1978.[31] Currently, all that can be seen in this area is the exedra marked out by a low, double-sided stone wall, with the rectangular area leading to it from the house outlined by hedges. This rectangular area is transected by another low stone wall, which is exactly in line with wall A behind the current farmhouse. Steps at either end and in the centre of this low wall lead down to the exedra. The nuns were responsible for this landscaping in the 1960s; the area served as their private garden and the girls in their care were not allowed to use it.[32] There were curved paths intersected with rockeries and two stone seats in the extant exedra stone wall.[33] These features are revealed in the aerial map of 1978, but the paths, rockeries and stone seats are no longer visible.

In 2012, I conducted resistivity surveys in three separate areas of the exedra garden using the same technique in each area. The east elevation of the house has a fifteen-metre-wide strip of asphalt running against it; this was used for parking during the 1980s and the first surveyed area had to start beyond it. The area measured thirty-eight metres (the full width of the garden) by fifteen metres. A grid of this area was marked out with string and divided into one-metre strips with tapes. Readings at one-metre intervals following the guiding tapes were taken using a resistivity meter. The data was then transferred to a computer to produce a plot in greyscale tones – light tones implying low resistance and dark tones, high resistance.

The first area has a large conifer that is visible on the 1978 photograph. It produced an area of high resistance surrounded by low resistance because of its root system, and can be discounted. The curved path that intersected with a centrally placed rockery is shown by the resistivity as an extant underlying structure – it lies about twelve centimetres below ground. There are also faint traces of another angled pathway (Figure 4.15). This corresponds to a compacted earth walkway, again constructed by the nuns; it led to an arbour near the modern brick apple store, just south of the chapel walls.[34]

Figure 4.14 *The nuns' exedra garden and alignment of garden walls, 1978.* Crown copyright: RCAHMW.

A second area measuring ten metres by fifteen metres was surveyed in the lower part of the exedra, further from the house. Again, the results reveal the underlying remains of the nuns' transecting pathway across the exedra garden area. A third surveyed area, close to the exedra's extant low stone wall, measured ten metres by twelve metres. The resistivity shows part of an extant perimeter path running against the wall. The nuns' two stone seats used to sit on this path.[35] No other underlying structures were revealed in the study; this might be expected if this area to the east of the house has been an orchard from at least Gillmore's map of 1712 until the time of the nuns (1904–77). Before their landscaping activity and during the 1950s, the nuns grew wheat in this area for their bread-making; they did not need to clear any trees to make this possible. Consequently, sometime between 1845, when the tithe map shows the area as orchard, and the 1950s at the very latest, either the trees were felled or they deteriorated to such an extent that their remains were removed.

Figure 4.15 *Overlay of the three areas' resistivity results with an aerial photograph taken during the nuns' occupation of Troy House.* Copyright: Ann Benson.

It is tempting to suggest that the nun's exedra garden is in the same position as those shown in the maps of Aram and Gillmore. Arguably, the nuns simply took what was there and embellished it with rockeries and bordering paths. Map overlays with MasterMap prove otherwise (Figures 4.16–17). These show that both the Gillmore and Aram exedra garden areas extend further to the east towards the river Trothy and further to the south in the direction of the current farmhouse than that of the nuns. However, the northern boundaries of the exedra gardens, which are parallel to the river, are in the same location for all three cases. This arrangement is shown most clearly with the Gillmore overlay.

In both overlays the walls A and B described in the area east of the farmhouse coincide with the southern edge of the Aram and Gillmore exedra gardens. This is best seen in Figure 4.17 using an overlay of Aram's map with that of the 1881 OS. The overlay shows these walls and the ruined gable end building all on the southern perimeter of Aram's 1765 exedra garden. This supports the view that walls A and B are likely to have been part of the seventeenth-century walled enclosures and makes it even more likely that they are those shown in Danckert's 1672 quadripartite garden. It appears that the decorative gardens of the house extended to

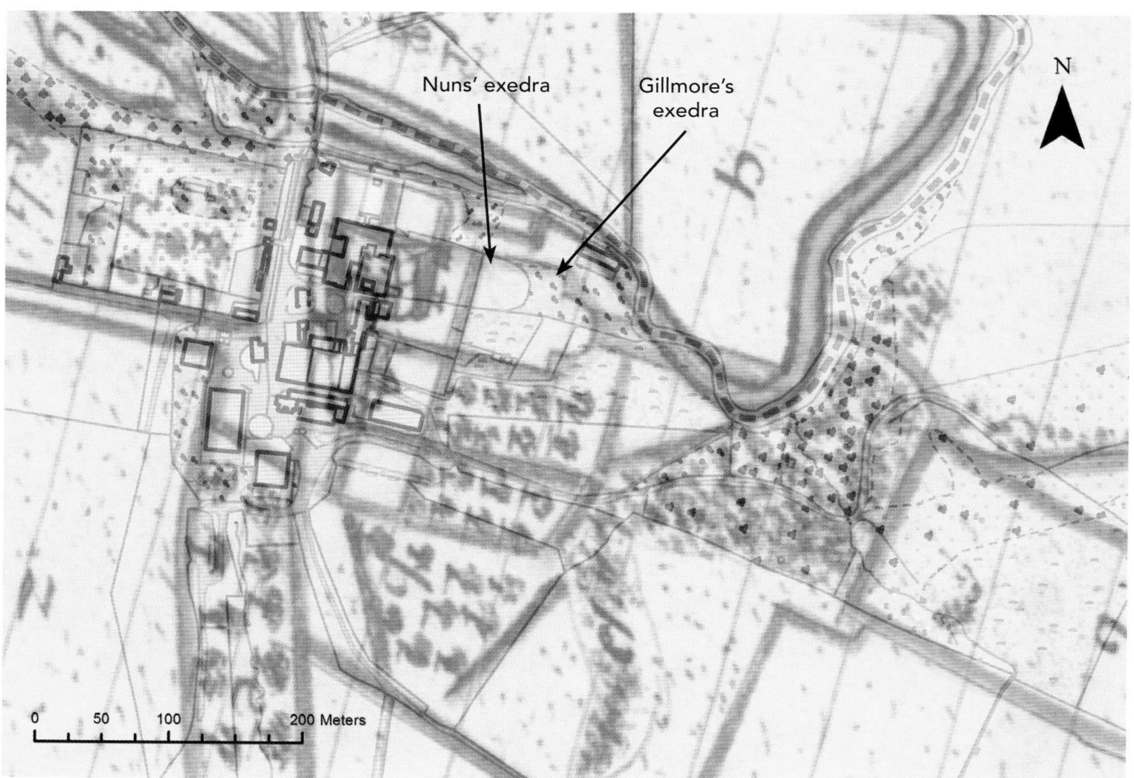

Figure 4.16
Overlay of Gillmore's 1712 map with MasterMap.
Copyright: Ann Benson.

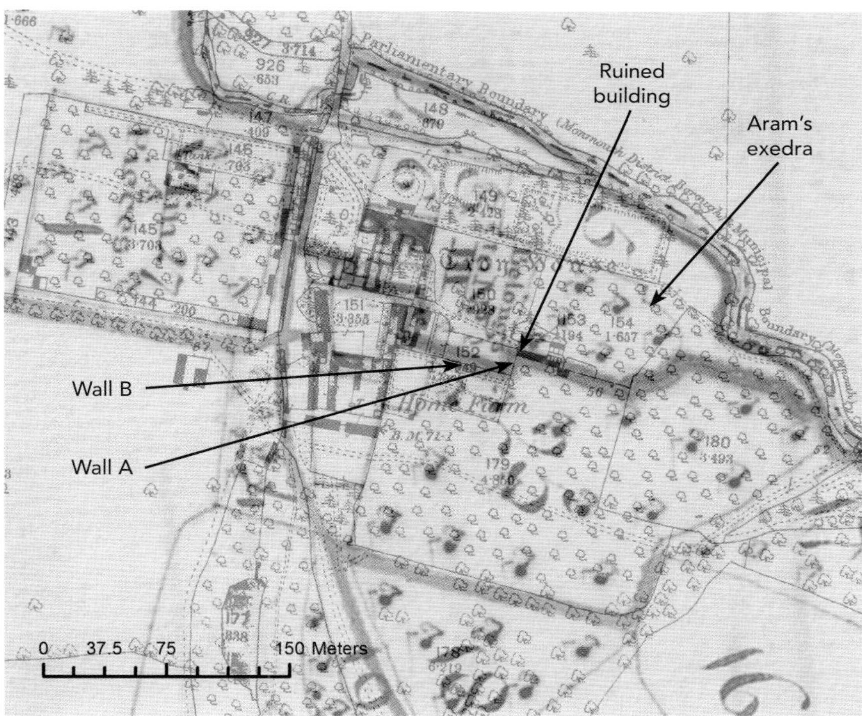

Figure 4.17 *Overlay of the 1881 OS map, which shows the position of garden walls, with Aram's 1765 map.*
Copyright: Ann Benson.

the east behind the current farmhouse during the early eighteenth century (the time of Gillmore's map) and most likely even earlier.

In architecture, an exedra is a semi-circular recess or plinth, often crowned by a semi-dome, which is sometimes set into a building's facade. It was the favourite form of Roman garden building. First revived in the Italian Renaissance, and then again in the period 1660–1710, when it became a particularly popular garden feature, it was often used as an ornamental curved screening wall to hide another part of the garden. Examples are at Belton House, West Wycombe Park, Prideaux Place and Stansted. Later examples by William Kent are at Chiswick and Stowe. An exedra can be used in landscape design to visually terminate a garden axis, as it does at Troy for views to the east from rooms of both the early and late seventeenth-century parts of the house. The exedra may have incorporated seating, as it did for the nuns, statues and fountains.

The exedra at Troy is most likely to have been created before 1680 and certainly no later than 1698, the time of Charles, Marquess of Worcester's fatal accident and of the house ceasing to be regularly occupied by Somerset family members. At Stansted a formal arrangement of flower beds existed within the area of its exedra, from which an avenue of trees stretched into the wider landscape, linking the formality of the garden

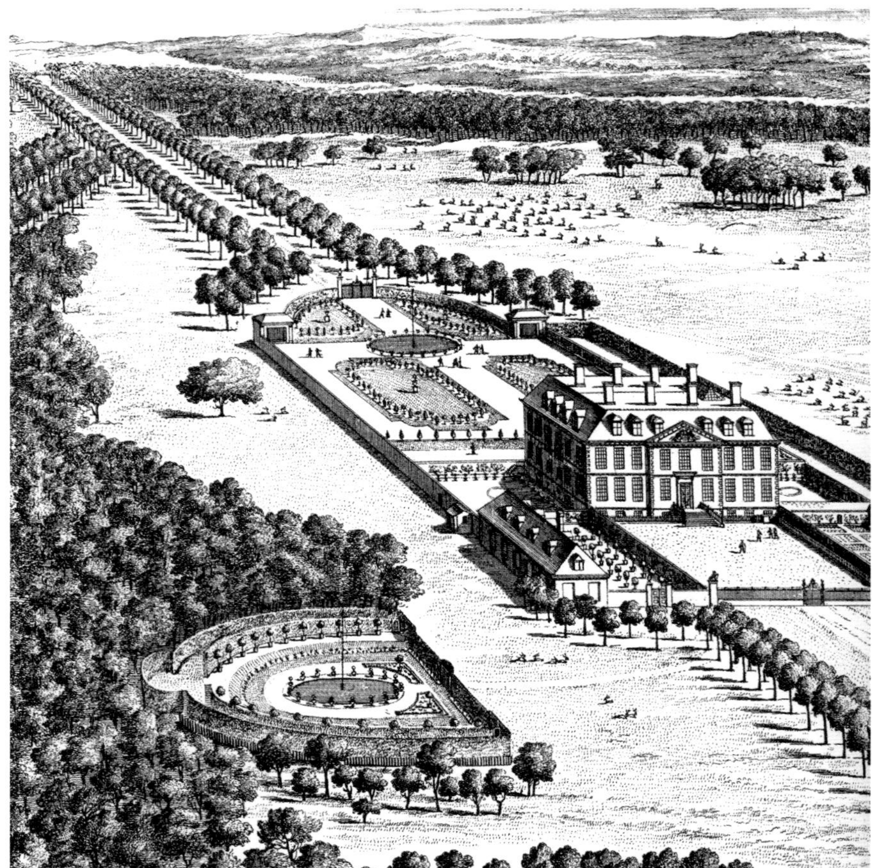

Figure 4.18 *Stansted's exedra leading to an avenue of trees in the late seventeenth century.*
Images by permission of The National Trust; author's copy of *Britannia Illustrata.*

with the untamed countryside. This arrangement is typical for the time and could have existed at Troy. In Gillmore's map (Figure 4.12) a shaded band is drawn from the end of the exedra towards the river and then strangely shown continuing on the other side without any indication of a bridge. This band might represent an avenue of trees that stretched out in the same manner as shown for Stansted (Figure 4.18),[36] despite the intervention of the river's course. This is possible, as *Britannia Illustrata* contains an early seventeenth-century etching of Swillington in the West Riding of Yorkshire showing an avenue of trees continuing in the same line on both banks of a river.[37] By the time of Charles, Marquess of Worcester's occupation of Troy in the early 1680s, the gardens close to the house would still have been prodigiously formal affairs, with clipped yews, gravel paths, pots, statues and fountains, similar in style to the gardens at Stansted.[38]

By the third quarter of the seventeenth century the knot gardens of Elizabethan and early Stuart times were coming under the influence of French designs with the creation of *parterres de broderie*. An example may be seen in the restoration of the late seventeenth-century gardens at Tredegar House, sixteen kilometres from Troy. Here, in the parterre in the Orangery Garden, as well as using flowers and grass in the design, different coloured materials such as sand, crushed coal and shells are used to create patterns. Such an effect could have been used within the garden area enclosed by the exedra at Troy, as due to its location, it could be seen at its best from the principal rooms of the house on the first and second floors.

The closeness of the river Trothy would have provided a continuous source of water for servicing fountains and other water features in the exedra garden east of the house – and better still, for gardens to the north. Even during the time of Sir Charles Somerset's occupation of Troy at the beginning of the seventeenth century, the means of lifting water to feed ponds and work fountains, including those of complex styles incorporating automata, was well known amongst the aristocracy. This was due largely to the work of the water engineers Salomon de Caus and his brother Isaac. Being a member of Prince Henry's inner circle, Sir Charles would have been well aware of the extensive gardens incorporating complex water features being planned by Mountain Jennings, Salomon de Caus, de' Servi and Inigo Jones for the prince's Richmond Palace.[39]

Figure 4.19 *Part of the* parterre de broderie, *Tredegar House, Newport, south Wales.* Copyright: Ann Benson.

This Mannerist alliance of science and art in garden design was in vogue before Sir Charles's departure on his European tour in April 1611.[40] At this time, a whole series of gardens, all making use of water, were created in the form of islands, rivers and fountains, for example Francis Bacon's Gorhamby, Robert Cecil's Hatfield and Sir Henry Fanshawe's Ware Park. In the diary Sir Charles kept during his tour of Europe, he makes twenty comments about the gardens he visited, and of these, thirteen refer to water features, which he describes enthusiastically and in detail.[41] Although not on the scale of those listed above, it seems inconceivable that Sir Charles would not have included ponds and fountains in his gardens at Troy during the first quarter of the seventeenth century.

Troy's 1901 auction catalogue refers to the house having lawns on the site of previous 'old fish ponds and Pleasance, which were renowned in the Jacobean period' and that these were 'screened from the North by a HIGH YEW HEDGE'.[42] The precise location of this yew hedge is not established, but the locations of the lawns belonging to the house have not changed since the 1901 auction; they are in the area of the exedra garden and to the north between the house and the river. This lends support to the argument that it is in these locations that ponds and fountains would have existed during the Jacobean period of Sir Charles Somerset's occupation.

The Art of Gardening. 53

flows by the Pipe A. *the Air iſſueth out at the Pipe* b b b. *the ends whereof make the Muſical ſounds in the Trough of Water at* C. *which is ſupplied with Water by the Pipe* D. *which in time dreins the Ciſtern, which waſte Water precipitates into* E. *and from* E. *into the common Drein.*

Theſe Waters are to be preferr'd for the irrigation of your Plants to any other, and in caſe you make your Ciſterns well, and cement the joynts of your Stone with *Pariſian Cement*, or with our own Lime compounded with Linſeed Oyl, they will retain the Water for a long time.

SECT. IV.

Of Water-works.

BEſides thoſe natural courſes that are propoſed, for the leading the water from the one place of your Garden to the other, after it is entred into its limits, there are ſeveral ways of ordering it, where it is either naturally or artificially advanced above the level of your Garden.

E 3 *The*

Figure 4.20 *John Worlidge,* Systema horticulturae, or, the Art of Gardening *(London, 1682).*

By permission of Llyfrgell Genedlaethol Cymru/The National Library of Wales.

Charles, Marquess of Worcester, married and began occupying Troy in 1682, the same year that the water engineer John Worlidge published his *Systema horticulturae*.[43] This publication gave a detailed account of different methods of bringing water into the garden for, he argued, 'a Garden [cannot] ever be said to be complete, nor in its full splendour and beauty, without this Element of Water'.[44] Worlidge also described seven types of fountain, including 'The Ball raised by a Spout of Water' and 'The Royal Oak with Leaves, Acorns, and Crowns dropping, and several small spouts round the top'.[45] These designs were amongst the fashions for fountains amongst the wealthy aristocrats towards the end of the seventeenth century and, given his status as the oldest son of Henry, first Duke of Beaufort, who was at this time creating the enormous gardens at Badminton, it is reasonable to suggest that Charles could have adopted them at Troy.

Gardens to the north-east of the house

The area north of the exedra garden and towards the house lies parallel and very close to the river Trothy. The 1765 Aram map shows this area as 'D° [ditto], part of Pleck meadow' (see Figure 4.13), whilst the 1712 Gillmore map shows an additional, distinct rectangular feature, labelled as R in Figure 4.21. No descriptions accompany the land around the house in Gillmore's map. It is suggested here that the shape R represents a rectangular stretch of water, referred to as a canal in garden history terms, running west to east, parallel to and fed from the river Trothy; the required overflow facility would also be provided by this river.

The existing topography in this area clearly shows landscaping to provide two extensive flat depressions that terminate at the north-east end with the nuns' 1960s covered games court near the river (Figure 4.22). These flat areas are bordered on either side by alternating wide and narrow single terraces, approximately one metre high. The two sunken areas are not entirely separate; they are currently partially separated by what appears to be a breached earth dam; there was possibly an earth walkway between the two depressions at some time.

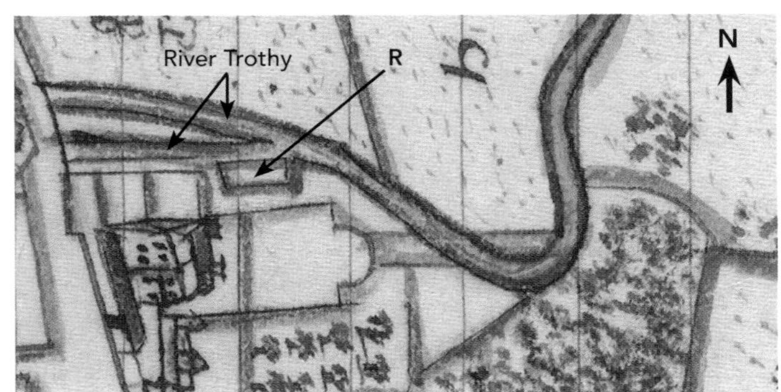

Figure 4.21 (left) *Detail, the 1712 Gillmore map showing a rectangular feature, R, close to the river.*

Map by permission of Llyfrgell Genedlaethol Cymru/The National Library of Wales; annotations: Ann Benson.

This would enable a person to walk across from one side of this area to the other without going down into one of the depressions. A measured field survey of the entire area is represented in a drawing using hachures in Figure 4.23; X marks the location of the remains of an earth dam.

Groundsmen, who worked at Troy for the entire twentieth-century period when the house was occupied, confirm that no landscaping took place in this area within their memory.[46] The 1881 OS map shows contours in this area but, largely due to its scale, lacks detail and simply implies a change in level between two sunken areas. Interestingly, the end of the area close to the current games building is shown as elevated above the surrounding ground, and thus indicates that the whole of the sunken area could be walked around on elevated ground (terrace). During the building of the covered games facility the surrounding ground was levelled and this part of the terracing was removed.[47] The 1845 tithe map (Figure 4.24) shows a curvilinear area in the same location as Gillmore's sunken rectangle; it is also shaded in the same manner as the river, implying it contained water. The tithe apportionments reveal no relevant information about this area. An alternative explanation to the existence of an artificial

Figure 4.22 (below) *Land to the north-east of the house. The river Trothy is below the tree-line on the left, the 1960s covered games court is in the distance, and the person stands at the breached earth dam.* Copyright: Ann Benson.

water feature is that the depression in the tithe map is an oxbow created from the river below as an alternative path, and then, as the flood has receded, left the area filled with water.

On balance, it is most likely that the tithe map shows the extant depressions filled with water, and no attempt has been made to draw the alternating walkways. This seems a reasonable assumption, given the lack of landscape detail shown on the rest of this map. The depressions could have been sunken gardens with parterres, so that their patterns could be admired from the terraces above. However, towards the end of the seventeenth century long canals became a particularly fashionable garden feature, reflecting the fashion for all things Dutch on the accession of William and Mary in 1689. Canals with terraces running alongside are commonly seen in etchings and paintings of this period (Figure 4.25).[48] A summer house placed at the end of the canal was also not uncommon, as for example in the Dutch water garden of 1696–1705 at Westbury Court, Gloucestershire, and the canal at Hall Barn, Buckinghamshire.[49]

Even at the beginning of the seventeenth century, canals and water parterres were features of the aristocracy's designed landscapes. Sir Baptist Hicks built Campden House in Chipping Campden in the early years of the reign of James I. Water parterres and canals some 350 metres in

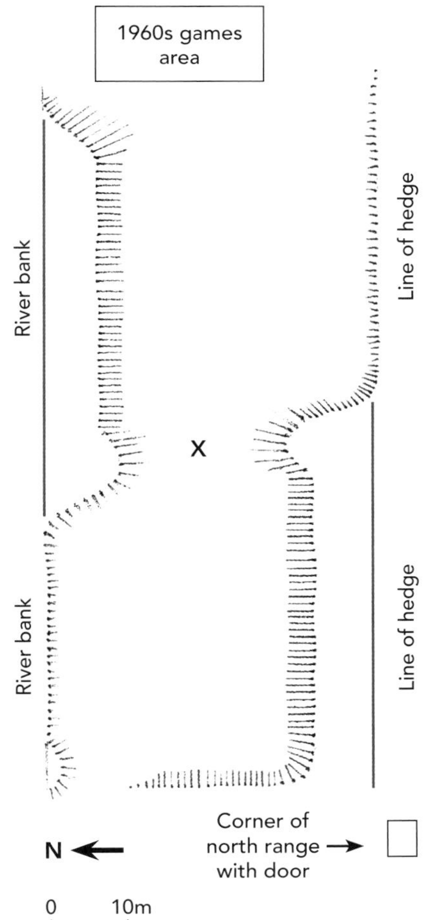

Figure 4.23 (above) *Topographical survey of the area to the north-east of the house.* Copyright: Ann Benson.

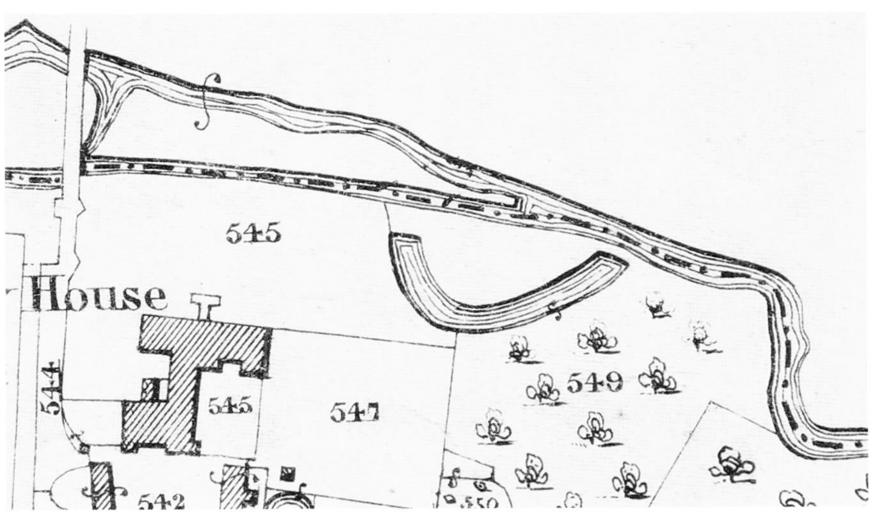

Figure 4.24 (left) *Detail, water feature on the 1845 tithe map.* By permission of Gwent Archives.

length, with alternating broad and narrow terraces and earthen causeways, stretched out across the valley east of the house.[50] These features are dated to the early 1610s and are thus contemporary with the period when, as argued here, Sir Charles Somerset was enhancing Troy on returning from his European tour. Paul Everson notes that Campden's 'linear layout extending the axis of the principal entrance looks back most obviously to Saint-Germain-en-Laye of 1577 onwards and that tradition represented in Britain by Hatfield and Moor Park'.[51] More relevant in family connections, the water parterre finds parallels with those at Wilton for the Somersets' distant relation, Philip Herbert, Earl of Pembroke, and even more closely with Raglan, the creation of Sir Charles Somerset's father and grandfather and his boyhood home. For this reason and the enthusiasm with which he describes the water features at Saint-Germain-en-Laye in his travel diary (1611–12), it seems inconceivable that he would not have created a canal and even a water parterre at Troy. The canal would

Figure 4.25 *The Canal and 'Great Room' at Hall Barn, Buckinghamshire, 1730.*
Image courtesy of *Country Life.*

have been a single stretch of water as shown for Hall Barn; a water parterre would have land rising up in decorative shapes within the stretch of water.

From what appears to be the remains of a breached earth dam and the hachure drawing, it is reasonable to suggest that at Troy there were at least two compartments of water divided by an earth causeway to enable a person to walk from one terrace across the water to the other side and on to its terrace, in short, a simple water parterre. It could have contained fountains and islands that have long since vanished. An extant door in the east elevation of the 1680s north range gives direct access within metres to one of the two broad terraces. Whatever existed in this area following the 1680s addition of the north range, it was clearly important enough to be accessed directly from this section of the house. The 1901 Troy estate auction catalogue describes this area towards the river Trothy as having 'a luxuriant growth of mature timber, copper beech, sweet chestnut, and lime', and that it had 'old Fish Ponds and Pleasance' in the Jacobean period.[52] Water features which originally served for the production of food would have been adapted to more aesthetically pleasing functions as the seventeenth century played out.

Gardens to the north and west of the house

The cost of building Troy's north range and melding it to the pre-existing house was carried by the first Duke of Beaufort. However, his son, Charles, Marquess of Worcester, was required 'to finish the house to his mind', which he did on marrying in 1682.[53] Garden creations during Charles's occupation of Troy until his death in 1698 were, therefore, also to his taste.

The principal reception rooms of the north range primarily overlook garden areas to the north and north-east of the house. The area to the west is forshortened by the closeness of the boundary wall. It may be for this reason that, from 1698, the west section of the house was consistently occupied by stewards; this arrangement also enabled close scrutiny of the nearby walled garden with its precious fruit and what became the main entrance to the house from the 1680s. As a consequence, the gardens on the west side of the house did not command as much attention from the Somersets as other areas.

Gillmore's estate map of 1712 shows the north range (Figure 4.26). The main focus of this map is on surveying the surrounding land and doubt remains about how accurately the house is represented. However, the correct number of bays and storeys are shown and the flights of steps are a valid representation of what is extant. The house is also shown with harling, which is known to have survived at least until 1802.[54] It seems

Figure 4.26 (right) *Detail, Gillmore's 1712 estate map showing the north range and its garden area.*

Map by permission of Llyfrgell Genedlaethol Cymru/ The National Library of Wales.

Figure 4.27 (below) *The procedural entrance to Tredegar House, Gwent, a late seventeenth-century house and garden.*

©National Trust Images/ Andrew Butler

reasonable to assume that in 1712 the garden area to the north of the house was as shown in Gillmore's map and consisted of a walled and railed enclosure with perimeter pathways, and a centrally placed round bed or pond set between geometric areas of grass. The paths may have been composed of hoggin, as Troy's estate accounts from the late seventeenth century include payments for re-laying paths with this material.[55] Due to the angle adopted in the map, the grass areas may have been in a quadripartite arrangement. Such a formal, simple design before the main entrance door is typical of seventeenth-century houses of quality (Figure 4.27).[56]

A 1720s painting of *Troy House from the Wye Bridge* by Thomas Smith shows the house with harling (stucco). However, in other respects the painting is questionable for its accuracy of representation. The land to the right of the house does not rise as shown and the walled garden is shown to the south with a curved wall and not as it should be, namely to the west. Certainly no such walled garden or exedra could exist in the position shown, as this is the area covered by the extant mediaeval farm buildings.

Figure 4.28 Troy House (View from the Wye Bridge), *by Thomas Smith, c.1720s.*

By permission of the Duke of Beaufort.

Perhaps the artist did not visit the site or the patron's vanity is at play here, because the walled garden would have still been famous for its fruit-growing after its production of apricots for King Charles I at Raglan Castle.[57]

Unlike Gillmore, Thomas shows a wall with pillars topped with finials either side of a bridge across the river Trothy, all in line with the steps leading up to the main door of the north range. These features imply the existence of a northern procedural route flanked by a double avenue of trees. Certainly, avenues of trees were popular for enhancing the approach to a house in the seventeenth and early eighteenth centuries and were much used by George London and Henry Wise for their patrons (Figure 4.29). Gillmore's map of 1712 and Danckerts's painting of about 1672 both show an incomplete double avenue of trees in the same location.

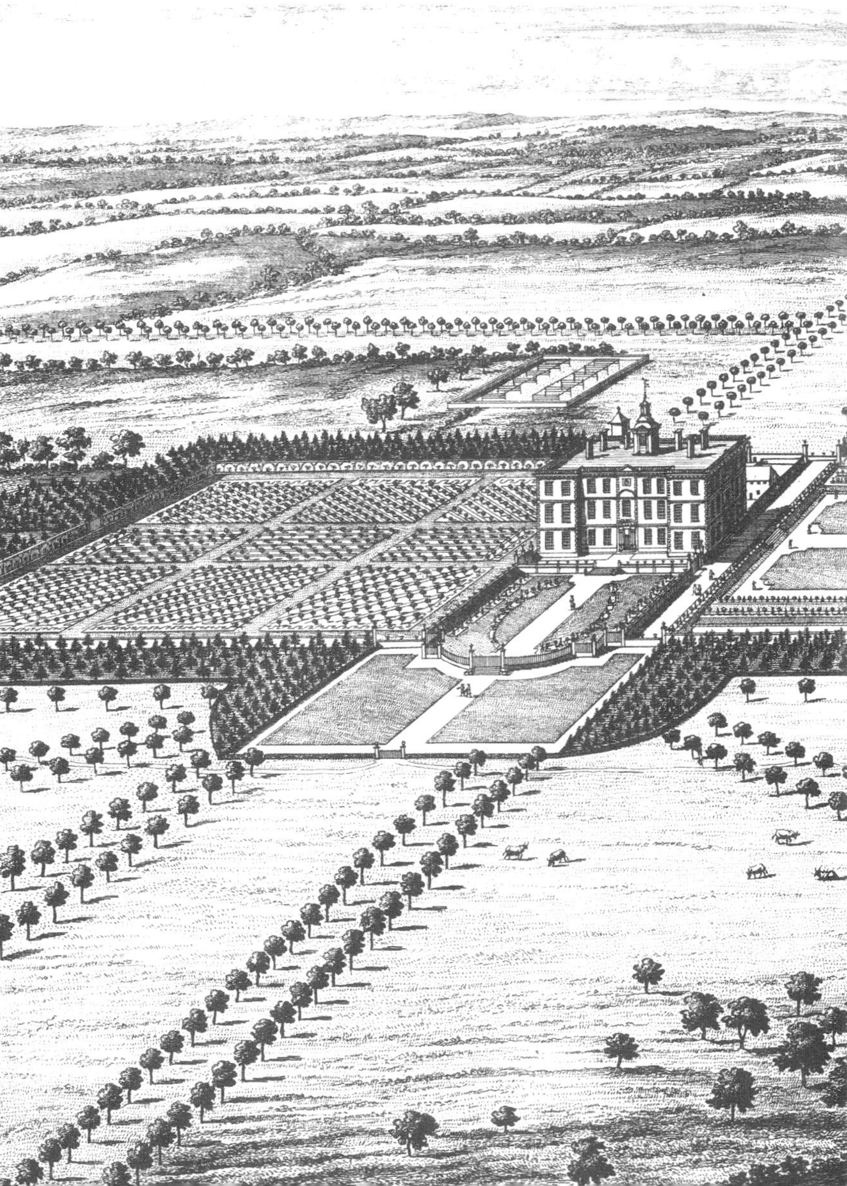

Figure 4.29 *Newby in the West Riding of the County of Yorke, c.1700, showing an avenue of trees lining the procedural route to the house.*

By permission of The National Trust; author's copy of *Britannia Illustrata.*[58]

However, it is unclear how the coach and horses in Thomas's picture would have accessed the house through the trees, particularly as the river Wye is in the foreground.

Details of gardens on the west side of the house before the early 1900s are not identifiable from estate maps or other sources. A photograph of this side of the house from about 1880 shows a gravel driveway leading to an entrance into part of the house pre-dating the north range; a lush growth of trees, shrubs, pampas grass, topiary and lawns complements gravel paths (Figure 4.30). Another photograph from the early 1900s, which is too grainy to reproduce here, shows the north range of the house neatly swathed in ivy to the second floor, and, before the range, a turning circle around a central flower bed. The Beaufort portcullis hangs on the pediment above the main door, so although labelled 'Troy Convent', the photograph pre-dates the nuns' replacing the portcullis with a figure of Our Lady.

An extract from Troy's 1901 auction catalogue describes the approach via 'a private road commanded by an Ornamental Lodge to the Inner Drive, enclosed by Iron Gates, and thence by a Circular Carriage Sweep to the Entrance Front'.[59] This 'private road' was flanked by Wellingtonia trees, which must post-date 1853, the year of the introduction of this type

Figure 4.30 *Troy House from the west, 1870–90.*

of tree to the United Kingdom; only three of these trees have survived along Troy's 'private road'. Two smaller driveways extend from the private road to the house; both are shown on the 1881 OS map. One leads directly to a turning circle (the 'Circular Carriage Sweep') before the 1680s north range, the other to the doorway in the west section of the house, which was the entrance to the steward's quarters. After 1881, the entrance of this second smaller driveway was sealed with a stone wall, and finally, during the 1960s, the nuns built a hostel and a teaching block on what had been the small garden area shown to the west of the house in Figure 4.30. The turning circle before the north range disappeared during the 1990s, and currently the inner drive only leads from the entrance gates to what was the steward's entrance.

Other than stretches of grass, which resemble meadows rather than lawns, gardens have now disappeared from around Troy House. But they were glorious from at least 1600 until 1901, when in the Somerset family's ownership.

Notes

1 Letter from Sister Jenny, The Priory, Northfield, Birmingham to Dr Ann Benson regarding archive material for Troy House School and Convent, 18 September 2012.
2 Paula Henderson, 'How to Research Garden History', lecture, Institute of Historical Research, 8 November 2012; Professor Timothy Mowl, MA Garden History lectures, University of Bristol, 2010–11.
3 Personal communications: Michael Tamplin, Troy's groundsman from about 1960 to 1977; ex-student and retired housemistress of Troy School.
4 Mitchel Troy Parish, 1845 Tithe Map, held at Gwent Archives, Ebbw Vale, Monmouthshire.
5 John Fitzherbert, *Book of Husbandry*, ed. Rev. Walter W. Skeat (1534; London: Trubner & Co., 1882 repr.).
6 Elisabeth Woodhouse, 'Spirit of the Elizabethan Garden', *Garden History*, 27/1 (Summer 1999), 11.
7 See Jill Francis, 'Order and Disorder in the Early Modern Garden, 1558–*c*.1630', *Garden History*, 36/1 (Spring, 2008), 22–35, for an account of horticultural literature and its inter-relationship with societal influences.
8 Thomas Hill, *The Gardener's Labyrinth*, 1577.
9 Timothy Mowl and Diane James, *Historic Gardens of Warwickshire* (Bristol: Redcliffe Press, 2011), p. 26.
10 Francis, 'Order and Disorder', 22.

11 Gervase Markham, *The English Husbandman* (London: printed by T.S. for John Browne, 1613).
12 Judith Roberts, 'The gardens of the gentry in the late Tudor period', *Garden History*, 27 (1999), 89–108, 95.
13 William Lawson, *The New Orchard and Garden* (1618), p. 36.
14 John Parkinson, *Paradisi in sole paradisus terrestris* (London: 1629), p. 3.
15 See Roy Strong, *The Renaissance Garden in England* (London: Thames and Hudson, 1979), pp. 39–42, for a history and examples of knot gardens.
16 Woodhouse, 'Spirit of the Elizabethan Garden', p. 25.
17 Sir Francis Bacon, *Selected Essays* (London: Zodiac, 1949), p. 47, from the essay *Of Gardening*.
18 Jeremy Musson, *How to Read a Country House* (London: Ebury Press, 2005), p. 224. See also Thomas Hill, *The Gardener's Labyrinth*, 1577.
19 Letter from Sister Jenny to Dr Ann Benson regarding archive material for Troy House School and Convent, 18 September 2012.
20 Susan Campbell, *A History of Kitchen Gardens* (London: Frances Lincoln, 2005), p. 60.
21 Personal communications: Michael Tamplin, Troy's groundsman from about 1960 to 1977; ex-student and retired housemistress of Troy School.
22 Personal communications: Michael Tamplin, Troy's groundsman from about 1960 to 1977; ex-student and retired housemistress of Troy School.
23 The building is listed as lot 153 (Pigsties) in the 1901 auction catalogue held at Monmouth Museum; recollection of Graham Long, Troy Farm owner 1960s to 2016.
24 Paula Henderson, *The Tudor House and Garden* (New Haven and London: Yale University Press, 2005), pp. 155–64.
25 See Jeremy Musson, *How to Read a Country House* (London: Ebury Press, 2007), pp. 223–4.
26 See Christopher Catling, *A Practical Handbook of Archaeology* (London: Anness Publishing, 2014) for a simple explanation of resistivity surveys.
27 Badminton: FmG 5/1.
28 See Mary Ann Wingfield, *Sport and the Artist, Vol. 1: Ball Games* (Woodbridge: Antique Collectors' Club, 1988) for a history of bowling.
29 *A briefe memorial of my voyage into France 1673–1674 Charles, Lord Herbert*, Badminton: FmG 4/1. This diary was transcribed by Ann Benson for David, eleventh Duke of Beaufort, and is now being edited.
30 Letter dated 13 January 1696 from Charles, Marquess of Worcester, to his mother, Mary, first Duchess of Beaufort, at Badminton. Badminton: FmF 1/3/2.
31 Exedra is the term used by garden historians for a semi-circular cultivated area.
32 Personal communications: Michael Tamplin, Troy's groundsman from about 1960 to 1977; ex-student and retired housemistress of Troy School.
33 Private communication, Troy ex-student and retired housemistress.

34 Personal communications: Michael Tamplin, Troy's groundsman from about 1960 to 1977; ex-student and retired housemistress of Troy School.
35 Personal communications: Michael Tamplin, Troy's groundsman from about 1960 to 1977; ex-student and retired housemistress of Troy School.
36 Leonard Knyff and Jan Kip, 'Stansted in the County of Sussex', in *Britannia Illustrata*, ed. John Harris and Gervase Jackson-Stops (Bungay: Paradigm Press, 1984), p. 80.
37 'Swillington in the West Rideing of Yorkshire', in *Britannia Illustrata*, p. 154.
38 See the very large Stoke Edith wall hanging, Victoria and Albert Museum, for a more detailed view of a garden typical of the late seventeenth and early eighteenth centuries.
39 Roy Strong, *Henry Prince of Wales and England's Lost Renaissance* (London: Thames and Hudson, 1986,) p. 107. See also Catharine MacLeod et al., *The Lost Prince: The Life and Death of Henry Stuart* (London: National Portrait Gallery Publications, 2012) for a richly illustrated account of the exhibition of the same title, containing plans of the Richmond garden.
40 The work was not completed due to the premature death of Prince Henry, aged 18, on 6 November 1612.
41 *A briefe memorial of my voyage into France 1673–1674 Charles, Lord Herbert*, Badminton: FmG 4/1.
42 Driver, Jonas and Co., *Troy House Estate Monmouth, To Be Sold on 27th March 1901* (London: Auctioneers Messrs Driver, Jonas & Co., 1901), p. 5. This auction catalogue is held at Nelson Museum, Monmouth.
43 John Worlidge, *Systema horticulturae, or the Art of Gardening* (London, 1682), p. 53.
44 Worlidge, *Systema horticulturae*, p. 42.
45 Worlidge, *Systema horticulturae*, p. 52.
46 Private communication with Michael Tamplin, the last groundsman to work at Troy until the nuns departed in the late 1970s, and whose father also worked and lived at Troy before him.
47 Personal communications: Michael Tamplin, Troy's groundsman from about 1960 to 1977; ex-student and retired housemistress of Troy School.
48 See *Britannia Illustrata* for further examples.
49 Although the source is not acknowledged, this image may also be found in Christopher Hussey, *English Gardens and Landscapes 1700–1750* (London: Country Life Ltd, 1967), facing p. 17.
50 Paul Everson, 'The Gardens of Campden House, Chipping Campden, Gloucestershire', *Garden History*, 17/2 (Autumn, 1989), 109–21.
51 Everson, 'The Gardens of Campden House', 118.
52 Troy House Estate 1901 auction catalogue, held at Nelson Museum, Monmouth.
53 Badminton: FmF 3/7.
54 Deduced from a painting of Troy dated 1801 held by Gill Davey of Mitchel Troy.

55 Badminton: FmG 5/1. Hoggin is a compactable ground cover, composed of a mixture of gravel, sand and clay that produces a buff-coloured bound surface.

56 See Nicholas Cooper, *The Jacobean Country House* (London: Arum Press, 2006) for other examples.

57 Thomas Bayly, Apophthegm 43, *The Golden Apophthegms of his Royal Majesty King Charles 1 and Henry Marq. of Worcester* . . . (London: John Clowes, 1660).

58 'Newby in the West Riding of the County of Yorke', in *Britannia Illustrata*, pp. 72–3.

59 Troy House Estate 1901 auction catalogue, p. 1. Held at Nelson Museum, Monmouth.

Five

The Walled Garden West of Troy House

THE WALLED GARDEN is rectangular in shape, measures 115 metres by 105 metres, and is of 1.6 hectares. Surprisingly, its original perimeter stone walls are almost entirely extant, with only a small amount of repair being conducted in the 1960s.[1] The walls are of rubble construction with dressed stone quoins on all four corners.

Figure 5.1 *Relative position of the walled garden.*

Currently, the interior consists of grass and a few fruit trees; it is divided into three parts, each being the garden of a private dwelling adjoining the perimeter wall. The main focus of this chapter is on the garden's structural elements, as these prove fundamental to understanding the history of the estate as a whole.

Entrances: service and ornamental

The 1881 OS map is used in Figure 5.2 to indicate the position of the garden's several entrances. The one in the south-east corner of the garden, close to Troy Farm, was blocked by the nuns during the 1940s.[2] It served as a service entrance between the garden and the farm; it has not been previously identified as an entrance in any survey and, from the alignment of the surrounding stones, appears to be original.

Another entrance some 2.6 metres wide, argued here as also original, is in the west wall close to the ancient route between Monmouth and Chepstow. The space between the pillars of this entrance was blocked with a stone wall by the nuns at an unknown date; they then turned the area inside this wall into a cemetery.[3] Five laywomen and twenty nuns are buried

Figure 5.2 *Walled garden: entrances and access routes. (Red line = position of stone walls; green line = oldest access route to the house from the ancient Monmouth to Chepstow road; dotted line = nineteenth-century route to Troy House.)*

By permission of The British Library Board; Mitchel Troy Parish, 1881 OS map. Image copyright: Ann Benson.

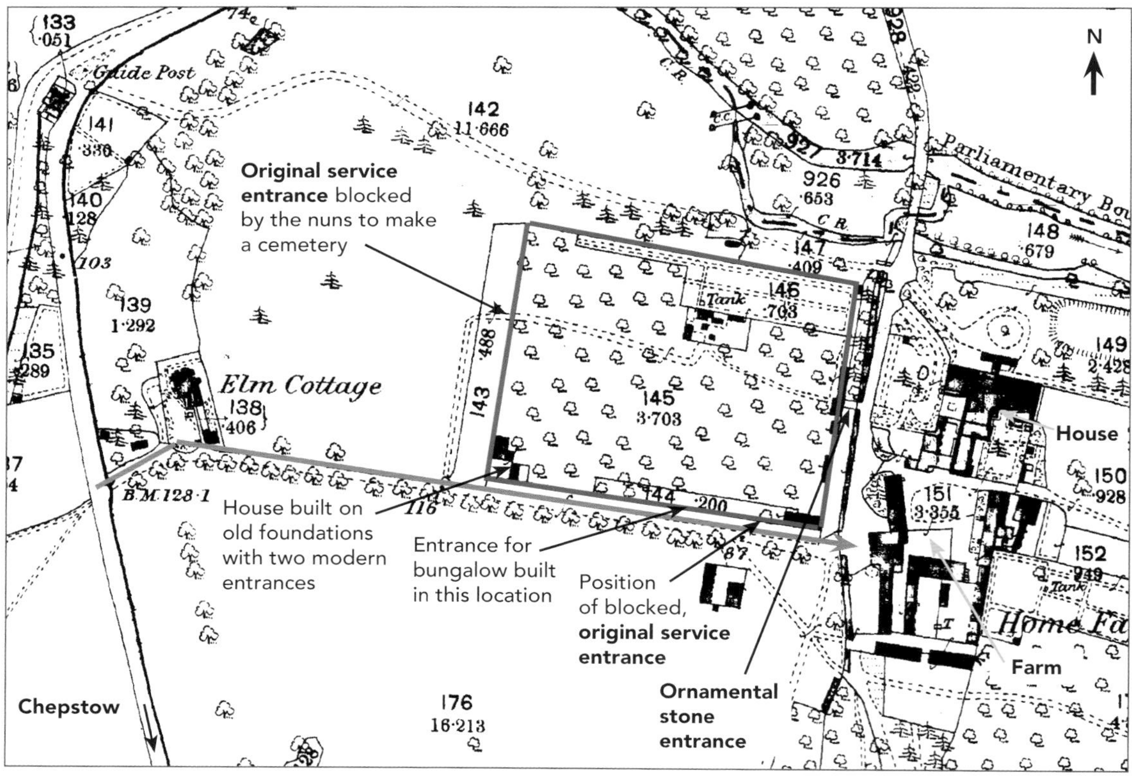

Figure 5.3 *The west wall's original entrance with pillars, infilled by the nuns to create a cemetery within the walled garden. Outside (above) and inside (right) the garden.*
Copyright: Ann Benson.

here, including Troy Convent's first Mother Superior, Sister Mary of the Blessed Sacrament Goullioud, who died on 27 August 1915. This blocked entrance does not lie in the middle of the west wall; classical symmetry does not appear to have influenced its design, a point returned to later when making the case for the garden's construction pre-dating Renaissance influences and Cadw's seventeenth-century attribution.

Running parallel to the east wall of the garden and outside of it is a canalised small stream with stone revetted sides, which in the 1901 auction catalogue is described as 'a Watercress Stream', now overgrown.[4] A small stone bridge crosses the stream and then a gently sloping path with five

Figure 5.4 *View of the ornamental entrance from outside the walled garden, 2015.*

Crown copyright: RCAHMW.

shallow stone steps leads to an ornamental stone entrance and lobby set within the wall. This entrance faces Troy House and, unlike the one on the west wall, lies exactly in the centre of its wall.

The ornamental entrance has a rectangular doorway surrounded by classically styled, dressed and moulded stonework with shallow rustication. The doorway has a double ovolo moulding terminating in an ogee stop. A wooden strap hinge is extant on the door. Above the doorway there is a triangular stone pediment with strapwork decoration on either side of a heraldic shield, on which the letters C, S and E are inscribed, with a simple flower. The initials refer to Sir Charles Somerset and his wife, Elizabeth. Charles was the fourth son of the fourth Earl of Worcester, and Elizabeth was the daughter of the earl's steward. They were shown in chapter 3 as residing at Troy House during the period 1612–28, having married about 1609. Cornucopias form the sides of the shield. The cornucopia, a symbol of abundance, refers to the bounty of nature that lies within the walled garden. Its meaning would have been understood by those with an understanding of the classics, and thus by the Somersets who occupied Troy during the sixteenth and seventeenth centuries.[5]

Cadw's report of 1994 is the earliest traceable claim that 'above the initials [CSE] there was originally a date of 1611 (? the date of the garden's construction), recorded in the early nineteenth century, but this has now worn off'.[6] Unfortunately, this statement is not referenced. Similarly, John Newman records 'a rectangular WALLED GARDEN, entered through a rusticated sandstone doorway with strapwork, a heraldic shield, the initials of Elizabeth and Charles Somerset – son of the fourth Earl of Worcester and his wife – and, formerly, the date 1611'.[7] However, no reference is given by Newman. The shield, let alone a date, is not even recorded by Joseph Bradney.[8] The top of the shield is some three metres from the ground and, when closely examined at eye-level from a platform, there is no evidence of any date ever being inscribed either on the shield or the pediment. Indeed, there does not seem to be space for any other inscription on the shield.

The area around the shield's edges appears intentionally smooth and is not large enough to accommodate numbers. The top of the shield appears to have its edges continue as two decorative loops, one on either side; these loops may have been taken to be a date of 1611. A date may have existed here but, given the scale of the rest of the shield, it seems unlikely that numbers small enough to fit here would have been used. Also, no date can be seen within the areas of strapwork on each side of the pediment. Horatia Durant, the chronicler of the Somerset family, writes 'over the stone entrance to the orchard where King Charles's dish of "apricocks" had been grown, are the faint initials C and E, and a

Figure 5.5 (above)
The moulding and ogee stop of the ornamental entrance's doorway, 2015.
Crown copyright: RCAHMW.

Figure 5.6 (left)
The pediment of the ornamental entrance, 2015.
Crown copyright: RCAHMW.

fainter S looped to the C'.[9] She makes no mention of any date, and given the detail she provides on all matters when writing about the Somerset family, it is reasonable to assume that there was no date. Possibly, speculation about the date of the gateway's creation has prompted an initial claim that has then been repeated in subsequent publications.

Strapwork is a stylized representation of straps or bands of curling leather, parchment or metal cut into elaborate shapes, with piercings and interweaving. It was particularly popular in Jacobean architecture.[10] The use of strapwork and the classically inspired design of the stone entrance is entirely in keeping with the status and aspirations of Sir Charles Somerset in the second decade of the seventeenth century. The date of 1611 is when Sir Charles embarked on his European tour. Before he left he probably married Elizabeth after the marriage settlement of 1609; she would have remained at Troy with her father and steward, Sir William Powell. It was not unusual for aristocrats to marry a younger woman and then engage in travel, only to return a few years later to a more mature wife.

The entrance door leads into a small lobby with a barrel-vaulted roof, diaper-flagged floor and a round-arched doorway on to the garden. On the garden's side of the entrance there is a symmetrical arrangement of

Figure 5.7 *The barrel-vaulted roof of the ornamental entrance's lobby, 2015.*
Crown copyright: RCAHMW.

Figure 5.8 (left) *View of the ornamental entrance from inside the walled garden, 2015.* Photograph: Crown copyright, RCAHMW; annotations, Ann Benson.

Figure 5.9 (below) *Detail of the ornamental entrance's classically inspired rusticated moulding, 2015.* Crown copyright: RCAHMW.

moulded rectangular, oval cabochon and lozenge stone shapes with rustication. This structure and decoration is clearly classically inspired, though relatively unsophisticated. Cadw's Monmouthshire register does not include any other building with similar features. Given the initials on the shield, it is reasonable to assume that the design is due to Sir Charles Somerset's influence.

As discussed in chapter 2, Sir Charles Somerset was the son of the learned courtier and royal favourite, Edward, fourth Earl of Worcester. Charles was well-educated, read French and Italian, moved in royal circles, and possessed an extensive library, covering the arts, philosophy and mathematics, amongst other subjects.[11] He also travelled extensively throughout Europe.[12] Most likely, he would have known the architectural treatise from Roman times, *Architectura*, by Vitruvius (*c.*80BC–*c.*15BC), and been familiar with the explosion of architectural expositions and handbooks that came during the Renaissance, including *De Re Aedificatoria* by Alberti (1404–72), published in 1485, and *Tutte l'Opere d'Architettura* by Sebastian Serlio (1475–1554), published over the period 1537–75. Serlio's book contained the first detailed work on the five classical orders and provided practical design patterns with copious illustrations.[13] It was written in Italian, whereas previous writings had been in Latin. As John Summerson notes: 'The books became the architectural bible of the civilised world. The Italians used them, the French owed nearly everything to Serlio and his books, the Germans and Flemings based their own books on his, and the Elizabethans cribbed from him.'[14]

Serlio's volumes were highly influential as a conveyor of the Italian Renaissance style, and quickly became available in a variety of languages. His plans and elevations of many Roman buildings provided a useful repository of classical images. Within five years of its original publication, the Flemish scholar, Pieter Coecke van Aelst, published adaptations of Book IV in Flemish and German in Antwerp; they served as significant vectors in the spread of Serlio's influence.[15] A Dutch version of Books I–V, released in Amsterdam in 1606 and based largely on Coecke van Aelst's work in Flemish, served as the basis for the English translation of Books I–V published by Robert Peake in London in 1611. This translation would have been eagerly sought by the royal court's favourites, of which Sir Charles Somerset was one. Book IV of Serlio's *Tutte l'Opere d'Architettura* contains an illustration of carvings similar to those seen on Troy's ornamental entrance.[16]

Jan Vredeman de Vries (1527–*c.*1607) worked as an architect but his importance rests on his numerous engravings used to popularise classic forms, which earned him the name of 'Flemish Vitruvius'. His last and greatest work is his *Perspective*, published in Latin in The Hague and in Leiden in 1604–5. The rusticated mouldings on Troy's ornamental gateway echo what is seen in de Vries's engravings and Serlio's publications, although in a less purely classical form.[17]

It is against this background of exponential growth in available information promulgating Renaissance architecture that the cultured Sir Charles Somerset returned to Troy from his European tour in May 1612.[18] Newly married to an heiress and with recent experience of Europe's Renaissance architecture, it is reasonable to assume that he would have been eager to put his mark on the Troy estate. Although Charles and Elizabeth's marriage settlement date is proven to be 1609, the date of the marriage is unknown.[19] Charles embarked on his travels in April 1611. Even if he had married in 1609, it would have given him little time to have the garden's

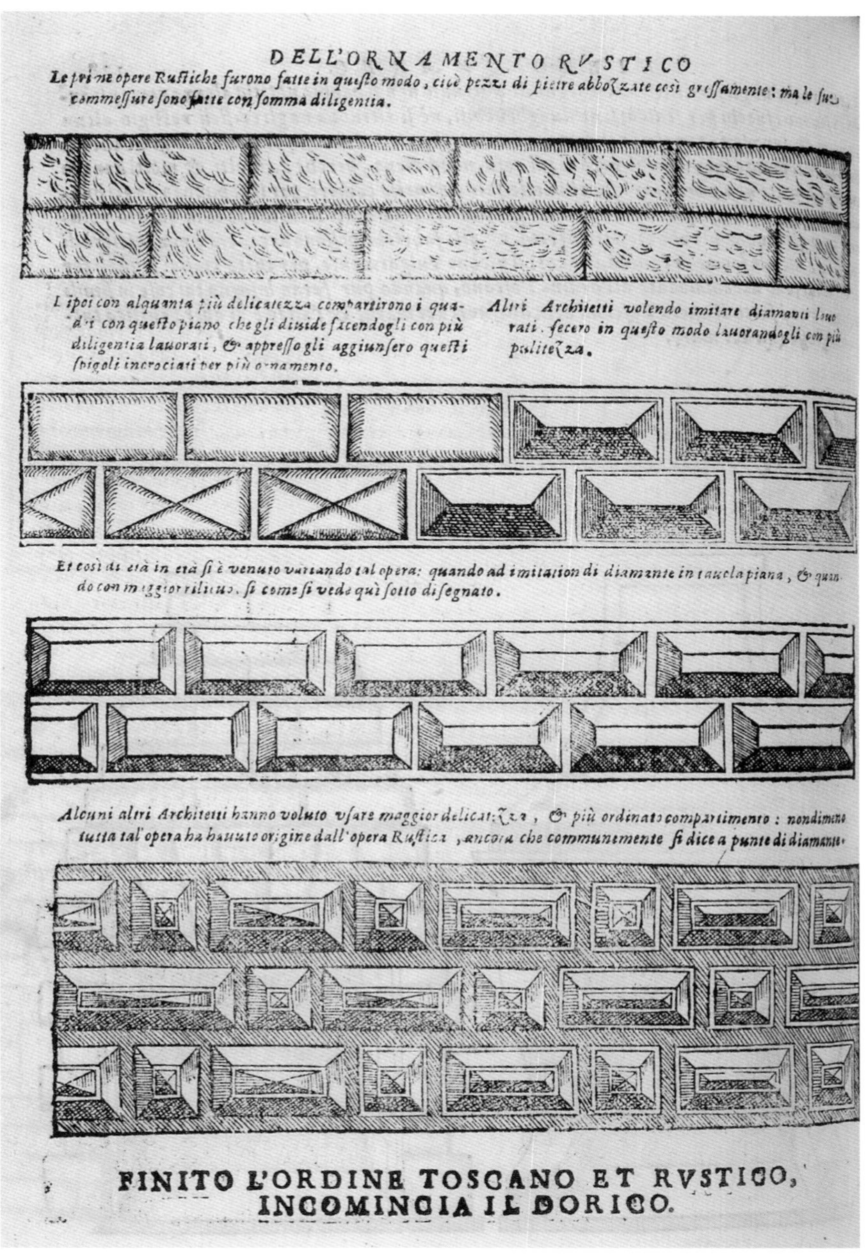

DELL'ORNAMENTO RVSTICO

Le prime opere Rustiche furono fatte in questo modo, cioè pezzi di pietre abbozzate così grossamente: ma le sue commessure sono fatte con somma diligentia.

I poi con alquanta più delicatezza compartirono i quadri con questo piano che gli divide facendogli con più diligentia lavorati, & appresso gli aggiunsero questi spigoli incrociati per più ornamento.

Altri Architetti volendo imitare diamanti lavorati, fecero in questo modo lavorandogli con più pulitezza.

Et così di età in età si è venuto variando tal opera: quando ad imitation di diamante in tavola piana, & quando con maggior rilievo, si come si vede quì sotto disegnato.

Alcuni altri Architetti hanno voluto usare maggior delicatezza, & più ordinato compartimento: nondimeno tutta tal'opera ha havuto origine dall'opera Rustica, ancora che communemente si dice a punte di diamante.

FINITO L'ORDINE TOSCANO ET RVSTICO, INCOMINCIA IL DORICO.

Figure 5.10 *Rustic work: Sebastian Serlio on architecture.*

By permission of the Bodleian Library.

walls and the ornamental entrance built to his design before his travels. As shown in chapter 3, the 1620 inventory of Troy in Charles's own hand shows that new building work on the house had been completed by that date, and the Jacobean plaster ceilings are also dated as no later than 1620. The addition of an ornamental entrance with contemporary architectural decoration could have been another of Charles's creations, and where

Figure 5.11
Vredeman de Vries: his use of rusticated stone mouldings in a classical setting (see top left-hand corner).
By permission of Dover Publications, Inc.

better to insert it, if driven by classical ideals, than in the centre of the walled garden's wall facing the house? It is argued here that Charles is responsible for the ornamental stone entrance in about 1612, but not for the garden's walls. So who is?

Dating the walled garden's construction and consequences for the estate's history

The walls of the ornamental entrance do not dovetail into the walls of the walled garden: they stand somewhat proud of the garden's walls, as if a later addition. At a distance of two metres south of the ornamental entrance, there is a bee bole set into the interior of the west-facing garden wall; another bee bole exists on the wall facing south but it has lost its middle shelf and is currently used as a memorial. A photograph was taken when the bee association came to register the bee boles in 1953; it shows the damaged bee bole intact and of a similar design to that on the garden's west-facing wall (Figure 5.13).

Both bee boles have overhead drip sills to keep rain off the skeps. The drip sills appear to be a designed part of the wall and the stones either side of the boles are evenly placed. Consequently, it seems that the walls and boles are contemporary. When these bee boles were first registered by the

National Beekeeping Museum[20] in May 1953, they were dated as 'certainly 16th century' (Figure 5.14).[21] Searches for boles of a similar design on the International Bee Register failed to reveal any matches.[22] However, the style of the overhead drip sill resembles the hood moulding seen above English windows of the late fifteenth and early sixteenth century and is thus in keeping with IBRA's attributed date.[23]

If, as reasoned here, the bee boles are contemporary with the wall and the ornamental entrance was inserted during the second decade of the seventeenth century, why place the entrance so close to potentially

Figure 5.12 (right) *West-facing bee bole near the ornamental entrance, 2015.*
Crown copyright: RCAHMW.

Figure 5.13 (below) *South-facing bee bole, 1953.*
Reproduced with permission from the International Bee Research Association (IBRA), Bee Boles Register.

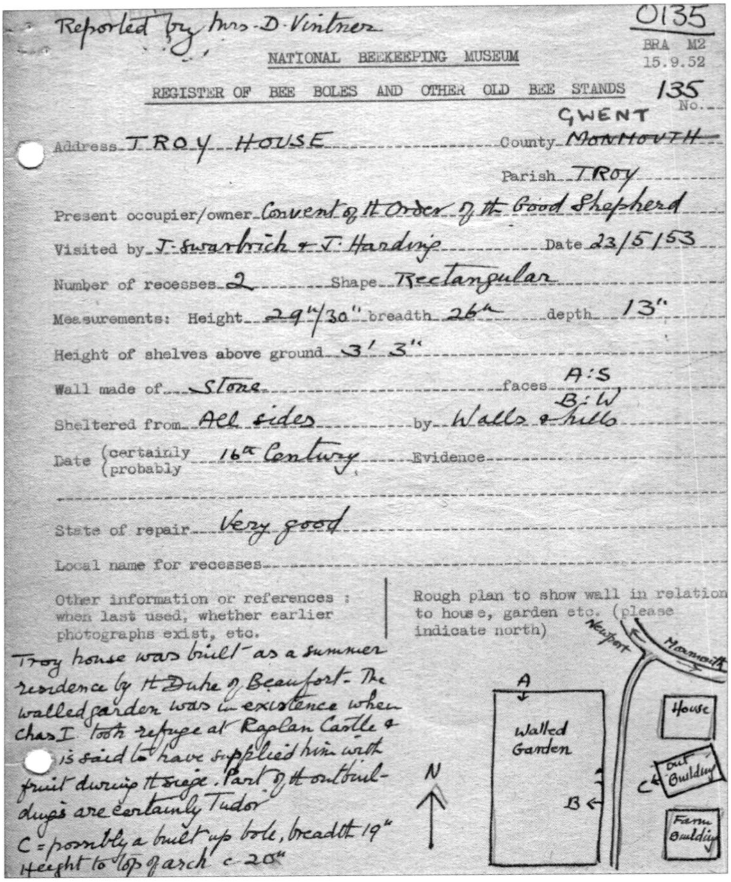

Reported by Mrs. D. Vintner

0135

BRA M2
15.9.52

NATIONAL BEEKEEPING MUSEUM

REGISTER OF BEE BOLES AND OTHER OLD BEE STANDS 135 No.

Address TROY HOUSE County ~~MONMOUTH~~ GWENT

Parish TROY

Present occupier/owner Convent of the Order of the Good Shepherd

Visited by J. Swarbrick & J. Harding Date 23/5/53

Number of recesses 2 Shape Rectangular

Measurements: Height 29"/30" breadth 26" depth 13"

Height of shelves above ground 3' 3"

Wall made of Stone faces A: S B: W

Sheltered from All sides by Walls & hills

Date (certainly / probably) 16th Century Evidence

State of repair Very good

Local name for recesses

Other information or references: when last used, whether earlier photographs exist, etc.

Troy house was built as a summer residence by the Duke of Beaufort. The walled garden was in existence when Chas I took refuge at Raglan Castle & is said to have supplied him with fruit during the siege. Part of the outbuildings are certainly Tudor

C = possibly a built up bole, breadth 19" Height to top of arch c 20"

Rough plan to show wall in relation to house, garden etc. (please indicate north)

Figure 5.14
Registration of Troy's bee boles, 1953.
Reproduced with permission from IBRA's Bee Boles Register.

dangerous bees? Placing the entrance exactly in the middle of the west-facing wall is likely to be classically inspired; this position also fulfils a pragmatic need to provide easy, procedural access to the walled garden from the oldest part of the house for the family and their favoured guests. Throughout the early seventeenth century it was the fashion of the wealthy to observe nature. A pastime for this class of society was to walk through a walled garden to sample its delights, including flowers that were sugared on the plant.[24] In 1618, William Lawson advocated the inclusion of bees in walled gardens to aid fruit pollination but also to provide both a pleasant sight and noise.[25] His publication, *A New Orchard and Garden*, contains a plan of an orchard with bee houses facing south.[26] Later horticultural publications by Francis Bacon (1625) and John Parkinson (1629) continued this mix of a profit and pleasure theme, but as the century progressed, and certainly after the Restoration, the literature took a greater interest in first spiritual and then scientific matters.[27]

If the walled garden does pre-date 1610, it is most likely from the sixteenth century when Troy was owned by Sir William Herbert (d.1524), illegitimate son of the first Earl of Pembroke, who had a chapel built within Monmouth Church and owned much property, or his son, Sir Charles Herbert (k. 1532), who was steward and receiver of the estates for the duchy of Lancaster, and MP for Monmouthshire in 1553.[28] Both had the wealth to build such a large stone structure, but which one had the horticultural interest?

A search of the estate maps enabled, for the first time, the identification of the walled garden as a cherry orchard in both 1765 and 1712. Certainly, as early as 1646, Troy had a reputation for its fruit-growing. For example, and as often quoted, apricots grown at Troy that year were

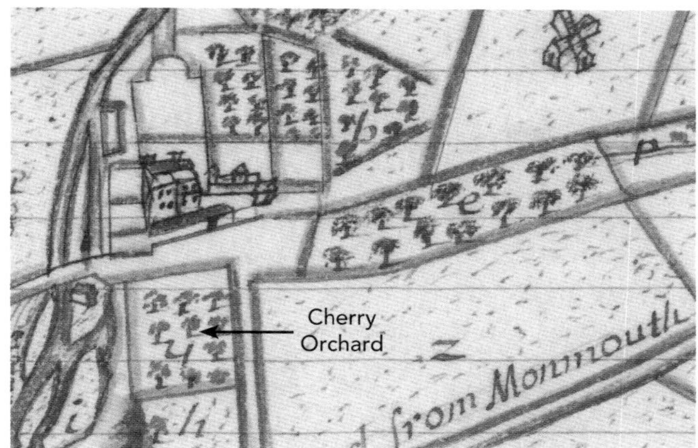

Figure 5.15 *Detail, Gillmore's 1712 map and its key showing the walled garden as a cherry orchard.*

By permission of Llyfrgell Genedlaethol Cymru/ National Library of Wales.

Troy in Monmouth-shire

Troy T grounds	Whole Quant in acres	Bounds Roads Ways	Meado	Pasture	Arab	Wood	Neat Convers			Value Annu
Troy House Gardens Orchards with a Small peece of Arable Ground lying above ye Kitchen Garden	13..3..17		13..3..17				28..0..0			
The Cherry Orchard	4..3..08		4..3..08							
Tump Close bounded South West and										

Figure 5.16 *Detail, Aram's 1765 map and its key showing the walled garden as a cherry orchard.*

By permission of Llyfrgell Genedlaethol Cymru/ National Library of Wales.

	Wm MORGAN Pt of Troy Farm				
1	Cherry Orchard		4..1..19		
2	Hither Loughton Field	19..1..39			
3	Middle Do.	27..0..12			
4	Levox Home Mead			15..1..14	
5	Meadow			17..2..16	
6	Park Orchard	11..2..18			
7	Horse Piece	5..3..00			
8	Yew Tree Piece	30..3..19			

presented by Sir Thomas Somerset to Charles I during his visit to Raglan Castle.[29] Whether the walled garden was used to grow the apricots in 1646 is unproven, but this garden's walls comply with the designs used to grow fruit in the sixteenth and seventeenth centuries.

A rectangle was the typical shape of a walled kitchen or orchard garden in the sixteenth and seventeenth centuries. The longest walls ran along an east–west axis to increase the length of the south-facing walls. This is the case with Troy's walled garden. The walls created a protected environment for the crops, both from the elements and from thieves. The height of the walls varied, but in order to provide enough growing space for the fruit trees trained against them, usually as fans, they needed to be at least three metres high.[30] Commonly, the south-facing wall was the highest, to allow sufficient space for vineries, lean-to glasshouses and the training of fruit that required the most protected, sunny location. At Troy the south-facing wall is the tallest, and the north-facing wall, which historically was usually the lowest or sometimes omitted altogether, is approximately the same height as the other three walls.

Cherries were a favourite fruit throughout Tudor and Stuart times.[31] They were also important as a symbol of innocence and virtue,[32] and often included in portraits of children, as in the 1596 portrait of Prince Henry, a contemporary and childhood friend of Sir Charles Somerset (Figure 5.17).[33]

The cherry trees in the sixteenth and seventeenth centuries were most likely free-standing and planted in a quincunx. Favoured varieties may have been trained alongside peaches, apricots and grapes on south-facing walls; trained apples, pears and plums would usually feature on west-facing walls.[34] The quincunx style of planting was introduced to England by Richard Harris, fruitier to Henry VIII, after being commanded to visit France and Flanders to learn how fruit was grown and to bring back new varieties; this led to the creation of the fruit orchards in Kent. It is recorded that Sir William Herbert (taken here to be 'of Troy'), in the reign of Henry VIII, also sent two men, Richards and Williams, to France and Flanders to study horticulture and to bring back vegetables and fruit trees.[35] As reasoned above, the walled garden pre-dates the time of Sir Charles Somerset at Troy. With this horticultural reference to William, it is reasonable to assume that it was William rather than his son, Charles, who created the walled garden. Nearly a century later, Sir Charles Somerset embellished it with a celebratory, ornamental entrance close to the house, and three hundred years after that, nuns ordered the sealing of its two service entrances.

Figure 5.17 Prince Henry Frederick (1594–1612), *by an unidentified artist, 1596.*

By permission of the Countess of Rosebery.

Pathways and a Victorian strip garden

Currently, no pathways are visible in the whole of the walled garden. During the time of Sir William Herbert of Troy, a perimeter path would have been laid at some distance from the walls, both for aesthetic reasons and in order to create generous beds for the roots of the wall-trained fruit trees.[36] A rule of thumb would be to place the path at the same distance from the wall as the wall's height. The most common material for paths was hoggin, which is a mixture of sand, gravel and binding-clay topped with gravel. This created a hard-wearing yet permeable surface. Paths were also made of cinders, bricks or cobbles. Grass was sometimes used, although this meant higher maintenance and would soon become muddy when wet. The 1881 OS map shows several pathways around what appears to be a heavily cultivated area close to the south-facing wall of the garden. This area corresponds to that seen in Figure 5.13 during the nuns' ownership. They had a greenhouse in this area, and used the water from an old stone tank (shown on the 1881 OS map) for irrigation. Furthermore, a pathway connected the ornamental entrance to the nuns' cemetery.

In 2012 I conducted resistivity surveys in the location of the walled garden to 'see' beneath the soil's surface.[37] Two areas were surveyed inside this garden. The first adjoined the ornamental stone entrance and measured twenty by twenty metres; the middle of this entrance's opening was used as the mid-point for the twenty-metre measurement. A second area, also measuring twenty by twenty metres, was surveyed in the location of the pathway shown on the 1881 OS map near the remains of this garden's ancillary service buildings, and in line with the blocked entrance and its cemetery. A grid of twenty by twenty metres was marked out with string and divided into one-metre strips with tapes. Readings at one-metre intervals following the guiding tapes were taken using a resistivity meter. The captured data was then transferred to a computer to produce a plot in greyscale tones; light tones imply low resistance and dark tones indicate greater resistance as might be offered by the buried foundations of a stone building. The results indicate the presence of underlying pathways offering low resistance. These two sets of results are superimposed on a map of the walled garden in Figure 5.18; a third surveyed area outside of the garden is also shown on this map and is discussed later.

The area adjoining the ornamental entrance shows a line of low resistivity (white line) approximately on the pathway shown in the 1881 OS map. This is crossed by a smaller line of low resistivity that is thought to be a water course, which emerges outside of the garden's east wall and empties into a small stream below.[38] There is no indication of lines of low or high resistance running parallel to the wall and consequently no indication of other pathways in the surveyed areas. The area in line with the blocked entrance of the nuns' graveyard also shows a line of low resistance, approximately on the pathway shown in the 1881 OS map, with regions of high resistance on either side, which are indicative of compaction of the surrounding earth. It is not possible to say when this pathway was constructed, but the resistivity shows that the effects its construction had on the surrounding earth are still detectable.

One might have expected the two identified pathways to be made of non-porous materials such as bricks, when lines of high resistance

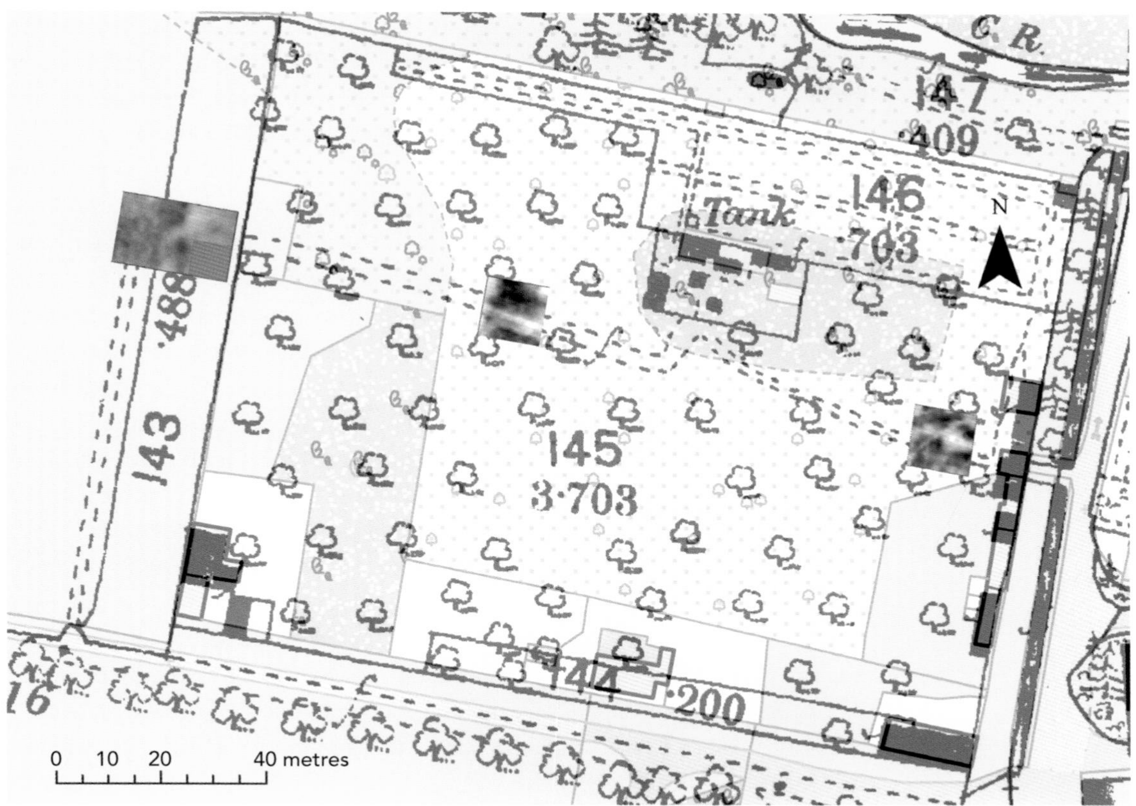

Figure 5.18
Resistivity results superimposed on a MasterMap of the walled garden. The purple square is where no readings were taken.
Copyright: Ann Benson.

(black lines) would have been produced. That lines of low resistance were obtained may be explained by porous materials being used in the paths' construction. During resistivity studies at Kenilworth Castle, Brian Dix found the pathways gave light-coloured resistance images, indicative of low resistance materials.[39] Excavation revealed the pathways to be constructed of cinders, which is a porous material and accounts for the low resistance results. The Somerset family at Troy House owned cinders as the refuse from the medieval forges that lay in quantity on Cinderhill, some 800 metres from the house. These were an important resource, as the family also had ownership of iron ore deposits on the estate (site unknown), and together they produced a highly tempered iron of commercial value.[40] Consequently, the low resistance shown by the two identified pathways within the walled garden may also be of cinders. Excavation to confirm this is planned. The lack of other identified pathways, particularly by the ornamental entrance, should not discount them as never having existed, rather, this small resistivity investigation has not detected them. The date of the construction of the identified pathways is unknown.

A line outside of and parallel to the west wall of the walled garden is shown on the 1881 OS map and the 1845 tithe maps, implying the presence of a wall or another structure. Currently, there is no evidence of any built remains in this location, although the aerial photograph of 1978 (Figure 5.19) shows a faint black line on the ground leading to a break in the hedge alongside the original access route to Troy.

The pathway running across the walled garden cuts across to this line and then continues alongside it to exit on to the route to the farm and the house (see Figure 5.18). The farmer owning the field in which this line can be seen can offer no explanation. except that he has noticed the soil in this section of the field as being much darker than the rest. Core sampling of the soil could illuminate this observation and a survey is in the planning stage. Resistivity was conducted in a dog-leg shape to maximize showing the remains of any foundations in line with the blocked entrance on the west wall and into the adjoining field. An area of low resistivity is shown in line with the blocked entrance and then as a narrow strip curving down to link with the route to the farm and house. This could indicate a pathway of similar porous material to that inside the walled garden, tracking across and then outside the narrow rectangle of land. No sign of high resistivity due to wall foundations is revealed.

It is unlikely that this strip of land was a historic bowling alley: a bowling green has already been identified as lying close to the east of the house, near the pleasure gardens. Whether horses awaiting shoeing at the smithy (now a private dwelling) in the south-west corner of the walled garden were accommodated in this area, is possible. However, given the farmer's reports

Figure 5.19 *Aerial photograph of the walled garden, 1978. Note the faint black line running parallel to the garden's west wall at the top of the photograph.*
Crown copyright: RCAHMW.

of dark-coloured soil in this strip of land, the most likely explanation is that the narrow rectangle of land is a 'slip garden'. A 'slip garden' was often created outside the walls of a walled garden. Sometimes enclosed itself, it provided space for the propagation and growing of the hardier, less fussy crops such as potatoes or cabbages.[41] The 'slip garden' was also the location for less attractive aspects of the garden, such as manure heaps, hot beds, cold frames and the like. The space encompassed was usually about nine metres wide; this is the width of the rectangular strip at Troy.[42] Darker-coloured soil than that of the surrounding land could result from this area having compost and manure added to it to encourage the growth of crops.

Slip gardens were originally created in the eighteenth century to take advantage of the outer sides of a walled garden, especially those facing south, east and west. From the presence of the line outside of the walled garden's walls on the 1881 OS and 1845 Tithe maps, but its absence on the Gillmore and Aram maps of respectively 1712 and 1765, the slip garden was possibly created between 1765 and 1845. A hedge would have been sufficient as a boundary and it is perhaps the remains of this hedge line, rather than a wall, that appears in the 1978 aerial photograph.

Notes

1 The repairs were conducted by the company Collins and Godfrey, which no longer exists. Gloucestershire Record Office carries some of this company's work records, but these mainly pre-date the 1960s.

2 Private communication with retired housemistress at Troy Convent School, August 2012.

3 Private communication with retired groundsman at Troy Convent School, May 2011.

4 Driver, Jonas and Co., *Troy House Estate Monmouth, To Be Sold on 27th March 1901* (London: Auctioneers Messrs Driver, Jonas & Co., 1901). An original copy of sales particulars may be accessed at Nelson Museum, Monmouth.

5 In classical mythology, a cornucopia was a horn containing food, drink, etc., in endless supply, said to have been a horn of the goat Amalthaea. See David Leeming, *The Oxford Companion to World Mythology* (Oxford: Oxford University Press, 2005), p. 13.

6 *Gwent, Register of Landscapes, Parks and Gardens of Special Historic Interest in Wales, Part 1: Parks and Gardens* (Cardiff: Cadw Welsh Historic Monuments, 1994), p. 155.

7 John Newman, *The Buildings of Wales: Gwent/Monmouthshire* (New Haven and London: Yale University Press, 2002), p. 392.

8 Joseph Bradney, *A History of Monmouthshire: The Hundred of Trelech*, Vol. 2, Part 2 (London: Academy Books, 1992).
9 Horatia Durant, *The Somerset Sequence* (London: Newman Neane, 1951), p. 124.
10 Timothy Mowl, *Country Walks Around Bath* (Bath: Millstream Books, 1986), p. 91.
11 Sir Charles Somerset, *An Inventorie of what is mouvable awe left at Troy the 20th of Octob. 1620.* Badminton Muniments: OC/2, RF/1. See also *The Travel Diary (1611–1612) of an English Catholic Sir Charles Somerset*, ed. Michael Brennan (Leeds: The Leeds Philosophical and Literary Society Ltd, 1993), pp. 1–39.
12 *The Travel Diary (1611–1612) of an English Catholic*, pp. 1–39.
13 Serlio's work also agreed with Alberti's on the ascendance of the circular form, but extended the range to include the Greek Cross and the oval, heralding the use of an ellipse in building designs from the sixteenth century onwards. See Paul Rosin, 'On Serlio's constructions of ovals', *The Mathematical Intelligencer*, 23/1 (2001), 58–69, for an account of Serlio's innovative work.
14 John Summerson, *The Classical Language of Architecture* (London: Taylor and Francis, 1963), p. 10.
15 Vaughan Hart and Peter Hicks (eds), *Sebastiano Serlio on Architecture Volume One: Books I–V of 'Tutte L'Opere D'Architettura et Prospetiva'* (New Haven and London: Yale University Press, 1996), pp. 32–3.
16 Hart and Hicks, *Sebastiano Serlio on Architecture Volume One*, p. 280.
17 Adolf K. Placzek, *Jan Vredeman de Vries Perspective – with a new introduction* (New York: Dover Publications, 1968), no page numbers given.
18 See Brennan, *The Travel Diary*, pp. 1–47, for an account of Sir Charles Somerset's education, interests and extensive library.
19 Marriage Settlement 1609, Sir William Powell of Llansoy. Badminton Muniments: OC/1. Private communication with archivist, Badminton House, September 2012, confirming that no date exists for the marriage between Elizabeth Powell and Sir Charles Somerset.
20 The Bee Museum of the 1950s is now referred to as the International Bee Research Association (IBRA).
21 IBRA, Bee Bole Register, Gwent, Troy House, No. 135.
22 The search included IBRA's international register of bee boles and P. Walker and W. Linnard, 'Bee boles and other beekeeping structures in Wales', *Archaeologia Cambrensis*, 139 (1990), 56–73.
23 Carol Davidson Cragoe, *How to Read Buildings* (London: Herbert Press, 2008), p. 185.
24 Hugh Platt, *Floraes Paradise*, 1608. Accessed at the Lindley Library of the RHS, London.
25 William Lawson, *A New Orchard and Garden*, 1618. See also Sandra Nicholson, 'The Role and Use of Fruit in the Seventeenth Century Garden' (unpublished MA dissertation, Architectural Association, London, 2004), 4–39.
26 Lawson, *A New Orchard and Garden*, p. 12.

27 Blanche Henrey, *British Botanical and Horticultural Literature before 1800, Volume One: The Sixteenth and Seventeenth Centuries History and Bibliography* (London: OUP, 1975).

28 Bradney, *A History of Monmouthshire*, p. 162.

29 In *Apopthegm 43* (Marquess of Worcester, 1645) Sir Thomas is credited as the grower of these fruits at Troy. Thomas inherited Troy from his father in 1628 and it appears that he then lived at Troy for a number of years, whilst his brother, Charles, moved with his wife from Troy to Rogerstone Grange (another Somerset property) near Chepstow.

30 *www.parksandgardens.org*. Accessed 10 February 2016. See also Nicholson, 'The Role and Use of Fruit in the Seventeenth Century Garden'.

31 Trea Martyn, *Elizabeth in the Garden* (London: Faber and Faber, 2008).

32 *www.tate.org.uk/art/artworks/lely*. Accessed December 2012.

33 Catherine MacLeod et al., *The Lost Prince: The Life and Death of Henry Stuart* (London: National Portrait Gallery Publications, 2012); exhibition autumn 2012.

34 See Nicholson, 'The Role and Use of Fruit in the Seventeenth Century Garden', 40–70.

35 J. Evans and J. Britton, *The Beauties of England and Wales XI* (London, 1810), p. 62.

36 *www.parksandgardens.org*. Accessed 10 February 2016.

37 See Christopher Catling, *A Practical Handbook of Archaeology* (London: Anness Publishing, 2014) for a simple explanation of resistivity surveys.

38 Private communication with Mr and Mrs Davey, long-time owners of the walled garden.

39 Brian Dix, 'Using archaeology to research a garden history', course at the Institute of Historical Research, October–December 2012.

40 John Sleigh, *Monmouth and the Somersets* (privately published; distributed by the Monmouth Field and Antiquarian Society, undated; ISBN 1870347005), p. 9.

41 Susan Campbell, A History of Kitchen Gardens (London: Frances Lincoln, 2006), pp. 26–9.

42 Campbell, *A History of Kitchen Gardens*, p. 26.

Six

Key Built Features of the Estate's Fieldscape

A mill, brick kiln, ice house, Keeper's Cottage and a deer-park wall

THE REMAINS OF AN ANCIENT water-driven mill are north-west of Troy House on an island close to the current Trothy Bridge. In 1712 Joseph Gillmore recorded the areas of land in this locality as: 'mill ham, a withy bed by ye mill, a small ground by ye Trothy Bridge and mill dam' and 'a breakey island by ye ware'.[1] During the Glyndŵr Rebellion, the mill was left ruined and unrepaired for some time.[2] Excavation of the area has revealed several eroded medieval pottery bowls.[3] All that now remains of the mill is a small section of a stone gable wall on the riverbank and a line of dressed stones forming a bridge to the mill's island.

Gillmore uses the word 'kiln' when surveying areas of land near Troy Orles Wood. A brick kiln existed in this location (Figure 6.1); it would have supplied the estate with building materials from at least the time of Gillmore's survey in 1712.[4] The remains of an eighteenth-century icehouse lie on rising ground some 10 metres from the Trothy and 300 metres south-east of the house. The chute is brick-lined and still accessible; the entrance used for obtaining the ice has suffered a landslide and the dressed-stone opening facing the river is now filled with earth.

Troypark Wood, the original deer park of the estate, is mentioned in the will of Sir Charles Herbert, dated 1512.[5] Substantial sections of the

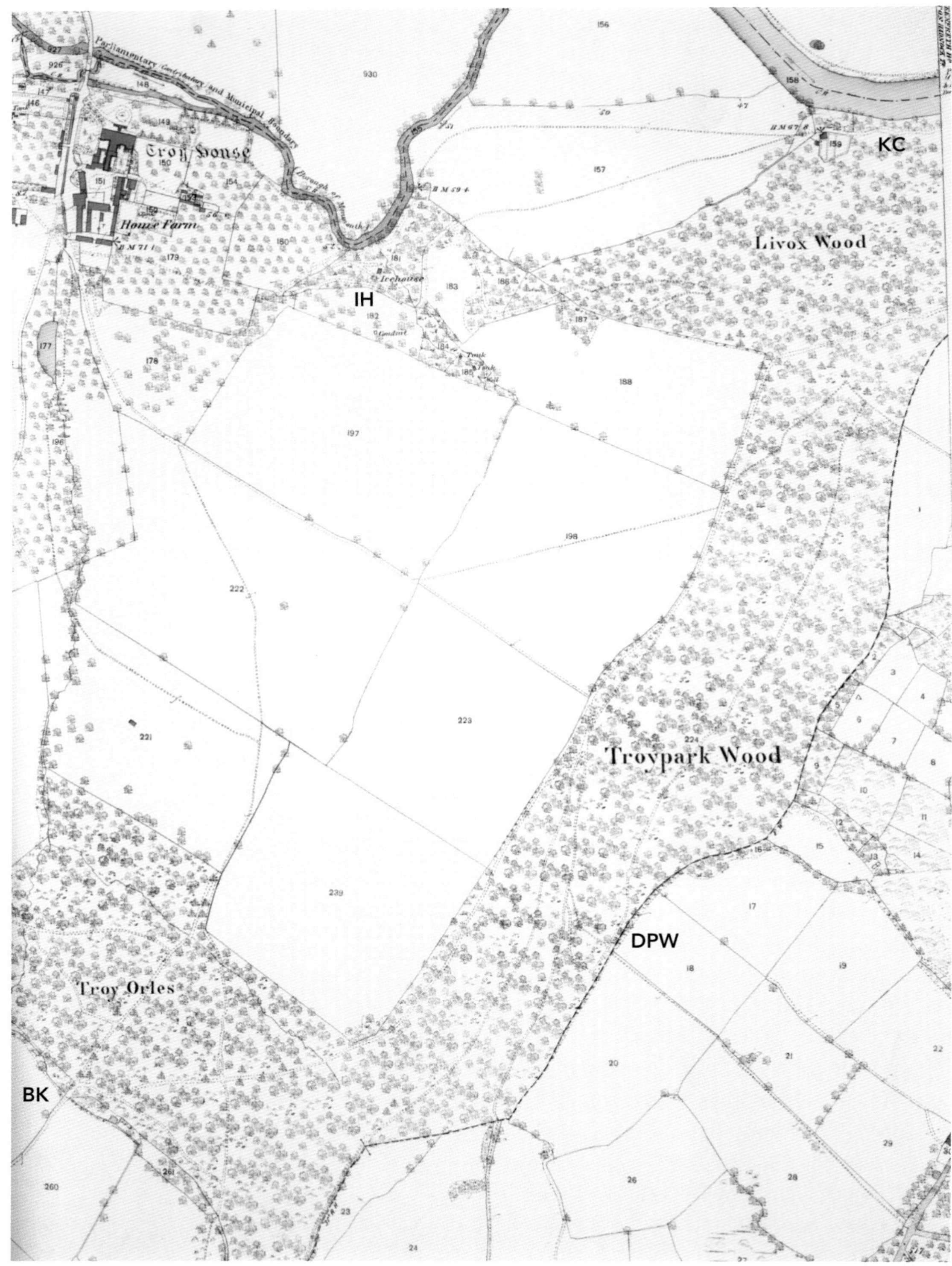
Troy House
House Farm
Icehouse
IH
KC
Livox Wood
Troypark Wood
DPW
Troy Orles
BK

deer-park wall survive and are formed from a mixture of old red sandstone and limestone, presumably sourced from the two quarries within Troypark Wood. The wealth of the estate's owners is reflected in having a stone wall, rather than a wooden rail and post fence, for enclosing the deer. A ruined building of stone and red brick construction is in the northern section of Livox Wood close to the river Wye. It is recorded for the first time as Keeper's Cottage on the 1881 OS map. The location of the cottage afforded a watchful eye, not just on the nearby deer park, but, in more recent times, on the Wye's salmon.

Figure 6.1 (opposite) *Locations of Keeper's Cottage (KC), brick kiln (BK), ice house (IH) and the deer-park wall (DPW) running along the eastern boundary of the woods.*

By permission of The British Library Board, Mitchel Troy Parish, 1881 OS map.

Cadw's 'game larder': a rare conduit house

Another ruined building lies within a meadow on a slope to the south-east and some 300 metres from Troy House and 50 metres south of the ice house (Figure 6.2). The east side of the building adjoins scrubland which blends into Livox Wood. After inspection in 1994 Cadw described the structure as follows:

> The most probable purpose for it is a game larder (confirmation for this could come from the fact that the atmosphere inside is very dry – a long-dead sheep inside was mummified at the time of the visit!). Date unknown, but possibly contemporary with the walled garden, in which case 17th-century.[6]

Cadw also noted: 'the "game larder" from its appearance seems to be older [than the nearby ice house, described as eighteenth or early nineteenth century], possibly late seventeenth century'.[7] There has been no subsequent publication about the 'game larder' by Cadw. It is proposed here that the date of this building's construction can be more accurately determined and that it was not designed as a 'game larder'.

The ruined building is very overgrown by ivy, which has dislodged large portions of the roof and some sections of the walls. What remains is a dressed sandstone, single-storey structure approximately 3 metres high and 2.5 metres square. A doorway some 1.6 metres high and with a Gothic arch lies on the south side. Depressions and an iron hinge in the stone of this entrance indicate that it was designed to take a wooden door.[8] Halfway up the building there is a moulded string course running all the way around the walls; this is level, except for being raised over the entrance. The facing stone remains on the south side, some survives on the west side, it largely exists on the east side, together with an intact wider plinth at the base, and some remains up to the string course on the north side.

Figure 6.2 *Cadw's 'game larder' seen from the south-east, 2015.*

Crown copyright: RCAHMW.

Troy's retired groundsman remembers the building well: the roof is recalled as being composed of roughly cut, overlapping stone slates, some 45 centimetres by 60 centimetres and of the same colour as the building's walls.[9] Inside there is an extant barrel roof with small, almost square, window openings high in the north wall and above the door on the south wall, the latter being blocked by the encroaching ivy. There are no remains of window mouldings or metal grilles. Close examination of the internal walls and ceiling does not reveal any evidence of shelves, depressions or hooks for the storage of game.

As shown in chapter 4, the ornamental stone entrance to the estate's walled garden also has a moulded stone string course. In the nature of its stone, colour, carved shape and dimensions, the moulding of the string course on this entrance is significantly similar to that seen in Cadw's 'game larder', to such an extent that it is reasonable to say they are the same and were most likely used in the same time period (Figure 6.5).

As argued in chapter 4, the ornamental entrance to the walled garden was most likely built between 1612 and 1620 by Sir Charles Somerset at the beginning of his residency at Troy as a married man.[10] A 1620 inventory of Troy in Charles's own hand shows that new building work had been completed by that date.[11] The Jacobean plaster ceilings within Troy House are also dated here as no later than 1620.[12] Troy estate rent rolls of 1612, again completed in Charles's own hand, show that his wealthy father-in-law and resident of Troy in 1600, Sir William Powell, had died in 1611.[13] Charles travelled throughout Europe between April 1611 and May 1612, and, as evidenced in his travel diary from this period, he had been inspired by the architectural achievements of mainland Europe.[14] The ornamental entrance to the walled garden is a coherent structure. It has a classically inspired design reminiscent of Jan Vredeman de Vries's treatise published in his last work, *Perspective*, in 1604.[15] It seems reasonable to suggest that Charles commissioned the ornamental stone entrance after his return from Europe in May 1612, along with other building work, to enhance the Troy estate.

Stylistically, the ornamental stone entrance appears at odds with the Gothic doorway of the 'game larder'. However, their creation during the same period reflects the aesthetic continuum of the time; Gothic, Renaissance, Baroque and Mannerism were all represented in a powerful combination.[16] It is possible that the well-travelled and cultured Sir Charles Somerset, who is shown here to have lived at Troy from 1612, would have chosen a classically inspired

Figure 6.3 (above)
Cadw's 'game larder' as it appeared in the 1960s.
Copyright: Michael Tamplin.

Figure 6.4 (left)
The north wall's window close to the barrel roof of Cadw's 'game larder', 2015.
Crown copyright: RCAHMW.

Figure 6.5 *A comparison of the moulded string courses: above, Cadw's 'game larder'; below, the ornamental entrance to the walled garden.*
Copyright: Ann Benson.

design promulgated by Vredeman de Vries for his ornamental entrance to his walled garden near the house to impress his guests, and a Gothic doorway design for a service building like the 'game larder'.

The elevated position of the 'game larder', which is within sight of the house, gardens and the river Trothy, might suggest that it was used for pleasure rather than as a service building. If this were so, there would be a window or door in the direction of the gardens and river to provide pleasant vistas. However, the two windows are set so high as to provide only views of the sky, and the doorway faces uphill, giving limited vision of any land beyond ten metres. Joseph Bradney in his *History of Monmouthshire* offers no indication of the building's use in his brief description, 'on a bank above is a curious square building of the seventeenth century, measuring 8 ft. by 8 ft. [2.5 metres by 2.5 metres], with a narrow door and a small window in each pine-end of the roof'.[17]

Searching maps for symbols and words that might indicate the use of this building revealed the word 'conduit' written on the Troy estate map of 1765 and the 1881 OS map in the location where the 'game larder' stands.[18] Both maps also show a square shape near this word, Aram's being larger than that of the OS. Aram also shows another square and the word 'conduit', east of the first. When these two maps are overlaid using ArcGIS, the conduit squares closest to the house almost coincide and certainly do so within the limits of error in overlaying historic estate maps. The second conduit of the Aram map lies close to where the OS map shows two water tanks and directly over the letter W, indicating the presence of a well.[19]

The coloured version of the 1881 OS map, with built structures shown in red, indicates two red water tanks and, some twenty-five metres distant from

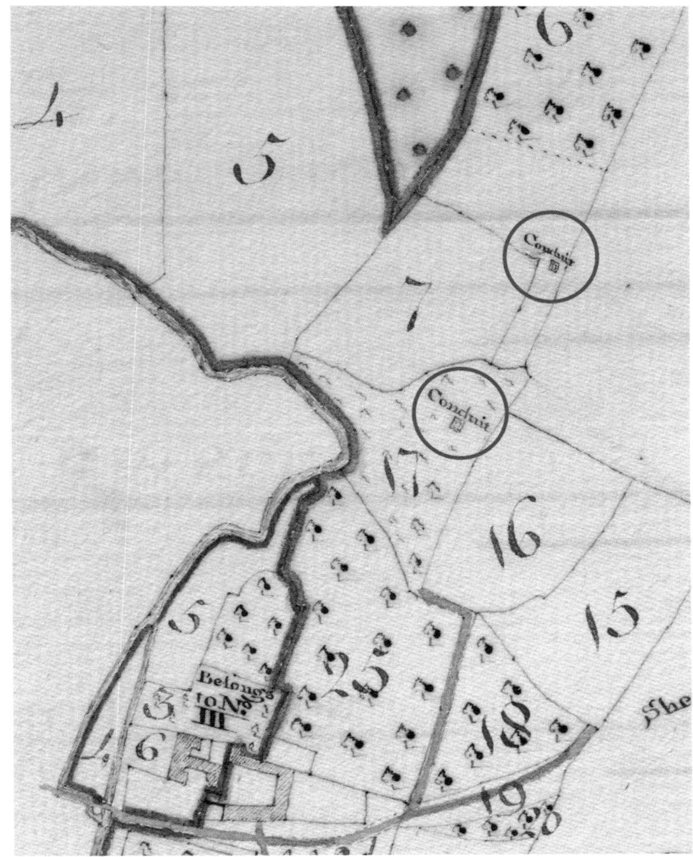

Figure 6.6 (right) *The two conduits on the 1765 Aram map.*

By permission of Llyfrgell Genedlaethol Cymru/The National Library of Wales.

these, the word 'Well', close to a field boundary.[20] Although labelling the conduit closer to the house, it does not colour the associated square red. Perhaps this omission explains why current OS maps do not represent this building and instead concentrate on the nearby ice house; the initial omission has possibly been perpetuated (Figure 6.8).

Coflein's website lists the 'game larder' building as NPRN 23108, Troy House Grotto, 'Game Larder', Monmouth, and describes it as: 'A single-storey, stone built structure, labelled as "conduit" on OS County series (Monmouth. XIV.8 1881), thought to have been a game larder, possibly 17th C'.[21]

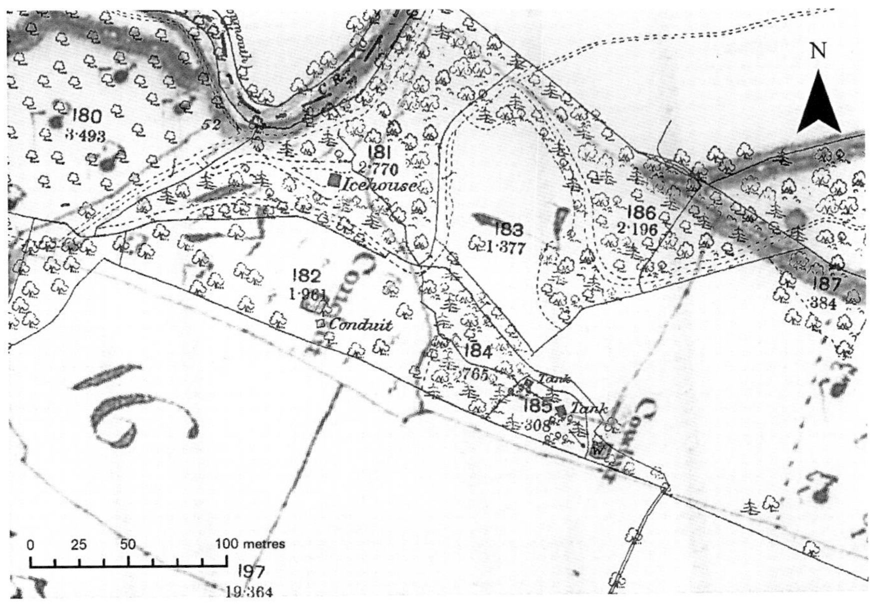

Figure 6.7 (left) *Overlay of enlarged sections of the 1765 Aram and 1881 OS maps.*

Copyright: overlay image, Ann Benson. Aram map, by permission of Llyfrgell Genedlaethol Cymru/The National Library of Wales; Mitchel Troy Parish, 1881 OS map, by permission of The British Library Board.

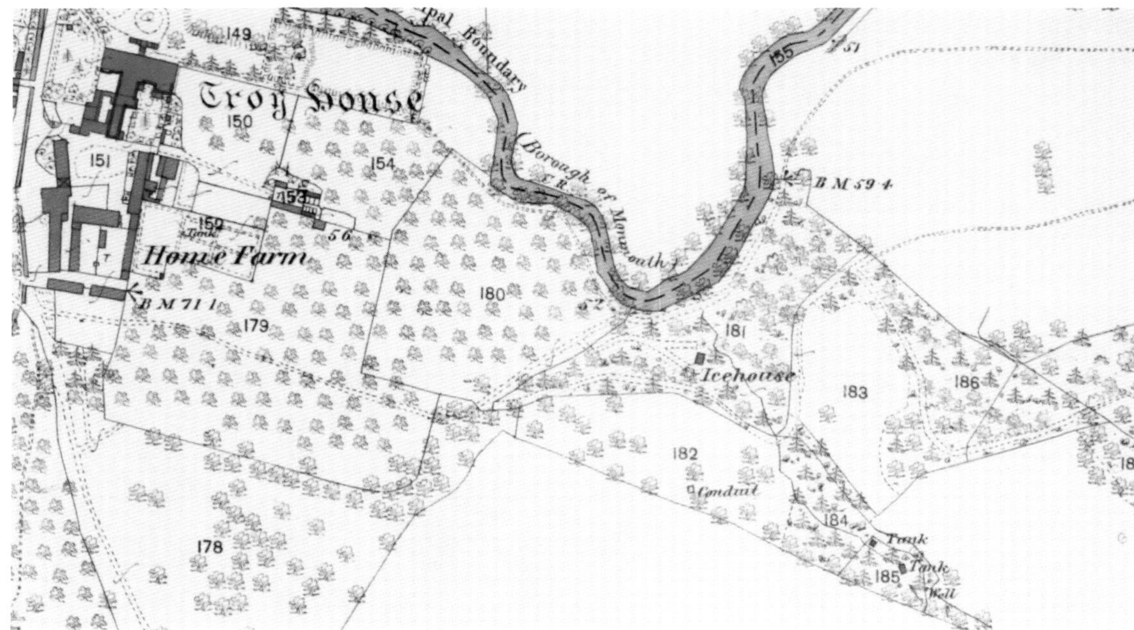

Figure 6.8 *Coloured Mitchel Troy Parish 1881 OS map with conduit label and red water tanks.*

By permission of the British Library Board.

Although the building is associated with an OS map's conduit label on the Coflein website, it is still described as a grotto or 'game larder' in its use. Searches for types of buildings that can be associated with the word 'conduit' revealed 'conduit houses'.[22] Their purpose can include protecting a water source such as a spring or well from animals, as may be the case in the Aram map's second 'conduit' square that coincides with W on the 1881 OS map. This location was checked for the remains of a building; one was found with stone foundations and part stone, part brick walls, and a square window opening with a crude wooden shutter (Figure 6.9). The rear of the building appears modern with brick walls and wooden bargeboards. Water issues from a pipe on the stone side of this building on to the ground below covered in loose, stone blocks. It is not possible to see inside due to the steepness of the surroundings and undergrowth. Perhaps the stone foundations were originally for a conduit house dating to the seventeenth century and the remains have subsequently been repaired with brick. Anecdotal evidence suggests repairs using bricks were made in the 1960s.[23]

The floor inside the 'game larder' building, which is the conduit close to Troy House, is compacted earth. When this was scraped away near the entrance a metal pipe approximately six centimetres in diameter and with a broken end was revealed three centimetres below the surface; it enters the building under the doorway's stone step and extends inside for approximately half a metre. A similar pipe in the ground near the opposite wall was also discovered; this arises from the floor and the broken, crimped end reaches to an opening between stones at the wall's base. Both metal pipes appear to be made of lead.

If this building was designed as a conduit house, it appears to be of the type that contains metal pipes connected to a tank made from lead or bricks; a source of water on higher ground than the building would be tapped and transported to it along lead pipes or hollowed-out tree trunks. The water would then be stored in the tank and allowed to flow along another pipe downhill towards Troy House, its flow rate being controlled by a tap within the conduit building. The water is thus transported by gravity to where it is needed. Sometimes one tank was placed above another inside the conduit house so that

Figure 6.9 (above) *West face of what may be Aram's second conduit house.* Copyright: Ann Benson.

Figure 6.10 (left) *Pipe bringing water into the conduit house.* Copyright: Ann Benson.

Figure 6.11 *Possible route of underground metal water pipes for Troy's conduit house. (Route shown with white tape: yellow spikes mark positions of detected metal.)* Copyright: Ann Benson.

debris could settle into the bottom of the top tank, before a pipe at its top then allowed the cleaner water to flow to the lower tank and, from the top of this one, out of the building to where it was required. At the Troy conduit house there is no evidence of any platform to support one tank above another and two tanks would also be unlikely, given the building's small size.

To further support the idea that this building is a conduit house and not a 'game larder', a metal detector was used to trace any pipework outside of the building. Metal was detected in a line of some 2.5 metres coming down the slope from the direction of the spring known to have fed the estate's water supply in the twentieth century.[24] Three random sites of metal were also detected near the doorway. Metal was detected downhill from the point where the metal pipe exits the building for some two metres towards Troy House. The metal detected at these points may indicate the continuation of the lead pipe found within the ruined building. The building stands within pasture, which has been ploughed in previous years.[25] The lack of traceable metal beyond two metres of the building may be due to disturbance caused by this ploughing.

Solid, stone-vaulted roofs were often used on conduit houses as they were impervious to decay, unlike timber.[26] This can be seen at the conduit house south-east of Bolsover Castle, Derbyshire, where the top roofing stone slabs are lost but not then masked by ivy, as at Troy. Just like Troy's conduit house, this one at Bolsover has closely fitting stones forming a barrel-vaulted roof interior. This design enables condensation to run down the inside walls rather than on to any water tanks below.

Figure 6.12 *The conduit house at North Hinksey, Oxfordshire.*

Crown copyright: Historic England.

Conduit houses were built for a number of country estates during the seventeenth century.[27] Usually unmanned and remote from the building they served, they had to be strong and secure to protect the water supply from pollution by animals or from other interference. They could be as simple as those at Bolsover in Derbyshire and North Hinksey in Oxfordshire, or a little more decorative as, for example, that at Chipping Campden in Gloucestershire, built for Sir Baptist Hicks in 1612, with an ogee arched roof, like his lodges by the church.[28] They could also be substantially larger and of a more unusual shape, as, for example, the hexagonal conduit house at Cowdray Castle in West Sussex.

Finally, it is unlikely that Troy's conduit house has ever been a game larder, as has been suggested by Cadw. Game larders are usually closer to the main residence than the 300 metres between the conduit building and Troy House. Troy's 1901 auction details also include the following statement when describing the parts of the House, indicating that a game larder was in use within its confines: 'and in a PAVED BACK YARD, Are Dairy, Game Larder, Coal House, and other Offices'.[29]

Notes

1 Joseph Gillmore, *Troy in Monmouth-shire, from The Mannor of Troy. Cophill Farme and Whitterns Farme in an[d] about Piercefield all in Monmouthshire Surveyed Anno MDCCXII*, National Library of Wales, WIAbNL002846217.

2 Arthur Clark, *The Story of Monmouthshire: From the earliest times to the Civil War* (Llandybïe: Christopher Davies Ltd., 1962), p. 121.

3 Steven Clarke, Monmouth Archaeology, private communication, September 2015.

4 Steven Clarke, Monmouth Archaeology, private communication, September 2015.

5 Sir Charles Herbert's will, TNA PRO 11/40/29.

6 Cadw/ICOMOS Register of Parks and Gardens of Special Historic Interest in Wales, PGW(Gt)16, The Park. Available at *www.Coflein.gov.uk/pdf/CPG268.* Accessed December, 2012.

7 *Register of Landscapes, Parks and Gardens of Special Historic Interest in Wales, Part 1: Parks and Gardens, Gwent* (Cardiff: Cadw, 1994), p. 155.

8 Michael Tamplin, a retired groundsman on the Troy Estate, recalls a wooden door being *in situ* during the period 1960–70. Private communication, 2011.

9 Michael Tamplin, a retired groundsman on the Troy Estate, recalls a wooden door being *in situ* during the period 1960–70. Private communication, 2011.

10 A. Benson, 'Troy House Estate: a Forgotten Landscape' (unpublished MA dissertation, University of Bristol, Bristol, 2013), 37–40, 88–103, 128.

11 Sir Charles Somerset, *An Inventorie of what is mouvable awe left at Troy the 20th of Octob. 1620.* Badminton Muniments: OC/2, RF/1. See the front cover of this inventory.

12 Benson, 'Troy House Estate: a Forgotten Landscape', 38–40.

13 Sir Charles Somerset, 'Booke of Rente-Rolls for 1612, 1621, and 1623 and Inventories etc. in 1622'. Badminton: OC/2.

14 Michael G. Brennan (ed.), *The Travel Diary (1611–1612) of an English Catholic Sir Charles Somerse*t (Leeds: Leeds Philosophical and Literary Society Ltd., 1993).

15 Adolf K. Placzek, *Jan Vredeman de Vries: Perspective* (New York: Dover Publications, 1968).

16 Placzek, *Jan Vredeman de Vries*, Introduction (no page numbers).

17 Joseph Bradney, *A History of Monmouthshire: The Hundred of Trelech*, vol. 2, part 2 (London: Academy Books, 1992), p. 165. Originally published 1913.

18 John Aram, *Plan of His Grace The Duke of Beaufort's Estates in the Manor and County of Monmouth, 1765*, National Library of Wales, WlAbNL004581355. First Edition 1881 OS, Mitchel Troy Parish, British Library, K 90134–98.

19 W represents a well on the OS Old list: see *www.ordnancesurvey.co.uk/oswebsite/.../understandingmapping.htm*. Accessed December, 2012.

20 Mitchel Troy Parish, Coloured First Edition 1881 OS, British Library, K90134–98.

21 *www.coflein.gov.uk/en/site/23108/*. Accessed March, 2014.

22 See the English Heritage website, *www.english-heritage.org.uk/.../conduit-house/history-and-research/* for further examples. Accessed October 2012.

23 Private communication with Troy Farm owner/occupier, April 2011.

24 Private communication, Michael Tamplin, groundsman at Troy Estate until 1977. This spring is still the main water supply for both the farm and house at Troy.

25 Private communication with Troy Farm owner, April 2011.

26 See the English Heritage website: *www.english-heritage.org.uk/.../conduit-house/history-and-research*.

27 See the English Heritage website: *www.english-heritage.org.uk/.../conduit-house/history-and-research*.

28 See Nicholas Pevsner, *Gloucestershire 1: The Cotswolds* (London: Penguin Books, 1970), p. 242.

29 Driver, Jonas and Co., *Troy House Estate Monmouth, To Be Sold on 27th March 1901* (London: Auctioneers Messrs Driver, Jonas & Co., 1901), p. 4.

Seven

Troy House Estate: its Historical Significance

BY USING A MULTI-METHOD APPROACH, the Troy House estate has been shown here to be of greater historical significance than previously recognized.

From the eleventh to the twentieth century Troy has either been owned or occupied by leading English and Welsh figures of the day. Few publications currently exist on Troy and they generally simply state that Troy has been the home of the Herberts and the Somersets. Here, for the first time, specific members of these families and those of the Scudamore and De Clare lines are identified and positioned for their connections with Troy and the influence they had in their lifetimes. In particular, Thomas Herbert the elder of 'Little Troye' and Sir William Herbert of Troy are shown to have had significant local and national significance during the late fifteenth and early sixteenth centuries whilst occupying Troy as their main residence. Due to Thomas's support of the House of York and his half-brother, William, first Earl of Pembroke, his trading activities, and his intimacy with the king as esquire of the body, he had considerable wealth and significant influence. Arguably, this accounted for Thomas's execution after Edgecote. Sir William Herbert of Troy made substantial changes to the estate during his tenure. These were of such a nature that Troy was deemed suitable for accommodating Henry VII and a heavily pregnant Elizabeth, Queen Consort, during their visit of 1502. Inventories are transcribed here for the first time to reveal the high quality of Troy's interior for this visit and also what existed during the seventeenth century when the Somersets owned and occupied Troy.

From at least the late medieval period, Troy is shown to have consisted of a main dwelling, an extensive farmstead, a water-driven mill, a walled orchard and a deer park. The deer park is confirmed as existing in the early sixteenth century and most likely even earlier, and its extant stone perimeter wall for enclosing the deer is shown for the first time. The use of a stone wall rather than a ditch with rail and post fencing reflects the wealth and status of Troy's owners across time.

The original approach to the house before the 1680s was from the south-west to an outer entrance courtyard, now a farmyard, surrounded by medieval buildings. This in turn connected to south-facing walled enclosures adjoining the medieval, Tudor and Jacobean parts of Troy House. Given that these enclosures were overlooked by rooms established here as of primary importance from at least 1612, they were designed for pleasure.

Robert Warren is identified for the first time as the person commissioned by the first Duke of Beaufort in 1679 for the plans of the north-range addition and enlargement of the house; simultaneously, Warren was also making changes to the duke's house in Chelsea. The work at Troy was completed by 1684 and resulted in a house that remains as a complex mix of medieval, Tudor, Jacobean and Carolean structures. From 1684 the orientation of the main approach to the house changed: rather than the old route from the south-west to the ancient parts of the house and farmstead, a more formal and impressive one from the north was established. This heralded consequent changes in the relative importance and function of the surrounding land.

From 1684, the outer entrance courtyard (current farmyard) became progressively more agriculturally orientated. By 1901, the south-facing walled enclosures adjoining the house were called a 'yard'. However, after this area was divided by cloisters and a chapel in the 1960s, part was retained as a private pleasure garden for use by the nuns. It appears that walled enclosures to the east of the current farmhouse existed at least as early as the Jacobean period and were associated with the house as pleasure gardens. It is proved that the house had a tower in 1620, adding credence to the validity of Hendrik Danckerts's painting of 1672. The walls of the quadripartite garden in this painting are shown as most likely being extant. Geophysics indicates that the compaction of soil caused by garden paths in the area further to the south-east, as shown on the 1881 OS map, is still detectable. Extensive orchards are shown to have bordered this area from at least 1712, when there is also evidence for the existence of a bowling green between them and the current farmhouse.

Gardens to the east of the house are identified for the first time to have included a large exedra-shaped garden area from at least 1712 and most likely even earlier. This garden extended eastwards towards the river Trothy and to the south behind the current farmhouse, thus supporting the view proposed here that this land was a pleasure garden for Troy House at this time. Map overlays reveal this arrangement to have continued up to Aram's 1765 mapping. They also prove that the exedral garden created by the nuns in the 1960s to the east of the house has the same northern boundary as its predecessor but is significantly smaller in other respects.

Geophysics in this area does not reveal any underlying structures pre-existing the nuns' landscaping, and map regression shows it having become an orchard by 1765. The date is consistent with the estate ceasing to be regularly occupied by Somerset family members following the fatal accident in 1698 of Troy's resident, Charles Somerset, Marquess of Worcester. Maintaining formal gardens was costly, and when they were no longer required for the family's enjoyment, transforming this ground into an orchard would have been a financial imperative.

Map regression and the extant topography indicate that from at least 1712, the land parallel and close to the river Trothy north-east of the house contained a canal or simple water parterre with alternating wide and narrow terraces. The two surviving large depressions in this area were originally linked by an earthen dam, now breached and eroded. Evidence indicates that water features were originally laid out in this area in Jacobean times by Sir Charles Somerset and that these may have been refashioned in the late 1680s by Charles, Marquess of Worcester. By the 1880s they had become sunken garden areas mainly given over to trees.

Due to the design of the bee boles, which are contemporary with their surrounding stone walls, and the estate's ownership history, the walled garden west of the house is proposed as dating from the sixteenth and not the seventeenth century, as reported by Cadw. An unrecorded entrance has been discovered and, with the now-blocked western entrance, they are suggested here as being the original ways into the walled garden. For the first time this garden is identified as a cherry orchard from both the 1712 and 1765 maps. It is most likely that the walled garden was created as an orchard by Sir William Herbert of Troy during the reign of Henry VIII after sending two men to France and Flanders to source and learn about the cultivation of fruit trees.

Close examination of the ornamental stone entrance does not show evidence of its ever having included a date, let alone that of 1611, as claimed in previous publications. Due to its architectural design, it is proposed that this entrance was inserted in pre-existing walls for Sir Charles

Somerset, most likely after his return from his European tour in 1612. This entrance cannot be dated to 1611 in celebration of the marriage of Charles to Elizabeth Powell, as previously claimed: their marriage date is unknown and the marriage settlement was in 1609.

The few existing reports of Troy's history concentrate on describing the north-range addition to the house in the late seventeenth century as the most expansive period of change in the estate's architecture and landscape. However, between 1612 and 1628, Sir Charles Somerset substantially modified the house and adorned the ceilings of its principal rooms with the latest fashions of plasterwork. The building assigned as a 'game larder' by Cadw is proven here to be a rare conduit house. The design of its stone string course is markedly similar to that of the ornamental entrance Sir Charles had inserted in the walled garden. Consequently, it is proposed that these two buildings are most likely contemporary and that whilst enhancing the aesthetics of the garden, he was also attending to the estate's water supply. Whether he is responsible for the building of the extant stone garden walls east of the current farmhouse, is not proven. Nevertheless, the beginning of the seventeenth century represents a major period of estate enhancement under Sir Charles Somerset's occupation that has not been previously recognized.

As a whole, the house and its pleasure gardens, the walled garden, the mill, the farmstead and the surrounding parkland, with its ruined conduit houses, brick kiln and stone quarries, is shown here as a rare surviving example, particularly in Wales, of a complete estate of medieval origin. With subsequent extensive Tudor, Jacobean and Carolean enlargement and enhancement, and owners of considerable influence at local and national levels, the estate deserves to be better recognized for its historical significance.

Appendix I

Troy's History: the Existing Literature, 2015

CADW HOLD RECORDS for the listed buildings, namely the gateway and gates to Troy House (25791), Troy House (2060), the walled garden (2886), a barn at Troy Farm (2088) and Troy Cottage (2734).[1] The descriptions accompanying the listings are brief: that for Troy House focuses on the seventeenth-century north range, although the house is stated to have been 'apparently built in three distinct phases, the first two of which are externally disguised by the third [the north range]' and the history section of the record states that 'A C16 manor house [was] built on the site of a medieval house'.[2] The interior is recorded as 'not seen' and the listing followed a visit in 1952.

The listed building record for the walled garden west of the house states that it is 'an exceptional example of a well-documented early C17 walled garden' and that 'notable features to the garden are two recesses that are probably bee boles; both have Tudor hoodmoulds and central shelves'.[3] The record does not say that the 'hoodmoulds' are merely Tudor in style, so unless they were dated to between 1601 and 1603, when the Tudor period ended, or they were Tudor originals inserted in the wall at a later date, the walled garden cannot be seventeenth century. Furthermore, this record states that the ornamental stone entrance carries 'the surviving initials ECS which refer to Elizabeth and Charles Somerset, the latter was the son of Henry, 1st Marquis of Worcester (of Raglan Castle), and 1611 was the date of their marriage'. Cadw claim this date was carved on the entrance but is now eroded. The date of this marriage is unknown,[4] and Charles was the fourth son of Edward, the fourth Earl of Worcester; Henry, first Marquess of Worcester, was Charles's older brother, not his father.[5] There has been no update of Cadw's records relating to the walled garden since the 1993 listing.

The entry for Troy House in Cadw's *Gwent Register of Parks and Gardens* has one page of text and one current OS map for reporting the structure and historical significance of the estate's park and gardens. It largely reiterates the content of the listed building record, provides only limited topographical information, and, other than the ornamental entrance, omits the recording of ways into the walled garden. In the Site Dossier (NPRN 266097), also written in 1994 by Cadw's Inspector for Parks and Gardens, there is speculation about a second entrance but no use is made of this information or any other to uncover the garden's design or uses across time. No archaeological work, other than a simple walking survey with brief reporting outcomes, has been conducted on the land surrounding the house or that within the walled garden by Cadw or the Glamorgan-Gwent Archaeological Trust (GGAT). The Cadw listed building record for the barn (Grade II) at Troy Farm offers a more detailed architectural account than that for Troy House. The barn is said to be 'probably a late C18 or early C19 rebuild of an earlier timber-framed structure', although no dates for the original build or fittings are offered.[6]

RCAHMW holds the National Monument Record (NMR), which is the national collection of information about the historic environment in Wales. Sites on the NMR are identified by a National Primary Reference Number (NPRN). This information may be accessed from the Coflein website administered by RCAHMW. The numbering system on this site refers to the organization that creates or holds the record, and there are a number of cross-overs between RCAHMW and Cadw. There are eight online images, including aerial photographs of parts of the Troy Estate, photographs of the staircase and plaster ceilings of the house taken in the early 1950s, and drawings of the house floor-plans from the late 1970s. Forty-seven associated collection records relate to material already described for Cadw. None of this information illuminates the history of the house before the construction of the seventeenth-century north range. The entry for the walled garden (NPRN 23109), like Cadw's listed building record, assigns its construction to the seventeenth century and also claims that the main entrance is inscribed with the date 1611. Amongst the six associated collection records is one written by Cadw's Inspector for Parks and Gardens when visiting the Troy estate in 1990.[7] It reiterates all that has been said in Cadw's listed building records but also mentions some additional features and historical points. For example, after briefly describing the north range, and without any supporting evidence for assigning a date of *c.*1660–70 to its construction, it states that 'There was a previous house on the site, the home in the first half of the 17th century of Henry, marquis of Worcester's brother Sir Thomas Somerset'. So there is an acknowledgement of a house pre-dating the north range, but it is not expanded upon.

There is speculation of a double tree avenue being planted between 1670 and 1706, leading from the north front of the house to the confluence of the river Wye and river Monnow to the north, and another 'extending from a wider enclosure to the east of the house to a bend in the river Trothy to the east'. Traces of terracing near the river and 'a rectangular grass sunken area' of an unknown date but which 'may go back to the building of the house in the seventeenth century' are also stated, but with only one reference to any measurement, namely for a raised walkway along the diverted channel of the river [river Trothy] being about half a metre above the sunken area. There is also a brief description of a surviving red-brick wall to the east of the farmhouse and a ruined building, thought to have been used as pigsties. Reference is made to the 1880s six-inch OS map as showing a walled kitchen garden to the east of the farm, and that a flower garden with lawns and gravel walks existed to the west of the house before this area was built upon. Low walls and paths of a derelict twentieth-century garden to the east of the house are noted. The structures of the ice house and 'game larder' are briefly described. Their construction dates are assigned respectively as eighteenth century and seventeenth or eighteenth century, although the latter is then speculatively said to be possibly late seventeenth century, and then qualified again as 'Date unknown, but possibly contemporary with the walled garden, in which case 17th-century'.[8]

The entry for Troy Farm (NPRN 20937) has a site description that only states it is 'Part of Troy House home farm. Associated with: Troy House (NPRN 20938) Barn (NPRN 43387)'. There are two associated collection records: they are sales particulars for the Troy House estate, one from 1901, the other from 1919, and both contain limited architectural and landscape history information. The dwelling built into the south-west corner of the walled garden and known as the Old Presbytery (NPRN 309119) is said to have been adapted and extended over the years, and is believed to have been accommodation for 'a local order of nuns'.

Of the four Welsh Archaeological Trusts holding the regional Historic Environment Record available at *www.archwilio.org.uk*, the Glamorgan-Gwent Archaeological Trust (GGAT) covers the Troy House estate area. GGAT's entries for Troy House (PRN 01271g), Troy House Walled Garden (PRN 04643g), Troy House Game Larder (PRN 09181g) and The Barn at Troy House Farm (PRN 01270g) are brief, refer to Cadw's listed building descriptions and offer little additional information. Three other items, which do not appear to be available from Cadw or RCAHMW, are for Troy Mill (PRN 01277g), which is simply described as a post-medieval mill with a NGR of SO505115, Troy Meadow (PRN 03876g) where a Mesolithic arrowhead was found in 2000, and Troypark Wood metal-working site (PRN 02966g), for an orally reported Roman bloomer site through the finding of smelting waste.

All of the above Cadw, RCAHMW and GGAT entries for the Troy House estate may be accessed and compared via the Historic Wales portal (*www.historicwales.gov.uk*). When GGAT is accessed directly online, more detailed accounts of the Historic Landscape Character Area (HLCA) are available for Troypark Wood (HLCA 036), Troy Farm Fieldscape (HLCA 037) and Troy House (HLCA 038). These records offer some history of ownership and usage which pre-dates the seventeenth century. For example, disused sandstone quarries of post-medieval and modern dates survive on the upper slopes of Troy Park ridge, although they are not depicted on historical maps. The barn at Troy Farm is said to incorporate stone-framed Tudor windows and an archway from the farmyard dating from the fourteenth century. Much of this information draws heavily on the earlier work of Sir Joseph Bradney, *A History of Monmouthshire.*[9] Bradney's main focus is on the genealogy of the owners of Troy House and Troy Farm and there is only a short, speculative account of the history of the gardens and parkland. Work conducted by other bodies and persons is very limited. John Newman's *The Buildings of Wales: Gwent/Monmouthshire* devotes one page to a description of the house, and with an emphasis on the importance of its staircase and plaster ceilings; five lines of text describe the walled garden, but only in terms of the appearance of the ornamental entrance's stonework.[10] The series, *Monmouthshire Houses*, has no reference to Troy House other than to state that 'A farm building incorporates a pointed archway of freestone'.[11] Wikipedia has a picture of the exterior of the house (the north range) and a short history of its ownership, as does the publication *Forgotten Welsh Houses*, which again appears to reiterate the work of Bradney.[12]

Notes

1 The numbers shown in brackets are Cadw's listed building reference numbers.
2 Cadw, listed building record, 2060.
3 Cadw, listed building record, 2886.

4 Archivist, Badminton House Muniments. The marriage settlement between Charles Somerset and Elizabeth Powell is dated 1609; the date of the actual marriage is unknown.
5 See the Somerset family tree on p. 6 of Michael Brennan's edited edition of *The Travel Diary (1611–1612) of an English Catholic Sir Charles Somerset* (Leeds: Leeds Philosophical and Literary Society Ltd, 1993), and here, in Appendix II.
6 Cadw, listed building record, 2088.
7 Cadw, *Troy House, Garden, Monmouth*, NPRN 266097.
8 Cadw, *Troy House, Garden, Monmouth*, NPRN 266097.
9 Joseph Bradney, *A History of Monmouthshire: The Hundred of Trelech*, vol. 2, part 2 (London: Academy Books, 1992), pp. 161–6. Originally published 1913.
10 John Newman, *The Buildings of Wales: Gwent/Monmouthshire* (London: Penguin Books, 2000), pp. 391–2.
11 Cyril Fox and Lord Raglan, *Monmouthshire Houses Part 1* (Cardiff: National Museum of Wales, 1954), p. 106.
12 Michael Tree and Mark Baker, *Forgotten Welsh Houses* (Llanrwst: Hendre House Publishing, 2008), pp. 158–9.

Appendix II

The Somerset Family Tree

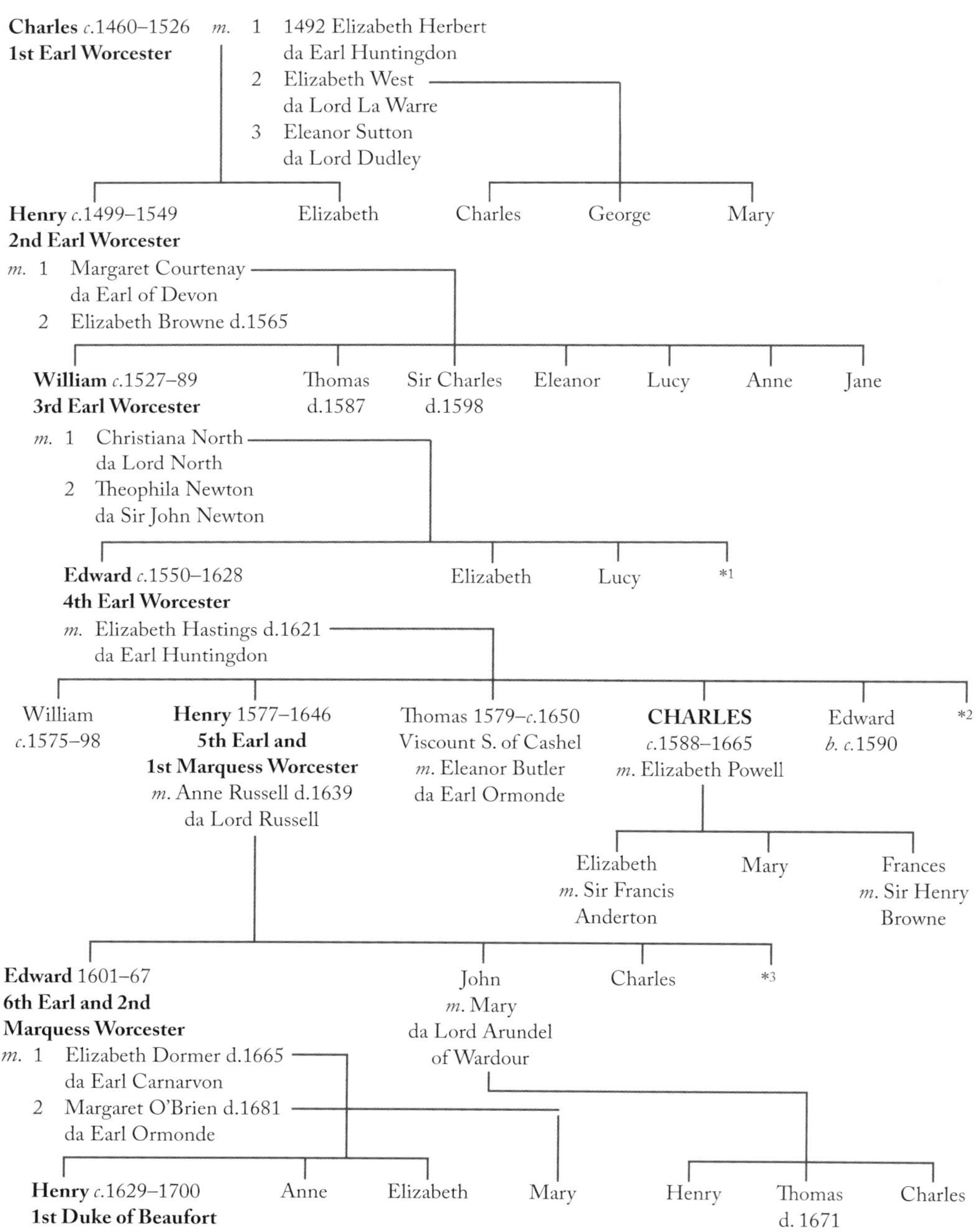

Notes

1 Three illegitimate daughters of the third earl are noted in the pedigree of the family in Joseph Bradney, *A History of Monmouthshire: The Hundred of Trelech*, vol. 3, part 1 (London: Academy Books, 1992), pp. 25–8.

2 The fourth earl had six surviving daughters: Elizabeth, m.1596 Sir Henry Guildford; Katherine, m.1596 William Lord Petre; Anne, m.1595 Sir Edward Winter; Frances, m. *c.*1611 William Morgan; Blanche, m.1606 Thomas, son of Lord Arundel of Wardour; Catherine, m. Thomas Lord Windsor. *Collins's Peerage*, vol. 1, p. 230, lists three other sons who died young (Charles, Francis and Christopher), and one daughter (Mary).

3 *CSP, Domestic*, 1639, p. 43, a certificate of the death of Anne, Countess of Worcester, who died on 8 April 1639, states that she had 'issue by the Earl nine sons and four daughters': Edward, John, Charles (and William, Henry, Francis, Frederick and James – all deceased – and another son who is named as Thomas in BL, MS Additional 39177, f.71v). Anne and Elizabeth (m. Viscount Montague of Cowdray) survived their mother's death (Elizabeth and Mary deceased).

The Somerset family tree, reproduced by permission of Professor Michael Brennan.

Select Bibliography

Aben, Rob and de Wit, Saskia, *The Enclosed Garden: History and Development of the Hortus Conclusus and its Reintroduction into the Present-Day Urban Landscape* (Rotterdam: 010 Publishers, 1999).

Airs, Malcolm, *The Tudor and Jacobean Country House: A Building History* (Godalming: Bramley Books, 1995).

Bacon, Francis, *Selected Essays* (London: Zodiac, 1949).

Bayly, Thomas, *The Golden Apophthegms of his Royal Majesty King Charles 1 and Henry Marq. of Worcester* . . . (London: John Clowes, 1660).

Benson, Ann, 'The Evidence for an Extant Conduit House on the Troy Estate', *The Monmouthshire Antiquary*, XXX (2014), 39–56.

Bradney, Joseph, *A History of Monmouthshire: The Hundred of Trelech*, vol. 2, part 2 (London: Academy Books, 1992).

Cadw, Gwent, *Register of Landscapes, Parks and Gardens of Special Historic Interest in Wales, Part 1: Parks and Gardens* (Cardiff: Cadw Welsh Historic Monuments, 1994).

Campbell, Susan, *A History of Kitchen Gardens* (London: Frances Lincoln, 2005).

Catling, Christopher, *A Practical Handbook of Archaeology* (London: Anness Publishing, 2014).

Charles, Lord Herbert, *A briefe memorial of my voyage into France 1673–1674*, ed. Ann Benson (published privately, Badminton: 2014).

Churchyard, Thomas, *The Worthiness of Wales a Poem* (London: Thomas Evans, 1776).

Cooper, Nicholas, *The Jacobean Country House* (London: Arum Press, 2006).

Cooper, Nicholas, *Houses of the Gentry 1480–1680* (New Haven and London: Yale University Press, 1999).

Coward, Barry, *The Stuart Age: England, 1603–1714* (London: Longman, 2012).

Davidson Cragoe, *Carol, How to Read Buildings* (London: Herbert Press, 2008).

Delano-Smith, Catherine and Kain, Roger J. P., *English Maps: A History* (London: British Library, 1999).

Durant, Horatia, *The Somerset Sequence* (London: Newman Neame, 1951).

Evans, C. J. O., *Monmouthshire: Its History and Topography* (Cardiff: William Lewis Ltd, 1953).

Evans, J. and Britton, J., *The Beauties of England and Wales XI* (London: 1810).

Fitzherbert, John, *Book of Husbandry*, ed. Rev. Walter W. Skeat (London: Trubner & Co., 1882).

Fletcher, John, *Gardens of Earthly Delight: The History of Deer Parks* (Oxford: Oxbow Books, 2011).

Foster Evans, Dylan, Lewis, Barry and Parry Owen, Ann (eds), *Essays on Guto'r Glyn and Fifteenth-Century Wales* (Aberystwyth: Centre for Advanced Welsh and Celtic Studies, 2013).

Fox, Cyril and Lord Raglan, *Monmouthshire Houses I, II, III* (Cardiff: National Museum of Wales, 1954).

Girouard, Mark, *Elizabethan Architecture: Its Rise and Fall 1540–1640* (New Haven and London: Yale University Press, 2009).

Girouard, Mark, *Robert Smythson and the Elizabethan Country House* (New Haven and London: Yale University Press, 1983).

Gotch, John Alfred, *Early Renaissance Architecture in England* (London: B. T. Batsford, 1901).

Griffiths, Ralph, Hopkins, Tony and Howell, Ray (eds), *The Age of the Marcher Lords, c.1070–1536* (Cardiff: University of Wales Press on behalf of the Gwent County History Association, 2008).

Hall, James, *Hall's Dictionary of Subjects and Symbols in Art* (London: John Murray, 1974).

Hanbury-Tenison, R., *The High Sheriffs of Monmouthshire and Gwent 1540–2000* (Bristol: Hanbury-Tenison, 2008).

Harley, J. B., *Ordnance Survey Maps: A Descriptive Manual* (Southampton OS, 1975).

Harris, John and Jackson-Stops, Gervase, *Britannia Illustrata* (Bungay, Paradigm Press, 1984).

Hart, Vaughan and Hicks, Peter (eds), *Sebastiano Serlio on Architecture Volume One: Books I–V of 'Tutte L'Opere D'Architettura et Prospetiva'* (New Haven and London: Yale University Press, 1996).

Heath, Charles, *Historical and descriptive accounts of the ancient and present state of the town of Monmouth: including a variety of particulars deserving the stranger's notice, relating to the borough and its neighbourhood* (Monmouth: Charles Heath, 1804).

Henderson, Paula, *The Tudor House and Garden* (New Haven and London: Yale University Press, 2005).

Henrey, Blanche, *British Botanical and Horticultural Literature before 1800, Volume One: The Sixteenth and Seventeenth Centuries History and Bibliography* (London: OUP, 1975).

Hill, Thomas, *The Gardener's Labyrinth* (London, 1577).
Howard, Maurice, *The Building of Elizabethan and Jacobean England* (New Haven and London: Yale University Press, 2007).
Howard, Maurice, *The Early Tudor Country House: Architecture and Politics 1490–1550* (London: Hamlyn, 1987).
Hussey, Christopher, *English Gardens and Landscapes 1700–1750* (London: Country Life Ltd, 1967).
Kenyon, John, *Raglan Castle* (Cardiff: Cadw, 1988).
Kissack, Keith, *The Making of a County Town* (London: Phillimore, 1975).
Laird, Mark, *The Formal Garden* (London: Thames and Hudson, 1992).
Lawson, William, *A New Orchard and Garden* with *The Country Housewife's Garden* (1618) (Totnes: Prospect Books, 2003).
Lloyd, Nathaniel, *A History of the English Country House* (London: Architectural Press, 1975).
MacLeod, Catherine et al., *The Lost Prince: The Life and Death of Henry Stuart* (London: National Portrait Gallery Publications, 2012).
Markham, Gervase, *The English Husbandman* (London: printed by T.S. for John Browne, 1613).
Martyn, Trea, *Elizabeth in the Garden* (London: Faber and Faber, 2008).
McClain, Molly, *Beaufort: The Duke and his Duchess 1657–1715* (New Haven and London: Yale University Press, 2001).
Michael, D. P. M., *The Mapping of Monmouthshire* (Bristol: RE Regional Publications, 1985).
Morgan, Luke, *Nature as Model* (Philadelphia: University of Pennsylvania Press, 2007).
Mowl, Timothy, *Gentlemen and Players: Gardens of the English Landscape* (Stroud: Sutton Publishing Ltd, 2000).
Mowl, Timothy and Earnshaw, Brian, *Architecture without Kings* (Manchester and New York: Manchester University Press, 1995).
Mowl, Timothy and James, Diane, *Historic Gardens of Warwickshire* (Bristol: Redcliffe Press, 2011)
Musson, Jeremy, *How to Read a Country House* (London: Ebury Press, 2005).
Newman, John, *The Buildings of Wales: Gwent/Monmouthshire* (London: Penguin Books, 2000).
Parkinson, John, *Paradisi in Sole Paradisus Terrestris* (London: 1629).
Placzek, Adolf K., *Jan Vredeman de Vries Perspective with a new introduction* (New York: Dover Publications, 1968).
Platt, Hugh, *Floraes Paradise* (1608).
Robinson, W. R. B., *Early Tudor Gwent 1485–1547* (UK: Robinson, 2002).
Sellers, Vanessa Bezemer, *Courtly Gardens in Holland 1600–1650* (Amsterdam: Architectura & Natura Press, 2001).

Somerset, Charles, *The Travel Diary (1611–1612) of an English Catholic Sir Charles Somerset*, ed. Michael G. Brennan (Leeds: Leeds Philosophical and Literary Society Ltd, 1993).

Summerson, John, *Architecture in Britain 1530–1830* (New Haven and London: Yale University Press, 1993).

Summerson, John, *The Classical Language of Architecture* (London: Taylor and Francis, 1963).

Taylor, A. J., *Monmouth Castle and Great Castle House, Gwent* (London: HMSO, 1951).

Tenth Duke of Beaufort, *The Duke of Beaufort: Memoirs* (Richmond upon Thames: Country Life Books, 1981).

Thomas, D. H., *The Herberts of Raglan and the Battle of Edgecote 1469* (Enfield: Freezywater Publications, 1994).

Williams, Glanmore, *Recovery, Reorientation and Reformation Wales c.1415–1642* (Cardiff: University of Wales Press, 1987).

Williams, Penry, *The Tudor Regime* (Oxford: Clarendon Press, 1979).

Worlidge, John, *Systema Horticulturae, or The Art of Gardening* (London: 1682).

Index

Abergavenny 15, 20, 22, 32
Aberystwyth Castle 26
Adam of Usk 19
Agincourt, battle of 21
Alberti, Leon Battista 113, 152
approach routes 7, **7**, 56, 73–4, **74**, 79, 81, 138–40, 182
apricots 48, 138, 156–8
Aram, John *see* maps
Archenfield 15, 16
Architectura (Vitruvius) 151–2
archways **78**, 78–9, 81, **82**, 117
Arnott, Edward 57
auction catalogues 76, 77, 120, **121**, 130, 135, 139, 177
Audley, Hugh d' 19
avenues of trees 56, 128, **138**, 138–40, 189

Bacon, Sir Francis 115, 130, 156
Badminton House 1–2, 9, 49–50, 51, 52–5, 56, 97, 100, 101, 106, 131
Bannockburn, battle of 19
banqueting houses 119, 120
Barnet, battle of 30
Baskerville, Jane 35
bathroom block 56, 95, 100
Bayly, Thomas 48
Beauchamp, Henry 22
Beaufort, Henry, 3rd Duke of Somerset 34, 39–40
Beaufort, Margaret 40
Beaufort House, Chelsea 52, 53, 93, 182
Belton House 127
Belvoir Castle 117
Berkeley, Elizabeth 21
Berkeley, Sir James 21
Blomfield, Reginald 115
Bluet, Sir John 21
Boke of Husbandrie (Fitzherbert) 113
Bolsover Castle 176, 177
Bosworth, battle of 32
Boteler, Nicholas 49
bowling green 122, 162, 182
Bradney, Joseph 15–16, 19, 22–3, 73, 81, 86, 149, 172, 190
Breteuil, Roger de, 2nd Earl of Hereford 16, 17
brick kiln 167, **168**, 184
Britannia Illustrata 128
Butler, James, Earl of Wiltshire 28
Byng, John 55

Cadogan House 83
Cadw 3, 5, 6, 8–9, 147, 148, 151, 169, 177, 183, 187–9, 190
Caerleon 15, 19, 25, 33
Caldicot 22
Camarthen Castle 26
Campden House 133–4, 177
canals 131–5, **134**, 183
Carroll, Peter 59
Cary Ddu 22, 89
Catchmay, Sir Alexander 15–16, 19
Catholicism 42, 44–7, 49, 106
Cecil, Robert 130
chapel 5, 59, 80, 104, 111, **112**, 117, 182
Charles I 48–9, 138, 157
Charles II 49, 50–1, 101
Charvet, Marie 59
Chepstow 15, 19, 25, 35, 37, 46

Chepstow Castle 25, 40, 44, **45**, 46, 50, 93–4
cherries 156–8, 183
Child, Sir Josiah 52
Chipping Campden 13–14, 177
Chiswick House 127
Churchyard, Thomas 38
Civil War 48–9, 102
clock face 86, **86**
cloisters 5, 80, 93, 104, 111, **112**, 182
Coecke van Aelst, Pieter 152
Coflein website 4–5, 173–4, 188
College of St Francis Xavier 45
Colonna, Francesco 113
Colvin, Howard 93
conduit houses 7–8, 169–77, **170**, **171**, **172**, **175**, **177**, 184, 189
Convent of Notre Dame de Charité du Refuge 57–9
Cormeilles Abbey 16
Cornewaile, Thomas 29
Courtney, Paul 13
courtyards 80–4, 111–12, 182
Cowdray Castle 177
Cromwell, Oliver 49, 50
cross wing 89–93, **90**, **91**, **92**, 104
Crouch, David 16
Cwm estate **45**, 45–7

Dafydd Gam 21
Danckerts, Hendrik 79, 96, 101–4, 116–17, 138, 182
David ap Philip 47
de Burgh, John 19
de Caus, Isaac 129
de Caus, Salomon 129
de Clare, Eleanor 19
de Clare, Elizabeth 19
de Clare, Gilbert, Earl of Gloucester and Hertford 19, 89
de Clare, Margaret 19
de' Servi, Constantino 129
deer park 38, 167–9, **168**, 182
Despenser, Hugh le 19
Devereux, Anne, Countess of Pembroke 25, 27, 30
Devereux, Robert, 2nd Earl of Essex 42
Devereux, Sir Walter 25, 26
Dineley, Thomas 52
Dissolution 40, 44
Dix, Brian 161
Durant, Horatia 55, 149–50

Ebboth 22, 33
Edgecote, battle of 29, 30, 181
Edward II 19
Edward IV 23, 25, 26, 28, 29, 30, 31, 89
Edward VI 36, 38, 40
Elizabeth I 36–7, 40, 42, 44, 113, 122
Elizabeth of York 35–6, 37, 83, 90, 181
Elms, The 57, 58, 59
English Husbandman, The (Markham) 114
entrance gates 3, 187
entrance lodge 3, 56, 187
Essay on Gardens (Bacon) 115
Everson, Paul 134
exedra gardens 123–8, **123–8**, 129, 183
external stone staircase **4**, 73, 105–6, **106**

Fanshawe, Sir Henry 130
Field of the Cloth of Gold 40
Fitzherbert, Anthony 113
FitzOsbern, William, 1st Earl of Hereford 16–17
Flanders 25, 152, 158, 183
Fontainebleau 98
Formigny, battle of 25
fountains 115, 129–31
France 17–19, 21, 28, 37, 49, 51, 57, 98, 158, 183
Francis I of France 98
Frecknall, Graham 80, 85, 87, 96–7, 103–4
'furniture door' 89–90, **90**, 104

'game larder' 7–8, 169–77, **170**, **171**, **172**, 184, 189
Gapper, Clare 98
garden walls 117–20, **118**, **119**, 184
Gardener's Labyrinth, The (Hill) 113, **114**
gardens 9–10, 52, 111–40, **117**, **118**, **120–7**, **131–3**, 182–3, 184, 189
George ap James ap Watkin 38, 39
Gerard, Fr John 47
Gillmore, Joseph *see* maps

Giovanni da Udine 98
Glamorgan 19, 22, 25, 26
Glamorgan-Gwent Archaeological Trust (GGAT) 9, 188, 189–90
Gloucester Castle 28
Gloucestershire Plot 50
Glyndŵr, Owain 19, 89
Glyndŵr rebellion 19, 23, 89, 167
Gorhamby House 130
Goullioud, Désirée Clotilde Marie 57, 58, 59, 147
Granville, John, Baron of Potheridge 53
Great Castle House 50–1
greenhouse 56, 160
Grosmont Castle 22, 34
Guto'r Glyn 20, 22, 34–5
Gwethenoc 17
Gwladus Gam 21, 23, **24**

Hall Barn 133, **134**
Hamelin de Ballon 15, 16
Hardwick Hall 83
Harlech Castle 27
Harris, John 80, 85, 87
Harris, Richard 158
Hatfield House 130, 134
Henderson, Paula 83
Henry IV 21
Henry IV of Castile 28
Henry V 21, 52
Henry VI 21, 22, 25, 26, 30
Henry VII 27, 30–2, 33, 34, 35–6, 37, 40, 83, 90, 104, 113, 129, 181
Henry VIII 40, 113, 158, 183
Henry Frederick, Prince of Wales 158, **159**
Herbert, Blanche (née Milbourne), Lady Herbert of Troy 35, 36–7, 91, 92
Herbert, Sir Charles, of Troy 36, 37–8, 90–2, 112–13, 116, 156, 167
Herbert, Cicill 37, 38
Herbert, Elizabeth 34, 40
Herbert, Elizabeth ap Rhys 38
Herbert, Joan 38
Herbert, Margery 35, 36
Herbert, Philip, 4th Earl of Pembroke 134
Herbert, Richard, of Coldbrook 28, 29
Herbert, Sir Thomas, of Wonastow 38, 47
Herbert, Thomas, the elder of Little Troye 22–3, 27–9, 83, 89, 181
Herbert, Thomas, the younger of Little Troye 27, 29, 31, 32, 33
Herbert, Sir Walter 31–2, 33, 34, 35, 36
Herbert, William, 1st Earl of Pembroke 23–4, 25–8, 29, 30, 89, 181
Herbert, William, 2nd Earl of Pembroke and Earl of Huntingdon 30–2, 33, 34, 40
Herbert, Sir William, of Troy 25, 31–7, 83, 90, 92, 104, 112–13, 116, 156, 158–9, 181, 183
Herbertorum Prosapia 28, 31
Hereford 26
Hermitage Cottage 119, **120**
Hicks, Sir Baptist 133, 177
Hill, Thomas 113
History of Monmouthshire (Bradney) 15–16, 19, 22–3, 73, 81, 86, 149, 172, 190
Hoesgyn, Frond Verch 32
hostel 5, 59, 140
hot walls 117
Howard, Thomas, 4th Duke of Norfolk 44
Humphrey, Duke of Gloucester 22, 25, 89
Hywel Dafi 23
Hypnerotomachia Poliphili (Colonna) 113

ice-house 7–8, 167, **168**, 189
Ireland 48, 49
Italy 49, 98, 152

James I 42, 44, 98, 122, 133
Jekyll, Gertrude 115
Jenkins, David 59–60, 106
Jennings, Mountain 129
Jesuits 44–7, 106
John of Gaunt 39
Jones, Inigo 129
Jones, Robert 45, 46, 47

Keeper's Cottage **168**, 169
Kenilworth Castle 161
Kent, Thomas 28
Kent, William 127

Killigrew, William 106
knot gardens 115

laundry 57–8, **58**, 86, 87
Lawson, William 114, 156
Lewys Glyn Cothi 25
Lewys Morgannwg 36, 40–2
Livox Wood 7, **8**, **168**, 169
Llannerch Park **84**, 84
Llanrothal 1, 45, 46, 52–3
Llantilio Crossenny 20
London, George 138
Louis XI of France 28
Luttrell, Sir James 30
Lutyens, Edwin 115
Lyre Abbey 16

Magor 22
main staircase **97**, 97–8, 100, 104, 188, 190
Malvern floor tiles 83, **83**
maps
- Aram's (1765) 73–4, **74**, 79, 81, **82**, 112, **113**, 121, 123, **124**, 126, **127**, 131, **157**, 163, 172, **173**, 174, 183
- Gillmore's (1712) 73–4, **74**, 79, 81, 121–3, **122**, **123**, 126, **126**, 128, 131, **131**, 135–8, **136**, **157**, 163, 167
- Ordnance Survey (1881) 56, 112, 119–20, **120**, 123, **127**, 132, 140, 146, **146**, 160, 162, 169, 172–4, **173**, **174**, 182
- Ordnance Survey (current) 7, **8**
- Tithe map (1845) 56, 112, 120–1, **121**, 123, 125, 132–3, **133**, 162, 163

Marcher lordships 13–17, **14**, 19, 21, 27
Markham, Gervase 114
Martel, John 19, 89
Mary I 36, 38, 40
Mary, Queen of Scots 44
Massie, Edward 48
Metamorphoses (Ovid) 113
Milbourne, Simon 35
Mitchel Troy 18, 33
Monmouth 15, 16–17, 22, 33–4, 35, 37, 50–1, 55, 102
Monmouth Castle 16, 52, 102
Monmouth Priory 17–18, 57, 83
Monnow, river 15, 17, 46, 189
Morgan, John Philip 38
Mortimer's Cross, battle of 26
Mulle, Sir William 28

Naseby, battle of 48
National Monument Record (NMR) 188–9
netball court 5, 59, 131, 132
Netherlands 25, 152
Netherwent 15, 17
Neville, Richard, Earl of Warwick 25, 26, 29, 30
New Orchard and Garden, The (Lawson) 114, 156
Newman, John 75, 76, 93, 96, 98, 148–9, 190
Newport 22
Nonsuch Palace 44
North Hinksey 177
north range **4**, 4–6, 52, 73, 85, 93–8, **94**, 100, 103–6, **106**, 117, 135, **136**, 139, 182, 184, 188

oak room 98–100, **100**
orchards 121–3, **121–3**, 125, 138, 149, 156–8, **157**, 182, 183
Order of Our Lady of Charity and Refuge 5–6, 57–9
Order of the Good Shepherd 58–9
Ordnance Survey *see* maps
Over Gwent 15, 16
Ovid 113
Owen, Nicholas 46–7, 106
Oxburgh Hall, Norfolk 106
Oystermouth Castle 19

Panorama of Monmouth (Danckerts) **79**, 79, 96, 101–4, **102**, **103**, **116**, 116–17, 138, 182
Paradisi in sole paradisus (Parkinson) 114
Parkinson, John 114, 156
parterres de broderie 128–9, **129**
Peake, Robert 152
Pembroke Castle 27, 31, 33, 35

Penalt 33
Percy, Sir Charles 42
Perspective (Vredeman de Vries) 152, **154**, 171–2
Philip IV of Spain 49
pigsties 119, **120**, 189
planning applications 5, 59, 60–1, 104–5
Plantagenet, Katherine 32
plaster ceilings 96, 98–101, **99**, 104, 153, 184, 188, 190
Pliny the Younger 113
Pontypridd 59
pottery finds 83, **83**, 167
Powell, Sir William 47, 83–4, 86, 150, 171
Power, Daniel 16
Powis Castle 19, 89
Prichard, Thomas 44
Prideaux Place 127
priest holes 46–7, 96, 106
Primaticcio, Francesco 98
Protestantism 44, 49

Raglan Castle 20–3, 25–7, 29–30, 32–6, 38, 40, 44–6, **45**, 48–9, 57, 89, 100, 134, 138, 158
Raphael 98
Re Aedificatoria (Alberti) 152
Rebellion of the Northern Earls 44
Register of Bishop Richard Clifford of Worcester 18, 79
Renaissance 98, 113, 127, 152
Restoration 49, 50
Richard III 30, 32, 33
Richard, Duke of York 21–2, 25, 26, 89
Richmond Palace 129
Rogerstone Grange 47, 48, 101
Rolls, John Etherington Welch 55
Rosso Fiorentino 98
Royal Commission on the Ancient and Historical Monuments of Wales (RCAHMW) 4–5, 9, 76, 85, 90, 92, 188–9, 190

St Briavels Castle 50
St Euphrasia's Convent School for Girls 5–6, 59
St Florent Abbey 17–18
St John the Baptist church, Troy 17–18, **18**, **79**, 79
St Michael's church, Mitchel Troy 17–18, **18**
St Wogan's 38
Saumur 17–19, 57
Scudamore, Sir Alan 15, 19
Scudamore, Jane (née Catchmay) 15, 16, 19
Scudamore, Sir John 19
Scudamore, Sir Philip 19, 89
Scudamore, Sir Titus 15, 19
Serlio, Sebastian 152
Severn, river 46
Shrewsbury 19, 89
Skenfrith Castle 22
slip gardens 162–3
Smith, Aaron 57
Smith, Thomas 93, 137–9
smithy 162
Somerset, Anne 44
Somerset, Sir Charles 42, 44, 48–50, 84, 98–102, 104, 112, 117, 129–30, 134, 148–54, 158, 170–2, 183–4, 187
Somerset, Charles, 4th Duke of Beaufort 53
Somerset, Charles, 1st Earl of Worcester 34, **39**, 39–40
Somerset, Charles, Marquess of Worcester 1–2, **2**, 50–3, 94, 102, 122–3, 127, 128, 135, 183
Somerset, Edward, 4th Earl of Worcester 39, 40–7, **43**, 49, 101, 106, 151, 187
Somerset, Edward, 6th Earl and 2nd Marquess of Worcester 49
Somerset, Elizabeth (daughter of Sir Thomas) 50
Somerset, Elizabeth (née Powell) 47–8, 84, 98, 100–1, 148–50, 184, 187
Somerset, Elizabeth (wife of 5th Duke of Beaufort) **54**, 54–5
Somerset, Henrietta 52
Somerset, Henry, 1st Duke of Beaufort 1, 2, 49–53, **51**, 93–4, 97, 101–3, 117, 131, 135, 182
Somerset, Henry, 2nd Duke of Beaufort 52, 53

Somerset, Henry, 5th Duke of Beaufort 54–5
Somerset, Henry, 8th Duke of Beaufort 55–7, **56**
Somerset, Henry, 9th Duke of Beaufort 2–3, 56–7, 100
Somerset, Henry, 10th Duke of Beaufort 97
Somerset, Henry, 2nd Earl of Worcester 37, 40
Somerset, Henry, 5th Earl and 1st Marquess of Worcester 48, 187
Somerset, Mary (née Capel) 50, 52, 53, 93–4
Somerset, Rachel (née Noel) 53
Somerset, Rebecca (née Child) 1, 51, 52–3
Somerset, Sir Thomas 42, 47–8, 49–50, 101–2, 158, 189
Somerset, William, 3rd Earl of Worcester 38, 40, 44
Somerset family tree 192
south wing 75, 80–1, **81**, 85–9, **86**, **88**, 104, 112
Spain 28, 49
Stafford, Lady Anne 34
Stafford, Edward, 3rd Duke of Buckingham 37
Stafford, Henry, 2nd Duke of Buckingham 32
Stansted 127–8, **128**
Stoke Gifford 56
Stowe House 127
Summerson, John 152
Swangrove Lodge, Badminton 106
Swansea Castle 19
Swillington House 128
Swynford, Katherine 39
Systema horticulturae (Worlidge) **130**, 131

Taster, Peter 28
teaching block 5, 59, 104, 140
Templeman, Graham 59–60
tennis court 120
Tewkesbury, battle of 30
theatre 5, 59, 87, 95, 104
Thomas, Inigo 115
Thornbury Castle 37
Tintern Abbey 40, 57
tithe maps *see* maps
Tockington 33
toll house 56
Torrington Diaries 55
tower 96, 101, 102–3, 182
Tower of London 26, 47, 50
Tredegar House 129, **129**, **136**
Tregrug 19
Trelech 15, 17, 33
Tretower 20
Triggs, H. Inigo 115
Trothy, river 2–3, 17, 45, 129, 131, 167, 183, 189
Troy Barn **76**, 76–7, **77**, 187, 188, 189, 190
Troy Cottage 3, 56, 187
Troy Farm
  aerial photographs **3**, **112**
  approach routes 7, **7**, 73–4, **74**
  archways **78**, 78–9, 81, **82**
  auction catalogues 76, 77
  barn **76**, 76–7, **77**, 187, 188, 189, 190
  building at west side of farmyard 79–80, **80**
  chapel 79
  current description 3, 7
  existing literature 187–90
  farmhouse **75**, 75–6, **82**, 117
  leased out 57
  maps **8**, 73–4, **74**, **82**
Troy House
  aerial photographs **3**, **112**, **117**, **118**, **125**, **145**, **162**, 188
  approach routes 7, **7**, 56, 73–4, **74**, 79, 81, 138–40, 182
  archways **78**, 78–9, 81, **82**, 117
  auction catalogues 76, 77, 120, **121**, 130, 135, 139, 177
  avenues of trees 56, 128, 138–40, 189
  bathroom block 56, 95, 100
  bowling green 122, 162, 182
  brick kiln 167, **168**, 184
  building costs 93, **93**
  building phases 85–106
  canal 131–5, 183
  chapel 5, 59, 80, 104, 111, **112**, 117, 182

clock face 86, **86**
cloisters 5, 80, 93, 104, 111, **112**, 182
commercial laundry 57–8, **58**, 86, 87
conduit houses 7–8, 169–77, **170**, **171**, **172**, **175**, 184, 189
as convent 57–9
as convent school 5–6, 59
courtyards 80–4, 111–12, 182
cross wing 89–93, **90**, **91**, **92**, 104
current description 2–9
Danckerts's painting of **79**, 79, 96, 101–4, **102**, **103**, **116**, 116–17, 138, 182
deer park 38, 167–9, **168**, 182
east elevation **96**, 96–7, 103, 135
eastern section **96**, 96–101, **99**, **100**, 103–4, 117
The Elms 57, 58, 59
entrance gates 3, 187
entrance lodge 3, 56, 187
exedra garden 123–8, **123–7**, 129, 183
existing literature 187–90
external stone staircase **4**, 73, 105–6, **106**
farm *see* Troy Farm
fountains 129–31
'furniture door' 89–90, **90**, 104
'game larder' 7–8, 169–77, **170**, **171**, **172**, 184, 189
garage 5, 59
garden walls 117–20, **118**, **119**, 184
gardens 9–10, 52, 111–40, **117**, **118**, **120–7**, **131–3**, 182–3, 184, 189
ground plans **5**, 85, **85**, **95**, **105**
Hermitage Cottage 119, **120**
historical significance 181–4
hostel 5, 59, 140
ice-house 7–8, 167, **168**, 189
inventory (1557) 35, 37–8, 91–2, 181–2
inventory (1620) 101, 102, 104, 153, 170–1, 181–2
and the Jesuits 45–7, 106
Keeper's Cottage **168**, 169
main staircase **97**, 97–8, 100, 104, 188, 190
maps of *see* maps
meadow 83, 190
mill 167, 182, 184, 190
netball court 5, 59, 131, 132
north range **4**, 4–6, 52, 73, 85, 93–8, **94**, 100, 103–6, **106**, 117, 135, **136**, 139, 182, 184, 188
oak room 98–100, **100**
orchards 121–3, **121–3**, 125, 138, 149, 156–8, **157**, 182, 183
ownership history 2–3, 13–61, 190
pigsties 119, **120**, 189
planning applications 5, 59, 60–1, 104–5
plaster ceilings 96, 98–101, **99**, 104, 153, 184, 188, 190
pottery finds 83, **83**, 167
priest hole 47, 96, 106
royal visit of Henry VII and Elizabeth 35–6, 37, 83, 90, 104, 181
Smith's painting of 93, **137**, 137–9
smithy 162
south wing 75, 80–1, **81**, 85–9, **86**, **88**, 104, 112
as special school for boys 6, 59–60
teaching block 5, 59, 104, 140
tennis court 120
theatre 5, 59, 87, 95, 104
toll house 56
tower 96, 101, 102–3, 182
Virgin Mary statue **92**, 113
walled garden *see* walled garden
water features 129–35, 183
watercress stream 147
west elevation **94**, 95, **139**
Whit Monday fêtes 55
woodlands 7, **8**, 38, 60, 93, 167–9, 190
Troy House from the Wye Bridge (Smith) 93, **137**, 137–9
Troy Meadow 83, 190
Troy Mill 167, 182, 184, 190
Troy Orles Wood 7, **8**, 93, 167, **168**
Troy School 6, 59–60
Troypark Wood 7, **8**, 38, 167–9, **168**, 190
Tudor, Edmund 25, 26
Tudor, Henry *see* Henry VII
Tudor, Jasper 25, 27, 28, 29, 30–1
Tunbridge Wells 53
Tutte l'Opere d'Architettura (Serlio) 152, **153**

Usk 15, 19, 21–2, 25, 27, 33

Valor Ecclesiasticus 37
Vatican loggia 98
Vaughan, Sir Roger 21, 31
Vaughan, Walter 26
Vergil, Polydore 31
Vitruvius 113, 151–2
Vredeman de Vries, Jan 152, 171–2

walled garden
- aerial photographs **3**, **112**, **145**, **162**
- approach routes 3
- bee boles 6, **151**, 154–6, **155**, 183, 187
- cemetery 7, 59, 146–7, **147**, 160
- current description 6–7
- dating of construction 154–8, 183, 187
- existing literature 187–8, 190
- greenhouse 56, 160
- leased out 57
- maps 146, **146**, 156, **157**, 160, **161**, 162, 163
- orchards 138, 149, 156–8, **157**, 182, 183
- ornamental stone entrance **6**, 6, **148–51**, 148–54, 160, 170, **172**, 183–4, 187–8, 190
- pathways 159–62
- service entrances 146–7, **146–7**
- slip garden 162–3
- in Smith's painting 137–8

Ware Park 130
Warleigh 60
Warren, Robert 93, 97, 106, 182
water features 115, 129–35, **134**, 183
watercress stream 147
Wellingtonia trees 56, 139–40
Wentworth Forest 50, 94
West Wycombe Park 127
Westbury Court 133
Whit Monday fêtes 55
White Castle 22
Whitney, George 37
Whitney, James 37
William I 15, 16
William II (William Rufus) 15
William III 133
William ap Thomas 20–4, **24**, 89
William John ap James 38, 91
William of Dol 17
Williams, David 17
Wilton House 134
Wise, Henry 138
Wonastow 37, 38
Woodhouse, Elisabeth 115
woodlands 7, **8**, 38, 60, 93, 167–9, 190
Woodville, Elizabeth 30
Woodville, Mary 30, 31
Worcester House, London 44, 49
Worcester Lodge, Nonsuch Palace 44
Worlidge, John 131
Wyatt, Osmond Arthur 57
Wye, river 15, 45–6, 139, 169, 189
Wyveswood 33